WORKING IN THE BIG EASY

The History and Politics of Labor in New Orleans

WORKING IN THE BIG EASY

The History and Politics of Labor in New Orleans

THOMAS J. ADAMS
AND
STEVE STRIFFLER

University of Louisiana at Lafayette Press
2014

Cover image credits: front, top image courtesy of the Library of Congress; front, middle image courtesy of Philip Gould; rear image courtesy of Christopher Porché West.

ISBN 13 (paper): 978-1-935754-33-6

http://ulpress.org
University of Louisiana at Lafayette Press
P.O. Box 40831
Lafayette, LA 70504-0831

Printed on acid-free paper.

Library of Congress Cataloging-in-Publication Data   Library of Congress Cataloging-in-Publication Data

Adams, Thomas Jessen.
  Working in the Big Easy : the history and politics of labor in New Orleans / Thomas Adams and Steve Striffler.
     pages cm
  ISBN 978-1-935754-33-6 (alk. paper)
  1. Labor--Louisiana--New Orleans--History. 2. Working class--Louisiana--New Orleans--History. 3. Labor unions--Louisiana--New Orleans--History. 4. New Orleans (La.)--Race relations--History. I. Striffler, Steve, 1967- II. Title.
  HD8085.N49A33 2014
  331.09763'35--dc23
     2014003524

Contents

Acknowledgments

This book arose out of a 2011 conference jointly hosted by the University of New Orleans and Tulane University. Generous funding for the conference and participant travel was provided by the New Orleans Center for the Gulf South at Tulane University, the Latin American Studies Program at the University of New Orleans, and the American Council of Learned Societies New Faculty Fellows Program. We wish to especially thank Larry Powell and Joel Dinerstein from the New Orleans Center for the Gulf South for their support in this project.

At the conference incisive commentary on many of the chapters here was provided by Emily Clark, Jana Lipman, Larry Powell, Bruce Boyd Raeburn, and Felipe Smith. Peyton Jones and Chris Willoughby helped with conference organizational tasks. Finally, we would like to thank Emily Mendenhall, Adolph Reed, Karon Reese, Matt Sakakeeny, and Nick Unger for their ongoing thoughts and conversations about New Orleans and labor that helped lead to this book.

Placing Labor in New Orleans History and New Orleans in Labor History

Thomas J. Adams and Steve Striffler

This book is a start. It is a start at rectifying two troubling historiographical, cultural, and analytic absences — the place of labor in the history of New Orleans and the place of New Orleans in the history of labor.

New Orleans stands as one of the most studied cities in the United States. From its founding as a malarial backwater of France's Atlantic empire in 1718 to the dislocations brought on by Hurricane Katrina and its aftermath nearly three centuries later, scholars of New Orleans have produced a wide-ranging and often brilliant corpus of work centered on the city. Analyses of racial formation, Atlantic World empire and colonialism, urban slavery, trans-Atlantic, Caribbean, and Mississippi political economy, urban geography, post-emancipation politics and life, the Great Society, and modern disaster have often been most effectively studied in the context of New Orleans.[1] Skating between the poles

1. On racial formation see Arnold R. Hirsch and Joseph Logsdon, *Creole New Orleans: Race and Americanization* (Baton Rouge: LSU Press, 1992); Gwendolyn Midlo Hall, *Africans in Colonial Louisiana: The Development of Afro-Creole Culture in the 18th Century* (Baton Rouge: LSU Press, 1995); Walter Johnson, *Soul By Soul: Life Inside the Antebellum Slave Market* (Cambridge, MA: Harvard University Press, 2001); Jennifer Spear, *Race, Sex, and Social Order in Early New Orleans* (Baltimore: Johns Hopkins University Press, 2008). On empire and colonialism see Emily Clark, *Masterless Mistresses: The New Orleans Ursulines and the Development of a New World Society, 1727-1834* (Chapel Hill: University of North Carolina Press, 2007); Ned Sublette, *The World That Made New Orleans: From Spanish Silver to Congo Square* (Chicago: Chicago Review Press, 2008); Shannon Lee Dawdy, *Building the Devil's Empire: French Colonial New Orleans* (Chicago: University of Chicago Press, 2009); Lawrence N. Powell, *Accidental City: Improvising New Orleans* (Cambridge, MA: Harvard University

of the city's exceptionalism embodied by its unique cultural formations and what one scholar has argued is its distinction as the only American city to produce "its own ethnicity" and its colonial, Atlantic, Caribbean, Southern, and American representativeness, the wealth of scholarship produced directly about the city has probably only been surpassed in the American context by New York, Chicago, and Los Angeles and only equaled by a smattering of other urban environs.[2] Despite this large, growing, and impressive body of scholarship on New Orleans, scholars of the city and south Louisiana have been relatively untuned to questions of labor history. Even in the context of scholarship on urban slavery, a subject that almost necessarily lends itself to analyses of work, the history of New Orleans has stood out for the lack of attention paid to the labors of slaves.[3] Scholars writing in this tradition have

---

Press, 2012). On expansion and political economy see Daniel Usner, *Indians, Settlers, and Slaves in a Frontier Exchange Economy: The Lower Mississippi Valley Before 1783* (Chapel Hill: University of North Carolina Press, 1992); Richard Follett, *The Sugar Masters: Planters and Slaves in Louisiana's Cane World, 1820-1860* (Baton Rouge: LSU Press, 2007); Adam Rothman, *Slave Country: American Expansion and the Origins of the Deep South* (Cambridge, MA: Harvard University Press, 2007). On geography see Peirce Lewis, *New Orleans: The Making of an Urban Landscape* (Chicago: Center for American Places, 1976); Craig E. Colten, *An Unnatural Metropolis: Wresting New Orleans from Nature* (Baton Rouge: LSU Press, 2005). Richard Campanella, *Bienville's Dilemma: A Historical Geography of New Orleans* (Lafayette: UL Lafayette Press, 2008). On post-emancipation politics see John Blassingame, *Black New Orleans: 1860-80* (Chicago: University of Chicago Press, 1973); Rebecca Scott, *Degrees of Freedom: Louisiana and Cuba After Slavery* (Cambridge, MA: Harvard Belknap, 2008). On the Great Society see Kent Germany, *New Orleans After the Promises: Poverty, Power, Citizenship and the Search for the Great Society* (Athens: University of Georgia Press, 2007); John Arena, *Driven From New Orleans: How Nonprofits Betray Public Housing and Promote Privatization* (Minneapolis: University of Minnesota Press, 2012).

2.   Campanella, *Bienville's Dilemma*, 1. For a cogent critique of polarity of New Orleans exceptionalism narratives see Matt Sakakeeny, "Privatization, Marketization, and Neoliberalism—The Political Dynamics of Post-Katrina New Orleans," *Perspectives on Politics* 10, no. 3 (September 2012): 723-26.

3.   Richard Wade's classic study *Slavery in the Cities: The South, 1820-1860*

often focused more on race making and the multitudinous identities and gradations between black and white produced in the seemingly peculiar context of antebellum New Orleans. At the same time, even as new work on urban slavery and the New Orleans-centered slave trade has forced slavery scholars to reevaluate the place of slavery in transnational networks of capital and a globally integrated market society, slavery as a relationship of forced labor between owned and owner has taken a backseat to the embeddedness of the institution in an antebellum world increasingly dominated by market principles.[4]

If scholars of New Orleans have a labor problem, then it is equally true that scholars of labor have a New Orleans problem. Despite a large and growing literature on work in the South dating back to the origins of the American variants of the "new labor history" four decades ago, Louisiana and New Orleans have been peculiarly underrepresented in this tradition.[5] A handful of articles and dissertations (virtually

---

(New York: Oxford University Press, 1967) as well as more recent works like Walter Johnson's *Soul By Soul* and Jennifer Spear's *Race, Sex, and Social Order in Antebellum New Orleans* spend little time on slavery as a system of ordering labor in favor of cogent analyses of racial domination and racialization.

4.   Johnson, *Soul By Soul*; Rothman, *Slave Country.*

5.   Key southern new labor history studies include: Michael Honey, *Southern Labor and Black Civil Rights: Organizing Memphis Workers* (Urbana: University of Illinois Press, 1993); Earl Lewis, *In Their Own Interests: Race, Class, and Power in Twentieth-Century Norfolk* (Berkeley: University of California Press, 1993); Alex Lichtenstein, *Twice the Work of Free Labor: The Political Economy of Convict Labor in the New South* (New York: Verso, 1996); Julie Saville, *The Work of Reconstruction: From Slave to Wage Laborer in South Carolina* (New York: Cambridge University Press, 1996); Tera Hunter, *To 'Joy My Freedom: Southern Black Women's Lives and Labors After the Civil War* (Cambridge, MA: Harvard University Press, 1998); Bryant Simon, *A Fabric of Defeat: The Politics of South Carolina Millhands, 1910-1948* (Chapel Hill: University of North Carolina Press, 1998); Jacquelyn Dowd Hall and Robert Korstad, *Like a Family: The Making of a Southern Cotton Mill World* (Chapel Hill: University of North Carolina Press, 2000); Steven Hahn, *A Nation Under Our Feet: Black Political Struggles in the Rural South From Slavery to the Great Migration* (Cambridge, MA: Harvard Belknap, 2005).

none of which have entered the canon of labor history) have combined with one classic study, Eric Arnesen's *Waterfront Workers of New Orleans*, to represent the entire corpus of labor histories of New Orleans.[6] Compared to various regions of Alabama, Virginia, and the Carolinas, let alone virtually every major northern, midwestern, and western city, this absence is striking both on its face and in relationship to the longer urban, regional, and metropolitan histories of New Orleans. Between New Orleans's existence as the only pre-Sunbelt urban metropolis in the entirety of the former Confederacy, the relatively early capitalization of a variety of wage labor intensive industries across the city, the diversity of both black and white populations in New Orleans vis-a-vis other southern, American, and Atlantic cities, and the nodal importance of the Gulf Coast and Mississippi River in the national and trans-Caribbean integration of American production, this absence is particularly striking. Furthering this absence has been what we might understand as the sociological imperatives of the historical profession. Labor history — as well as other subfields like African American urban history and indeed, the whole of urban history in fact — while generally more in tune with what

6.   Eric Arnesen, *Waterfront Workers of New Orleans: Race, Class, and Politics, 1863-1923* (Urbana: University of Illinois Press, 1994). Studies that have not entered into broader American labor historiography include: Roger W. Shugg, *Origins of Class Struggle in Louisiana: A Social History of White Farmers and Laborers During and After Slavery* (Baton Rouge: LSU Press, 1939); David Williamson, "Adaptation to Socio-Cultural Change: Working Class Cubans in New Orleans," *Caribbean Studies* 16, no. 3 (January 1976): 217-27; Daniel Rosenberg, *New Orleans Dockworkers: Race, Labor, and Unionism, 1893-1923* (Albany: SUNY Press, 1988); Claude Jacobs, "Benevolent Societies of New Orleans Blacks During the Late Nineteenth and Early Twentieth Century," *Louisiana History* 29, no. 1 (Winter 1988): 21-33; Michael D. Pierson "'He Helped the Poor and Snubbed the Rich:' Benjamin Butler and Class Politics in Lowell and New Orleans," *Massachusetts Historical Review* 7 (2005): 36-68. The most complete corpus of scholarship on New Orleans labor history has been produced at the University of New Orleans where students of Joseph Logsdon, Arnold Hirsch, and Michael Mizell-Nelson have written a wealth of master's theses on aspects of New Orleans labor history.

we can understand as the labor question—that is, who does the work and under what historical conditions—has been a decidedly northern, midwestern, and to a lesser extent, Pacific Coast affair. This snowballs on itself, as studies grounded in Chicago or New York or Detroit produce their own next generation of scholarship while normatively defining the broader American labor experience in relationship to these cities' specific histories.

All of this begs the questions: how does the history of labor change our understanding of the history of New Orleans, and how does the history of New Orleans shift our understanding of the history of labor? The essays that follow in this book provide a variety of starting points to this question.

Eric Arnesen starts the collection with a broad look at the historiography on race and labor through a discussion of a theatrical play about New Orleans, his own groundbreaking book on the port city (*Waterfront Workers of New Orleans*), and the broader scholarly literature. How has scholarship on race and labor developed since the 1960s? And, has it mattered? Arnesen finds that from the 1980s onward labor historians began to produce increasingly sophisticated accounts of work and race, studies that delved into the daily lives of black and white workers with much greater nuance and detail than an earlier generation of scholarship. He nevertheless concludes that despite all this fine work, scholars of race and labor "have done remarkably little to alter the broader contours of the historical narrative." The dominant currents within southern history and American labor history remain largely unaltered by the proliferation of scholarship on race and labor.

The rest of the book moves chronologically through New Orleans's rich labor history. Celine Ugolini starts with a look at the earliest efforts by the French and others to physically establish the city of New Orleans. As we will see, there was nothing routine about attempts to build a city on a site that was not only continually hit by storms and fires throughout the 1700s, but also struggled to attract a population. Forced laborers, including convicts and slaves, were instrumental in the city's early construction.

Demetri Debe focuses more directly on slave labor, concentrating in particular on the remarkable mobility of skilled, enslaved, black women. As he shows, in a city where (by the 1730s) slaves outnumbered free people by nearly two to one, and slaves constituted almost the entirety of the labor force, enslaved black women were central to life in New Orleans. In order to increase their own wealth, slave owners gave black women considerable mobility, responsibility, and autonomy as market women, domestics, and saleswomen. They were literally everywhere, running errands, managing businesses, and otherwise sustaining New Orleans's economy.

In chapter 4, Michael Mizell-Nelson looks into the world of black public utility workers during the early 1900s by exploring an interesting moment. In 1918, white streetcar union officers decided to include African American railway and utility workers into their union, a remarkably early effort at interracial unionism. Mizell-Nelson attempts to understand this decision and what it meant for black workers and organizing efforts more broadly.

In the following chapter, Kodi Roberts examines the work and "bisness" of Voodoo practitioners, providing a fascinating window into the world of Depression-era New Orleans. Operating in the context of growing consumerism and economic hardship, Voodoo practitioners adjusted their business model to meet the needs of clients who were struggling to find jobs, run small businesses, or boost their luck in gambling. What the reader is left with is not only a nuanced treatment of Voodoo, but a rich portrait of life and economy in New Orleans during the Great Depression.

Like Roberts's placement of Voodoo in the context of the market, Elizabeth Manley shows how another key facet of New Orleans culture—music—cannot be divorced from relationships of labor. Manley follows the everyday integration of musical commerce and performance in the city in the years before its segregated locals of the American Federation of Musicians officially integrated. Focusing closely on the iconic Preservation Hall, she demonstrates that the stage and the recording studio, like the assembly line and the shop floor, were contested spaces of labor that were utterly transformed by the civil rights movement and local and national politics.

Chanda Nunez then traces the rich history of one of New Orleans's most iconic workers. As her research makes clear, the actual work and life of "praline mammies" was much more complex than stereotypes of the subservient, ever-loyal, black servant suggest. As street vendors, black women were able to carve out a degree of independence from the white world that most other available occupations did not allow. What Nunez does so well is weave together the history of the mammy stereotype with the actual lives of praline vendors.

In chapter 8, Nancy Dixon explores work within the New Orleans service industry. Through a fascinating discussion of the author's own personal history as a server/bartender, Dixon's chapter provides an outline of the city's post-war political economy and demonstrates how broader forces continually re-made the service sector. It simultaneously explores how literature on New Orleans has represented the labor and lives of service workers.

In chapter 9, Aurelia Murga turns attention to the Latin American immigrants who arrived in the aftermath of Hurricane Katrina to participate in the reconstruction of New Orleans. As Murga shows, the first immigrants were initially welcomed by everyone from local contractors to the National Guard because they were willing to work long hours under extremely difficult conditions for relatively low wages. They played a central role in making the city livable again. What Murga's chapter ultimately charts, however, is how this relatively favorable reception quickly transitioned into a less welcoming one, and how immigrants navigated, resisted, and organized within the context of an increasingly hostile terrain.

Our final chapter, by Aaron Schneider and Saru Jayaraman, provides a sobering look at working conditions within the restaurant and construction industries, the two sectors of the city's economy that provide the most jobs. The portrait is both clear and grim. Although workers within these industries were not treated particularly well prior to Katrina, their conditions have deteriorated since the storm. Race, gender, and legal status shape an individual's ability to succeed within these industries, but most workers are treated poorly, have relatively little chance for advancement, and are earning less than a living wage.

Collectively, then, the chapters cover some four hundred years of history, from slavery to post-Katrina New Orleans, and include many of the city's most iconic and important workers, from slaves, dock workers, mammies, and Voodoo practitioners to bartenders, servers, dishwashers, and construction workers. Building on the research of other scholars, the historical and topical breadth of the collection provides a glimpse of what a more robust New Orleans labor history might look like.

Yet, the volume provides more than just breadth. Through local case studies of particular forms of work, the chapters challenge scholarly and popular understandings of what it meant, in particular times and places, to be a female slave selling goods in the local market; a Voodoo practitioner meeting the needs of changing clientele; a black dockworker or railway worker trying to navigate white-run unions; a praline mammy selling her treats to a largely white clientele; or an immigrant construction worker navigating post-Katrina New Orleans. Together, then, these chapters not only begin to help us understand how a deeper exploration of labor will ultimately transform our understanding of New Orleans, but how a closer look at work in the Crescent City might shift our understanding of labor history more broadly.

1 | The Peculiar Waterfront: The Crescent City and the Rewriting of the History of Race and Labor in the United States

ERIC ARNESEN

In the depths of the Great Depression of the 1930s, an original play opened in New York to widespread attention and even, in some circles, critical acclaim. *Stevedore*, one black press account explained, was a theatrical drama whose theme—"trouble on the New Orleans waterfront"—moved "from one-punch-like climax to another at such a rate the audience and actors both are gasping when the final curtain falls." "No music. No brilliant stage setting. No display of dangling robes," explained an editor. "None of these greet you as the curtain in 'Stevedore' rises." And yet it was the "Finest Play on [the] American Stage."[1] One attendee of a performance in Cleveland concluded that it was "so forceful and profound, that all words used to describe [it] . . . are lost in the profundity of the story."[2] Ethel Waters, who attended *Stevedore* at least three times, described it as "[o]ne of the most thrilling plays" she had "ever witnessed."[3] *Stevedore* "has a way of jarring the white man's conscience," a black journalist noted, taking as his example the progressive novelist and white southern expatriate Erskine Caldwell. Approached by the reporter in the lobby of Chicago's Selwyn Theatre, Caldwell

1. James W. Woodlee, "'Stevedore': Finest Play on American Stage, Says Editor, of Drama Union Show," *Chicago Defender*, January 19, 1935.

2. "Ministers' Fight to Stop 'Stevedore' Fails as Play Continues with Crowds," *Cleveland Call and Post*, March 16, 1935.

3. Ethel Waters, "Ethel Waters Thinks 'Stevedore' is Fine Play," *Chicago Defender*, December 15, 1934.

was "still trembling from the violent impact of 'Stevedore's' last scene." The play was "honest and courageous enough" to show that "Negroes and white men are essentially one . . . [and] that there is no important difference between the races."[4] The Harlem-based tap dancer Bill Robinson, attending a performance at the Civic Repertory Theatre, seemingly forgot he was attending the theater. Caught up in the drama of the third and final act, the well-dressed Robinson "leaped out of his seat . . . took the stage steps three at a time," and joined actors behind the barricade on the set and "hurled bricks with the rest." With "no conscious notion of what had transpired at the time," he later explained it was "purely a matter of reflex" that was "unapologetic, [sic] unrestrained."[5] He was hardly the only member of an audience to participate in such a manner. "I'm telling you, it kind of shook us up," recalled Joe Staton, a cast member in the Seattle Federal Theatre Project's production of Stevedore. At a special performance before local longshoremen and African Americans, those in attendance "became so engrossed in that last scene that they came up on stage and helped us build a barricade."[6]

Stevedore got its message across far and wide. Initially produced by the Theatre Union, a left-wing operation in New York, it was given new life by the New Deal's Federal Theater Project. The FTA's Negro Repertory Company won the title of "Seattle's History Making Negro Theatre" for its rendition of the drama in the late 1930s.[7] Cleveland's Gilpin Players staged another production. (Efforts by that city's Interdenominational

---

4.   "Southern Writer Declares Race Hatred is Not Natural," *Pittsburgh Courier*, February 2, 1935.

5.   "Bill Robinson Forgets All to Join 'Stevedore,'" *Chicago Defender*, July 7, 1934.

6.   Errol G. Hill and James V. Hatch, *A History of African American Theatre* (Cambridge: Cambridge University Press, 2003), 327-28. Also see Susan Quinn, *Furious Improvisation: How the WPA and a Cast of Thousands Made High Art out of Desperate Times* (New York: Walker & Co., 2008), 96.

7.   "'Stevedore' to Play Return Engagement," *Northwest Enterprise*, March 19, 1937.

Ministerial Alliance and the Baptist Conference to shut down the play on the grounds of its profanity proved futile).[8] The show opened in Boston, Los Angeles, Chicago, Philadelphia, and even London, where Paul Robeson performed the lead role in a cast of largely non-professional actors.[9]

What was it about this "sensational drama of the New Orleans waterfront" that impressed many critics at home and abroad?[10] Its central attraction was its depiction of racial oppression and African American challenges to it. In the play, the overworked, underpaid, and at times cheated dock employees of the fictional Oceanic Steamship Company begin to complain and organize; a paternalistic but racist manager has police remove one of their spokesmen, Lonnie Thompson, who is then falsely implicated in the rape of a white woman. Before a lynch mob can kill him, Lonnie manages to escape. Fast forward to the third and final act: Lonnie rallies his compatriots to take a stand for justice, exhorting them to pursue the route of unionization and resistance, not the route of accommodation promoted by another docker or that of Christian forbearance

---

8.   "Ohio State News: Cleveland, Ohio," *Chicago Defender*, December 11, 1937; "'Stevedore,' Hailed by Public as Great Play, Fought by Clergymen," *Cleveland Call and Post*, March 9, 1935; "Ministers' Fight to Stop 'Stevedore' Fails as Play Continues with Crowds," *Cleveland Call and Post*, March 16, 1935. Profanity troubled more than just the Cleveland ministers. Critic Ralph Matthews observed that *Stevedore*, with its considerable "cussing and swearing," was a "play with the worst manners Broadway has seen since Mae West went high-hat and tamed her producers down to meet the requirements of the movie censors." Ralph Matthews, "Looking at the Stars," Baltimore *Afro-American*, May 12, 1934. In a hearing of the House Un-American Activities Committee in 1938, the conservative southern congressman Martin Dies fumed over the profanity and the taking of the Lord's name in vein in *Stevedore*.

9.   "'Stevedore' Scheduled for Boston Showing This Fall," *New York Age*, August 10, 1935; Hannen Swaffer, "English Critic Writes of 'Stevedore' and the South," *Chicago Defender*, September 22, 134; "'Stevedore' is Sensation on Pacific Coast," *Pittsburgh Courier*, October 27, 1934; Martin Duberman, *Paul Robeson: A Biography*, 192.

10.   "'Stevedore,' With Harlem Cast, Here for Holidays," *Chicago Defender*, December 22, 1934.

advocated by a black minister. "What you gwine fight with," a resigned black worker, Jim Veal, asks Lonnie. "White man own dis country. White man rule it. You can't fight against him. White man make de law and you can't fight de law. You try it and dey just shoot you down. Dey wipe you out — dey wipe out de whole black race."[11] The preacher seconds that belief. "Lonnie's talk just lead you to conflict and violence," he declares. "And dat's all wrong. De black man got to walk humble in de eyes of de Lawd. De Lawd say, 'Blessed are dey date are meek, for dey shall inherit de Kingdom of Heaven.'" [12]

Lonnie will have none of it, and he counters their pessimism with a forceful call to arms: "We can't wait fo' de judgment day. We can't wait till we dead and gone. We got to fight fo' de right to live," he retorts. "Now — now — right now."[13] And he carries the day. The embattled black workers build a barricade in the alley to hold off an advancing white mob as they prepare to engage in combat on their own behalf. "You all know what we hyar for," Lonnie continues in an inspirational vein. "We hyar to defend our homes. We hyar to fight fo' our lives. And we hyar to show 'em dat we ain't gwine be kicked around, and starved and stepped on no mo.' We hyar to show 'em we men and we gwine be treated like men." And lest one thinks that this is merely a local affair, Lonnie puts it all in context: "And remember we ain't only fighting fo' ourselves. Dar black folks all over de country looking at us right now: dey counting on us, crying to us: 'Stand yo' ground . . . You fighting fo' all of us." Just as the violence is about to erupt, help arrives in the form of Lem Morris, the radical — the "red" — union organizer and a small but welcome band of fellow white workers, who take a stand with their black brothers. (Mike Gold, Communist literary critic, characterized Morris as a "cool, strong Leninist

11.   Paul Peters and George Sklar, *Stevedore: A Play in Three Acts* (New York: Covici, Friede, Publishers, 1934), 107.

12.   Ibid.

13.   Ibid., 109.

leader" in his review in *New Masses*).[14] Pistols are fired; the white mob retreats, pursued by the interracial union activists. Lonnie is shot on the penultimate page and dies on the last, but his cause lives on.

This saga of resistance on the part of long-suffering black workers and of the possibility—even imperative—of interracial working class unity attracted considerable praise. "All of this is virile material, portrayed in the sharp, staccato manner of the best modern theater. The scenes are etched and the melodrama is deft," critic Bessye J. Bearden insisted.[15] The "Theatre Union has started something," an excited William Pickens exclaimed. The educator and National Association for the Advancement of Colored People (NAACP) official complemented *Stevedore* as a "breaker of precedents, a violator of traditions," prompting him to conclude that the stage was "the best spot on earth on which to get over correct and effective propaganda for the American Negro," excelling the "pulpit, platform and editorial columns." Indeed, he predicted, black "actors may become our emancipators."[16] To Communist literary critic Mike Gold, *Stevedore* was "one of the best, if not the best, revolutionary dramas that has yet appeared in this country." Plays like this, he maintained, "have a profound effect, in that they teach a great revolutionary lesson by driving it deep into your bones." All New York workers, he advised, should "go to see it."[17] (Not every proletarian in New York

---

14.   Michael Gold, "Stevedore," *New Masses*, May 1, 1934, 28.

15.   Bessye J. Bearden, "Critic Says 'Stevedore' is Play for Race," *Chicago Defender*, April 28, 1934.

16.   William Pickens, "Stevedore," *New York Amsterdam News*, May 5, 1934. The Theatre Union also rejected any aspect of segregation in its internal operation. "There is no Jim Crow in the Theatre Union," co-author George Sklar explained. "Negro actors share dressing rooms with white actors" and "Negroes sit everywhere in the audience." George Sklar, "Negro Actors in The Theatre Union Play, 'Stevedore,'" *Daily Worker*, May 9, 1934.

17.   Michael Gold, "'Stevedore,' the Play: Critics in New York Argue over Class of Drama about Lynching," *Chicago Defender*, May 5, 1934. *Stevedore* was, he stressed, "the most successful attempt at a proletarian drama we have yet

caught the show, but a battered truck transported twenty-four African Americans from Philadelphia to see a performance; black and white textile workers from Providence also made the trip to the city for the same purpose; and the Theatre Union distributed some three hundred tickets weekly to the unemployed, largely in Harlem).[18] To another reviewer, one of the characters — Black Snake Johnson — "personified the young men of the incoming generation who will throw off the yoke of cowardice and passiveness and who will demand and get all the rights that every citizen has guaranteed to him by the Constitution of the country in which he lives."[19] "'Stevedore' is more than a mere play — it is a portrayal of real life as it exists in the South," yet another reviewer explained, for the drama brought home "to disinterested parties the story of how the Race is treated in the South. Not in propaganda, but fact — that is what 'Stevedore' does in a big way."[20]

Not propaganda, but fact? From the distance of eight decades, *Stevedore*'s agitprop sensibility is impossible to miss. The playwrights and performers did little to hide their political sympathies. As playwright George Sklar explained in 1935, "In America, it's time we had a theatre with courage enough to present on the stage the life issues and realities which confront the twelve million Negroes in this country everywhere." For him,

had in America." At "last the American revolutionary movement has begun to find itself expressed adequately on the stage." Gold, "Stevedore," *New Masses*, May 1, 1934, 28-29. Another Communist critic, Harold Edgar, concurred. *Stevedore* was "[a]ltogether a very encouraging occasion in the history of the American revolutionary theatre." Harold Edgar, "Audience Roused by Theatre Union Production of 'Stevedore': Play of New Orleans Negro Longshoremen Seethes with Struggle," *Daily Worker*, April 20, 1934.

18.   "Jobless Motor Here for Play," *New York Amsterdam News*, May 19, 1934. Also see "Jobless to Get Tickets to Play," *Los Angeles Sentinel*, October 18, 1934.

19.   Woodlee, "'Stevedore': Finest Play on American Stage."

20.   Rob Roy, "'Stevedore' is Real Life Down South Scribe Says," *Chicago Defender*, December 29, 1934.

Stevedore was just such a play.[21] "We believe that the solution of the Negro problem lies in the unity of black and white workers," Sklar and Peters explained on another occasion. Happily for the authors and their Communist supporters, they discerned that "under the pressure of starvation of black and white alike," the unity they valued was "being welded . . . much more rapidly than most people dream."[22] The false accusation of rape conjured up explicit images of the Scottsboro case. Indeed, the play's authors—Paul Peters (the pseudonym of Harbor Allen) and Sklar—were committed Marxists. Peters had worked with the International Labor Defense (ILD)—the CP-affiliated group defending the Scottsboro Boys—as an editorial board member of its journal, *Labor Defender*, and as its publicity director. Lest there be any doubt as to the connections between that frame-up and the drama, the theater company "entertained" Mamie Williams, Ida Norris, Viola Montgomery, Josephine Powell, and June Patterson, mothers of several Scottsboro defendants attending one of the New York performances of this self-proclaimed "anti-lynch play" in the Spring of 1934, while Ruby Bates—one of the young white women who initially raised the rape charge—and officials of the International Labor Defense, attended as well.[23] The CP's black vice presidential candidate, James W. Ford, called *Stevedore* "another Scottsboro, connecting

21.   Sklar quoted in Rena Fraden, *Blueprints for a Black Federal Theatre 1935-1939* (New York: Cambridge University Press, 1994): 88. According to Errol Segal, the authors were determined that *Stevedore* be an "authentic social commentary for the audience." This led them to consult with "eyewitnesses and leaders of mass organizations on the problems raised by the play"; its original director, Mike Blankfort, "spent time on the docks and in the working-class sections of New Orleans and saw film footage of longshoremen at work." Errol Segal, "George Sklar: Playwright for a Socially Committed Theatre" (PhD diss., University of Michigan, 1968), 172; Michael Blankfort, "Behind Scenes of 'Stevedore,' a Play for Negro Rights," *Daily Worker*, April 27, 1934, 5.

22.   Paul Peters and George Sklar, letter, quoted in John Anderson, "Collaborators Act upon Theory . . ." *New York Journal*, April 28, 1934, quoted in Segal, "George Sklar," 191.

23.   "Scottsboro Mothers Have Day in East," *Chicago Defender*, May 19, 1934.

up economic exploitation of Negro workers with the whole system of national oppression of the Negro people."[24]

But what about its basis in reality? To what extent was *Stevedore* factual? One of its authors, Paul Peters, responded to doubts raised about the drama's authenticity in early 1935. "Such things have actually happened, not once, but many times in the South," he insisted. The year Peters claimed to have spent working on the New Orleans docks informed an earlier play which appeared in the pages of *New Masses* (on whose staff he worked) as "Wharf Nigger" and "On the Wharf" in 1929 and 1930.[25] He noted that New Orleans's waterfront experienced some "three important strikes" since 1913, all of which "involved brickbat and pistol clashes between company guards and longshoremen and were broken by strikebreakers." The "significant thing about these strikes, however, is that Negro and white 'dock wallopers' stood shoulder to shoulder in the battle against injunctions and physical attacks." Peters was even aware that in the 1880s, the city was "the scene of impressive parades of black and white, who joined together and for a time paralyzed the city," presumably a reference to the 1892 general strike. But the playwright's New Orleans political morality tale drew on more than a reading of New Orleans history. Peters walked his readers through the 1919 Bogalusa strike and the mine war in West Virginia's Mingo County. Providing further positive examples of interracial solidarity were black and white demonstrations on behalf of the imprisoned black

24.   James A. Miller, *Remembering Scottsboro: The Legacy of an Infamous Trial* (Princeton: Princeton University Press, 2009), 22, 104; "Southern Scribe Praises 'Stevedore,' Broadway Hit," *Chicago Defender*, June 2, 1934; Sender Garlin, "Paul Peters, Revolutionary Playwright—An Interview," *Daily Worker*, May 15, 1934. Peter's colorful career combining the arts and politics included working with the Suitcase Theatre, a one-act play group, along with the black poet and playwright Langston Hughes and the Communist journalist and spy (and future anticommunist) Whittaker Chambers. "'Stevedore' Premiere Scheduled; 'Peace on Earth' Closing Today," *New York Amsterdam News*, March 17, 1934.

25.   Miller, *Remembering Scottsboro*, 22, 104.

communist, Angelo Herndon, in Georgia and the rise of left-led sharecropper unionism in Alabama, both at the time the play debuted. As for its portraits of white violence, the co-author explained that the drama drew upon the 1917 East St. Louis race riot and the 1919 Chicago riot. Another account noted that the case of Ossian Sweet, the black Detroit doctor whose forcible resistance to white rioters attempting to drive his family out of its home in a white neighborhood, was also woven into the drama's plot.[26]

Paul Peters's insistence on historical grounding raises important questions about the play's use of history, on the one hand, and the nature of historical memory, on the other. If "[s]uch things have actually happened, not once, but many times in the South," as Peters claimed, their recounting in *Stevedore* represented a creative amalgamation of incidents and trends, not a faithful depiction of the New Orleans waterfront. Peters was absolutely right about the impressive interracial parades of the 1880s, but there were certainly more than "three important strikes" since 1913; there may have been fewer pistol clashes than he suggested; and not all strikes, at least not the multiple strikes prior to 1923, were "broken by strikebreakers." One could argue that the history of the New Orleans waterfront and race relations in the Crescent City were more complex—and interesting—than Peters let on. More important, perhaps, was his portrayal of black dock workers. His African American figures, prior to their political epiphany at the climax, are oddly disconnected from the city and its black social and political infrastructure. Waterfront labor conditions may have deteriorated dramatically following the collapse of the Dock and Cotton Council in 1923, but black social and political organizations hardly vanished. *Stevedore*'s black protagonists seem to know nothing of their city's labor history, maneuvering

---

26.   Paul Peters, "'Stevedore' Based on Facts, Says Its Authors," *Chicago Defender*, January 19, 1935; "Did 'The Man from Baltimore' Go Home?," *New York Amsterdam News*, December 1, 1934; "'Stevedore' for U.S., London and Moscow Theatres," Baltimore *Afro-American*, September 22, 1934.

in a racist world devoid of black political organization outside of the black church, whose anti-agitation gospel the play rejects. It was only with the arrival of "the union" — it has no name but comes with white radical leadership — that black dock workers begin to challenge, at first tentatively and then militantly, the conditions that have stripped them of their dignity. As it turns out, when unionization again swept the docks later in the 1930s, off the stage and on the real waterfront, the left-led International Longshoremen's and Warehousemen's Union (ILWU) brought in its version of Lem Morris to preach the gospel of interracial unionism only to find itself at a competitive disadvantage. In a repressive atmosphere, the ILWU lost, as Bruce Nelson has shown, to the biracial, segregated International Longshoremen's Association (ILA). For all its corruption and acceptance of segregation, the ILA had a much deeper history in the black community. In this instance, black workers stuck with an institution that, however imperfect, offered them a measure of autonomy in an all-black local.[27]

However well-meaning its intentions, *Stevedore* drew poorly from history. New Orleans provided merely a backdrop for the larger political lessons of the mid-1930s Communist left: In the Jim Crow South, black workers were exploited as workers and exploited as blacks; their racial subordination was inextricably intertwined with their class subordination; the former made the latter that much easier. Without the benefit of a union, they were at their employers' mercy; following the path of accommodation got them nowhere. Nor did taking the advice of traditional leaders like preachers, whose dreams of otherworldly deliverance explained away suffering in the here and now. But resistance was not futile. Unionization — working-class unity and particularly unity across racial

---

27.   Garlin, "Paul Peters, Revolutionary Playwright"; Bruce Nelson, "Class and Race in the Crescent City: The ILWU, from San Francisco to New Orleans," in *The CIO's Left-Led Unions*, ed. Steve Rosswurm (New Brunswick: Rutgers University Press, 1992), 19-45.

lines — was key. "He's a member of the union and we've got to help him get away," the leftist organizer Lem Morris tells his white compatriots about Lonnie, who by that point was in deep trouble. When one white dockworker objects to coming to the aid of a black man, Lem sets him straight: "We've had this out before. The only way we can tie up this river front is by organizing these black boys, and you know it. There are three of them to every white man on these docks. And if you think you're going to pull a strike . . . without them, you're crazy."[28] Without interracial labor solidarity, it's divided we fall. Now that was a lesson that black and white dock workers in New Orleans had learned the hard way decades before. And it constituted, at least for longshore labor in a racially divided labor force, an imperative that scholars have appreciated. Testifying before the President's Committee on Fair Employment Practices in 1943, the industrial relations specialist Herbert Northrup put forth the formula with regard to the white railroad brotherhoods: The lily white union could "admit the Negro into the union" and "teach him and educate him" to "present a solid front against the employer" or "force the railroads to eliminate the Negro from train and engine service." Less than a decade later, in 1951, the eminent historian C. Vann Woodward borrowed that formulation and broadened it to encapsulate labor's racial dilemma: The choice of southern unionists was simple, Woodward argued: "eliminate the Negro as a competitor . . . or take him in as an organized worker."[29] The only qualification, as it pertains to New Orleans, is an important one: It was less a matter of white unions "taking in" blacks or teaching and educating them; rather, in the pre-1920s era, black workers seemed as likely to embrace trade unionism as their white counterparts

28.   Peters and Sklar, *Stevedore,* 60-62.

29.   Herbert R. Northrup, "The Negro in the Railway Unions," *Phylon* 5 (2nd Quarter 1944), 160; C. Vann Woodward, *Origins of the New South 1877-1913* (1951; repr. Baton Rouge: Louisiana State University Press, 1971), 229.

and, in some instances, even more likely to embrace it.[30]

This raises a larger issue about race and labor history and the place of the New Orleans story in that historiography and in the larger historiography of the Jim Crow South. Today, race and labor is a subject with which every labor historian is familiar, if not wholly conversant. When I launched the project that was to become *Waterfront Workers of New Orleans* just over three decades ago, in 1981, that was by no means the case. Indeed, the field was fairly barren or at least undeveloped. The so-called old labor history of the Commons School often approached union history in a top-down, institutional manner; it shared, to an extent, the views of the leaders of the American Federation of Labor regarding black workers as a threat and understood the AFL's exclusionary barriers as a logical response to that threat. Approaching the matter from a very different political perspective, a number of social scientists condemned the labor movement's racial policies. Charles Wesley, Sterling Spero and Abram Harris, Lorenzo Greene and Carter G. Woodson, and, in the 1940s, Herbert Northrup, all charted, often in a union-by-union, economic sector-by-economic sector manner precisely how white-dominated trade unions excluded or otherwise marginalized black labor.[31] In the midst of the Second World War, the African American scholar Rayford Logan simply and directly declared that the "'solidarity of labor' is [just] another

30.   Eric Arnesen, *Waterfront Workers of New Orleans: Race, Class, and Politics, 1863-1923* (New York: Oxford University Press, 1991); Daniel Rosenberg, *New Orleans Dockworkers: Race, Labor, and Unionism 1892-1923* (Albany: State University of New York Press, 1988); Eric Arnesen, "Biracial Waterfront Unionism in the Age of Segregation," in *Waterfront Workers: New Essays on Race and Class*, ed. Cal Winslow (Urbana: University of Illinois Press, 1998).

31.   Charles H. Wesley, *Negro Labor in the United States 1850-1925: A Study in American Economic History* (New York: Vanguard Press, 1927); Sterling D. Spero and Abram L. Harris, *The Black Worker: The Negro and the Labor Movement* (1931; repr., New York: Atheneum, 1969); Lorenzo J. Greene and Carter G. Woodson, *The Negro Wage Earner* (New York: Russell & Russell, 1930); Horace R. Cayton and George S. Mitchell, *Black Workers and the New Unions* (Chapel Hill: University of North Carolina Press, 1939).

myth as far as the history of American labor is concerned." In so arguing, Logan was arriving at no novel conclusion, for he was merely drawing upon the experiences of countless black workers as well as the scholarly indictment of a generation of black social scientists who had been chronicling, in copious detail, blacks' long, negative encounter with the trade union movement. Black workers and intellectuals alike could agree that much of organized labor proved itself generally hostile to African Americans, with dozens of unions barring blacks from membership while others granted them only "limited rights" through second-class auxiliary unions. Discriminatory white unions, in Logan's eyes, deserved the same epithet that they directed at Big Business: they were merely "soulless corporations."[32]

For its part, the new labor history was a bit slow out of the gate when it came to race. In retrospect, some of the early new labor scholarship was romantic; scholars embraced a bottom-up history and celebrated the resistance of workers and their communities to the onslaught of industrial capitalism. Race was not exactly absent; it just was not a central focus, outside of a small number of scholars.[33] Between the minimal attention and the coverage that it did receive, Nell Irvin Painter charged in 1989 that the new labor history had "downplayed or completely overlooked racism." Endorsing the views of the

---

32.   Rayford W. Logan, "The Negro Wants First-Class Citizenship," in *What the Negro Wants*, ed. Rayford W. Logan, (Chapel Hill: University of North Carolina Press, 1944), 12.

33.   Paul B. Worthman, "Black Workers and Labor Unions in Birmingham, Alabama, 1897-1904," *Labor History* 10 (Summer 1969): 375-407; Alexander Saxton, *The Indispensable Enemy: Labor and the Anti-Chinese Movement in California* (Berkeley: University of California Press, 1971); James Green, "The Brotherhood of Timber Workers 1910-1913: A Radical Response to Industrial Capitalism in the Southern U.S.A.," *Past and Present*, no. 60 (August 1973): 161-200; Jervis Anderson, *A. Philip Randolph: A Biographical Portrait* (New York, 1972); Peter J. Rachleff, *Black Labor in Richmond 1865-1890* (1984; Urban: University of Illinois Press, 1988); Dolores E. Janiewski, *Sisterhood Denied: Race, Gender, and Class in a New South Community* (Philadelphia, 1985).

NAACP labor secretary-turned-industrial-relations-scholar Herbert Hill, she charged the field with having a serious race problem."[34] It was a view that David Roediger, Noel Ignatiev, and Bruce Nelson, among others, would reiterate and amplify in the late 1980s and 1990s. As late as 2001, Bruce Nelson was denouncing the "widespread tendency of labor historians to portray the working class as white . . . either to minimize the importance of race in writing the history of American workers or to assign it a distinctly secondary role as an explanatory factor."[35] These charges were, to a considerable extent, exaggerated, more the product of politics than informed historiographical consideration. Even while Hill, Roediger, and Ignatiev were leveling their attacks, labor historians were producing article after article, book after book, dealing with race and labor. But however one evaluates the field's treatment of race in the late twentieth century, by the opening decade of the twenty-first century it was evident that the quantity and quality of the new literature has made it easy to retire labor history's "race problem" question once and for all.[36]

34.   Nell Irvin Painter, "The New Labor History and the Historical Moment," *International Journal* of *Politics, Culture, and Society* 2, no. 3 (Spring 1989): 369

35.   Bruce Nelson, *Divided We Stand: American Workers and the Struggle for Black Equality* (Princeton: Princeton University Press, 2001), xxii; Noel Ignatiev, *How the Irish Became White* (New York: Verso, 1995), 180-81; Noel Ignatiev, "The Paradox of the White Worker: Studies in Race Formation," *Labour/ Le Travail* 30 (Fall 1991), 33-40; David Roediger, "'Labor in White Skin': Race and Working-Class History" in *Reshaping the U.S. Left: Popular Struggles in the 1980s*, eds. Mike Davis and Michael Sprinker (London: Verso, 1988), 289; David Roediger, "Notes on Working Class Racism," *New Politics* 11, no. 3 (Summer 1989), 61-66; David Roediger, *The Wages of Whiteness: Race and the Making of the American Working Class* (London: Verso, 1991).

36.   A sample of the new work includes Michael Honey, *Southern Labor and Black Civil Rights: Organizing Memphis Workers* (Urbana: University of Illinois Press, 1993); Robin D.G. Kelley "'We Are Not What We Seem': Rethinking Black Working-Class Opposition in the Jim Crow South," *Journal of American History* 80 (June 1993): 75-113; Rick Halpern, *Down on the Killing Floor: Black and White Workers in Chicago's Packinghouses, 1904-1954* (Urbana: University

The sense of intellectual excitement that produced the first substantial wave of the new labor history in the 1970s similarly informed those working on race and labor in the 1980s and 1990s. That was certainly my experience with the subject. The project that became *Waterfront Workers of New Orleans* began as

of Illinois Press, 1997); Roger Horowitz, *"Negro and White, Unite and Fight!": A Social History of Industrial Unionism in Meatpacking, 1930–1990* (Urbana: University of Illinois Press, 1997); Joe Trotter Jr., *Coal, Class, and Color: Blacks in Southern West Virginia, 1915–1932* (Urbana: University of Illinois Press, 1995); Kevin Boyle, "'There Are No Union Sorrows That the Union Can't Heal': The Struggle for Racial Equality in the United Automobile Workers, 1940–1960," *Labor History* 36 (Winter 1995), 5-23; Tera W. Hunter, *To 'Joy My Freedom: Southern Black Women's Lives and Labors after the Civil War* (Cambridge, MA: Harvard University Press, 1997); Melinda Chateauvert, *Marching Together: The Women of the Brotherhood of Sleeping Car Porters* (Urbana: University of Illinois Press, 1997); Karin Shapiro, *A New South Rebellion: The Battle Against Convict Labor in the Tennessee Coalfields, 1871-1896* (Chapel Hill: University of North Carolina Press, 1998); Daniel Letwin, *The Challenge of Interracial Unionism: Alabama Coal Miners, 1878-1921* (Chapel Hill: University of North Carolina Press, 1998); Timothy J. Minchin, *Hiring the Black Worker: The Racial Integration of the Southern Textile Industry, 1960–1980* (Chapel Hill: University of North Carolina Press, 1999); Eric Arnesen, *Brotherhoods of Color: Black Railroad Workers and the Struggle for Equality* (Cambridge, MA: Harvard University Press, 2001); Brian Kelly, *Race, Class, and Power in the Alabama Coalfields, 1908–1921* (Urbana: University of Illinois Press, 2001); Beth Tompkins Bates, *Pullman Porters and the Rise of Protest Politics in Black America, 1925-1945* (Chapel Hill: University of North Carolina Press, 2001); William P. Jones, *The Tribe of Black Ulysses: African American Lumber Workers in the Jim Crow South* (Urbana: University of Illinois Press, 2005); Eric Arnesen, ed., *The Black Worker: Race, Labor, and Civil Rights since Emancipation* (Urbana: University of Illinois Press, 2007); Paul D. Moreno, *Black Americans and Organized Labor: A New History* (Baton Rouge: Louisiana State University Press, 2006); Theresa A. Case, *The Great Southwest Railroad Strike and Free Labor* (College Station, TX: Texas A & M Press, 2010); Robert H. Zieger, *For Jobs and Freedom: Race and Labor in America Since 1865* (Lexington: University Press of Kentucky, 2007); Clifford Farrington, *Biracial Unions on Galveston's Waterfront, 1865-1925* (Austin: Texas State Historical Association, 2007); Philip Rubio, *There's Always Work at the Post Office: African American Postal Workers and the Fight for Jobs, Justice, and Equality* (Chapel Hill: University of North Carolina Press, 2010). Also see Robert H. Zieger, "Recent Historical Scholarship on Public Policy in Relation to Race and Labor in the Post-Title-VII Period," *Labor History* 46, no. 1 (February 2005): 3-14.

a masters thesis in Yale's Afro-American Studies program in the early 1980s. It was Herbert Gutman's 1968 essay on black labor activist Richard Davis that first drew me to the world of the waterfront. Gutman's call to develop a ground up social history of working-class race relations appealed to me, as did the questions he posed of the "Age of Booker T. Washington and Samuel Gompers." Richard Davis, the African American coal miner and union leader, had no obvious place in the historiography, and yet not only did he exist, but the paper trail he left allowed for a detailed reconstruction of relations between blacks and whites as well as insights into the evolving worldview of a black organizer committed to both union and racial advancement. Gutman's larger programmatic call drew me in: the "absence of detailed knowledge of the 'local world' inhabited by white and Negro workers,"[37] he said, was a serious absence; it could be addressed when social historians dug deeper and reconstructed those local worlds. What was needed was a social history of working-class race relations, a history based not on the proclamations of white union leaders and black elites but, rather, on the daily experiences of black and white workers living in specific communities. It was only in the 1980s that historians finally heeded Gutman's call. *Waterfront Workers* was only one of a number of responses to Gutman's challenge.

I was led to the world of the New Orleans waterfront by a desire to reexamine race and labor in the age of Booker T. Washington and Samuel Gompers. What particularly attracted me was the existence of numerous black and white longshore unions, alternating moments of collaboration—I did slip in the word solidarity from time to time—and hostility across racial lines, and, of course, extremely rich sources. (The

---

37.   Herbert Gutman, "The Negro and the United Mine Workers of America: The Career and Letters of Richard L. Davis and Something of Their Meaning: 1890-1900," in *The Negro and the American Labor Movement*, ed. Julius Jacobson (Garden City, NY: Anchor Books/Doubleday & Company, 1968), 117.

location had something to recommend it for the purposes of carrying out research, but lest that sound too selfish a reason, let me confess that my first two research trips to the Crescent City took place in the month of August, a time when no one in their right mind would want to visit.)

What I found in New Orleans made for a dramatic story. The docks witnessed the rise and fall of two interracial labor federations—the Cotton Men's Executive Council in the 1880s and the Dock and Cotton Council in the first two decades of the twentieth century. They were also the site of a number of massive, interracial strikes, as well as brutal and bloody race riots in which white dock workers sought to drive their black competitors off the docks. But what explained both the interracialism *and* the violence? How was it that New Orleans dock workers managed alternately to both uphold *and* violate the tenets of the emerging Jim Crow order in the South? *Waterfront Workers of New Orleans* sought to answer these and other questions. As I learned, I was hardly the first to explore race and labor relations on the city's docks. If it was Gutman's concluding section in his Richard Davis essay that first alerted me to interracialism on the waterfront, I soon discovered terrific material in master's theses and dissertations on the city; Sterling Spero and Abram Harris had investigated the port in the late 1920s; and Jim Stodder and Dave Wells's 1976 *Radical America* essay highlighted joint action between black and white dock workers.[38] These works chronicled the story of the ups and downs of waterfront unionism and provided an indispensable guide to my own research. All of them came

---

38.   For examples see Raymond Arthur Pierce, "The Rise and Decline of Labor in New Orleans (master's thesis, Tulane University, 1938); Carroll George Miller, "*A Study of the New Orleans Longshoremen's Union* From 1850 to 1962" (master's thesis, Louisiana State University Press, 1962); David Paul Bennetts, "Black and White Workers: New Orleans, 1880-1900" (PhD diss., University of Illinois at Urbana-Champaign, 1972); Sterling Spero and Abram Harris, *The Black Worker: The Negro and the Labor Movement* (1931; repr., New York: Atheneum, 1969); Dave Wells and Jim Stodder, "A Short History of New Orleans Dockworkers," *Radical America* 10, no. 1 (January-February 1976).

out of an earlier historiographical and political tradition; none drew inspiration from the new labor history or addressed Gutman's desire for a history of race and labor relations at the grassroots level. The works provided a roadmap that allowed me to pursue a different set of issues.

So to return to my earlier questions: What explained both the interracialism *and* the violence? How was it that New Orleans dock workers managed alternately to both uphold *and* violate the tenets of the emerging Jim Crow order in the South? One answer that was not persuasive was that of "New Orleans Exceptionalism" — the notion that the city of jazz was somehow profoundly different, somehow more open to the promiscuous intermingling of the races, leading to interracial collaboration. To some extent, yes, the lines dividing black and white were more fluid, as they were in a number of older cities examined by C. Vann Woodward so many decades ago, at least until the 1880s and 1890s. But New Orleans whites could be as vicious as their counterparts in the rest of the New South; they rioted, lynched, segregated, and otherwise excluded African Americans in much of the period I examined. The answer, I suggested, was rooted not so much in "culture" but in the politics and economics of the South's most important port city.

On the politics front, a Democratic Party machine, heavily dependent upon the votes of the city's white working class, extended a degree of support — or at least neutrality — to the city's white unions, allowing them to violate certain tenets of the emerging segregationist order if it was to their advantage to do so. My book also made the case that the existence of large and strong black unions was a crucial variable: they forced unskilled whites to negotiate equitable deals or risk the consequences of not doing so. Black longshore labor's availability, ability, and determination to work, coupled with employers' incentive to retain a racially divided labor force, made it impossible for whites to seek the solution that so many other white unionists had resorted to: the exclusion of blacks from their trades altogether. The only alternative to division and powerlessness lay in inter-trade and biracial collaboration.

So New Orleans dock workers established biracial labor associations. But what, precisely, did that mean? This gets us "solidarity" question. Biracialism did not mean "equality" by any stretch of the imagination. Although dock workers' interracialism was impressive compared to the racially exclusionary tendencies of the city's white craft union federation, white union members were hardly immune to the ideology of white supremacy. On the plus side: in a number of waterfront crafts, whites and blacks divided available work equally; belonging to separate unions, they nonetheless received identical wages and observed identical work rules; they met regularly to debate strategy and ratify contracts. There were limits, however, beyond which whites would not go. Blacks may have served as vice presidents and secretaries of the Dock and Cotton Council, but whites always held the federation's presidency and held onto a majority of foremen's jobs. At no time would anyone admit of even a hint of "social equality," and whites certainly failed to support black workers' struggles against segregation and disfranchisement. There were elements of solidarity, but it was a highly circumscribed, imperfect solidarity, largely born of pragmatism, not idealism. That, I would argue, should hardly be surprising. In *Waterfront Workers* and in a variety of articles exploring biracial unionism elsewhere in the South,[39] I made a case for evaluating biracial unionism not in romantic terms or from the perspective of the late twentieth-century political

---

39.   Eric Arnesen, "Following the Color Line of Labor: Black Workers and the Labor Movement before 1930," *Radical History Review*, no. 55 (Winter 1993): 53-87; Arnesen, "'What's on the Black Worker's Mind?': African-American Labor and the Union Tradition on the Gulf Coast," *Gulf Coast Historical Review* 10, no. 1 (Fall 1994): 7-30; Arnesen, "'It ain't like they do in New Orleans': Race Relations, Labour Markets, and Waterfront Labour Movements in the American South, 1880-1923," in *Racism and the Labour Market: Historical Studies*, eds. Marcel Van Der Linden and Jan Lucassen (Bern: Peter Lang, 1995), 57-100; Arnesen, "Biracial Waterfront Unionism in the Age of Segregation," 19-61.

sensibilities, but rather for evaluating it from the perspective of black workers themselves. They were hardly unmindful of the inequalities it codified, but their goals did not include integration — as some historians seemed to believe. Instead, they appreciated biracial unionism for the opportunities it afforded and critiqued it for its inadequacies. What they did *not* do — at least not before the 1930s — was condemn it for its sanctioning of separate unions for blacks and whites.[40]

Waterfront Workers was one of many histories of race and labor and African American workers to emerge in the 1990s. One of the exciting things about working on the project was the company one kept: In graduate school, others were pursuing these issues in other geographical areas or economic sectors: Daniel Letwin explored miners in the Birmingham district, Karin Shapiro focused on miners and convict labor in East Tennessee, and Tera Hunter unearthed the world of domestic laborers in Atlanta. Simultaneously — and subsequently — others were engaging in comparable projects: Daniel Rosenberg's book on New Orleans labor preceded my own; Brian Kelley also took on Alabama miners; Alex Lichtenstein and Mary Ellen Curtin addressed southern convict labor; Kimberley Phillips explored black workers in Cleveland, while Joe Trotter did the same for Milwaukee, West Virginia, and elsewhere; Roger Horowitz, Rick Halpern, and Paul Street provided us with accounts of packinghouse workers and their unions; Michael Honey published several books on Memphis labor; Robin Kelley rehabilitated the Communist party in Alabama; Robert Korstad offered a fine-grained portrait of tobacco worker unionism in Winston Salem; and Timothy Minchin authored many books on more recent southern labor. That is but a very partial portrait; I have left off more names than I've included. My point is a simple one: Scholarship on race and labor has very much come of age.

This raises another question: What has that new literature

40.   This is an argument I developed most thoroughly in Arnesen, "Following the Color Line of Labor."

done to alter or enrich our understanding of southern or American labor history? That is a harder matter to assess, but my impressionistic view is that, for all of the richness of the scholarship, scholars of race and labor have done remarkably little to alter the broader contours of the historical narrative.

A place to start is American history textbooks. In what follows, I focus on the years between Reconstruction's demise and the Great War, a period well explored by the monographic literature on black workers, race, and labor. Most texts contain the obligatory "New South" section; industry and agriculture are described, as are "race relations." In most accounts readers will encounter references to "the nadir" and Booker T. Washington and W. E. B. Du Bois make their appearance, their "debate" framing the outlines of black politics in the age of segregation. Interracialism may come up in the brief considerations of southern Populism and the People's Party, but rarely in other contexts. Let me offer several specific examples. *Liberty, Equality, Power: A History of the American People* contains a section on "African American Labor and Community" which consists of a few paragraphs on late nineteenth-century sharecropping, a mention of black workers in industrial pursuits and in service jobs, and a reference to black businessmen and women. It then jumps forward in time to the World War I era Great Migration. Period. The more recent *American Stories* by H. W. Brands, et al., mentions the NAACP and employment discrimination; we learn that "[f]ew blacks belonged to labor unions."[41] Period. The Darlene Clark Hine, et al., text, *The African-American Odyssey*, does have a chapter entitled "Black Southerners Challenge White Supremacy."[42] Booker T.

41.   H. W. Brands, T.H. Breen, R. Hal Williams, and Ariela J. Gross, *American Stories: A History of the United States* (New York: Pearson Longman, 2009), 599.

42.   Darlene Clark Hine, William C. Hine, and Stanley Harrold, *The African-American Odyssey*, 2nd ed., vol. 2, *Since 1865* (Upper Saddle River, NJ: Prentice Hall, 2003): 335-63.

Washington and Tuskegee Institute figure prominently, as do black churches, Buffalo Soldiers, black cowboys, blacks in the Navy and in the Army in the Philippines, black businesspeople and entrepreneurs, black professionals, black musicians, and blacks athletes. And black labor is not wholly ignored—the subject gets a page. Readers learn that the Knights of Labor counted among its members 70,000 black workers, the United Mine Workers maybe 20,000. The Reconstruction-era black labor activist Isaac Myers receives a sentence, as does the Progressive Era Industrial Workers of the World. In one of the four paragraphs devoted to strikes, we learn that black "stevedores" "periodically went on strike in Charleston, Savannah, and New Orleans."[43] Presumably drawing (weakly) on Tera Hunter's fine study of black women in Atlanta, the section concludes: "Though the strike [of washerwomen in 1881] gradually ended without having achieved its goal, it did demonstrate that poor black women could organize effectively." How failure to achieve goals and the subsequent disintegration of the very short-lived union constitute an "effective" demonstration of organization is never explained.[44] The following chapter on "Conciliation, Agitation, and Migration" in the early twentieth century tells us a lot about Booker T. Washington again, his rival Du Bois and the NAACP, and, to round things out, the black club women's movement. Here black workers are mentioned specifically in a sentence as the strikebreakers whose presence provoked the 1917 East St. Louis race riot and, in a paragraph on the black sharecroppers who fell victim to the massacre and legal repression in Elaine, Arkansas, in 1919.[45] The Clayborne Carson, et al., text, *African American Lives: The Struggle for Freedom*, contains a page and a half on unions, including three paragraphs

---

43.   Ibid., 354.

44.   Ibid., 355. Also see Hunter, *To 'Joy My Freedom*.

45.   Ibid., 387. The brief section on black migration to the urban North during World War I does quote one black South Carolinian about his ability to make more money in the North and one short paragraph mentions black workers in Chicago meatpacking plants in 1919, job competition, and the ensuing riot. (p. 392)

on the Knights of Labor, whose black membership now drops to 60,000, as well as three paragraphs on Lucy Parsons and the Haymarket bombing and trial (an extremely odd selection, given limited space). This top-down account features a few atypical individuals and union policy; *nothing* reflects the aspirations, visions, or practices of black laborers themselves.[46] For the early twentieth century, there is a bit of coverage of black club women, black soldiers, Du Bois and the NAACP, a bit on culture, the National Urban League, churches, sports, and charismatic leaders; the page and a half on "New Charismatic leaders" offers a paragraph on the black radical A. Philip Randolph.[47] Finally, there is the latest edition (the 9th) of John Hope Franklin's classic *From Slavery to Freedom*, with Evelyn Brooks Higginbotham as the new co-author. Chapter 12, "The Color Line," explores the post-Reconstruction Era, though it only has one paragraph on "employment and unions" in a subsection called "Confronting the Urban Color Line," and one sentence

46.   Clayborne Carson, Emma J. Lapsansky-Werner, and Gary B. Nash, *The Struggle for Freedom: A History of African Americans* (New York: Pearson Longman, 2007), 300-302.

47.   Carson et al, *The Struggle for Freedom*, 311-38, 332. As a biographer of Randolph, I confess to more than a little discomfort with the mangling of his biography in the single paragraph devoted to him here and cannot resist mentioning some examples. Randolph graduated from Cookman Institute in Jacksonville, not Daytona; he did not teach economics at City College; his belief that the "U.S. economy needed overhauling—but not overthrowing" is a mischaracterization; his wife was hardly a "wealthy widow" and she at times worked for, but was not a partner of, Madame C. J. Walker; and Randolph had not yet "built a small but dedicated following by 1915." (p. 332) The subsequent chapter covering the World War I years to the Great Depression mentions southern migrants seeking economic opportunity and new economic opportunities in the North. It mistakenly places the 1917 East St. Louis race riot in 1916 (p. 346) and mentions A. Philip Randolph as an example of rare black support for radicalism and the formation of the Brotherhood of Sleeping Car Porters in 1925 (p. 348)—although, for comparative purposes, I should note that this occurred after the period I am discussing here. The claim that "[in] many unions, the members embraced the communist belief that socioeconomic differences posed a far greater problem than racial differences did" would have been a surprise to both union members and communists alike. Ibid.

incorrectly tells us that "[o]nly" two unions— the cigarmakers and mine workers—"seemed to welcome African Americans into membership." In the following chapter on the "Era of Self-Help," we learn about philanthropy, women's activism, intellectual and cultural endeavors, and social and economic striving. That coverage of economic striving consisted of yet more on Tuskegee, the Exodusters of 1879, interest in African colonization, entrepreneurs and bankers, and two paragraphs on black workers in the industrial pursuits of the New South and service jobs. From this account, a reader would never know that a generation or more of rich scholarship on race and labor or on African American workers' aspirations and activism even existed.[48]

Perhaps the problem comes from the textbook format: So much information, so few pages. (And, as faculty members will complain, fewer and fewer, for over the years, they discern a tendency for students to read less and less, a tendency addressed by the increased popularity of abridged or concise editions of textbooks). Perhaps textbook authors might respond that they just can't fit it all in. Given page limits insisted on by publishers, this would undoubtedly ring true. But it's an argument that those who believe that issues of race and labor are not merely afterthoughts would reject. In the larger scheme of things, the complicated black labor tradition

---

48.   John Hope Franklin and Evelyn Brooks Higginbotham, *From Slavery to Freedom: A History of African Americans*, 9th ed. (New York: McGraw Hill, 2011), 308. The following chapter, "In Pursuit of Democracy," mentions black migration and new urban jobs and, in a sentence, mentions that "African Americans organized several unions of their own" and citing one example—the shortly-lived, obscure, and inconsequential Associated Colored Employees of America. It misleadingly states that the AFL in 1917 "began to express sympathy for workers of all races" though accurately notes that black leaders' deliberations with the AFL came to naught. (p. 349) In a paragraph on the *Messenger* magazine's opposition to World War I, the ninth edition wrongly asserts that Randolph and Chandler Owen were sentenced to two and a half years in jail for the publication of an anti-war essay. (p. 346) The Industrial Workers of the World, the radical union which rejected all racial barriers, is erroneously called the "International Workers of the World." (p.369)

that embraced tens of thousands of African American workers strikes me as deserving more treatment than Buffalo Soldiers, as important as they are.

What about scholars writing for other scholars or the educated public whose work is not hemmed in by textbook publishers' global word limits; can we expect more of them when it comes to absorbing the most recent scholarship? Here too you can look and, alas, strain your eyes. Edward Ayers wasn't much interested in black labor per se in his grand sweeping study of the New South. Leon Litwack's magisterial *Trouble in Mind* offers a few pages at most to acknowledge a generation of scholarship, tagging it on to his story, while Pulitzer Prize winner Steven Hahn is more interested in proto-nationalists in the agrarian South whose forms of resistance are less organized and more subterranean and, presumably, radical.[49] Historian Stephen Tuck's sweeping 2010 study, *We Ain't What We Ought to Be*, is a little more attentive to labor issues, acknowledging that in the post-Reconstruction era, black southerners "continued to challenge the economic and political order." In a chapter entitled "Resisting the Juggernaut of White Supremacy, 1878-1906," we find passing reference to an 1877 washerwomen's strike in Galveston, a joining together of black and white coal miners in Alabama for "higher pay and against convict leasing," an 1880 sugar workers' strike in Louisiana, and the 1881 Atlanta washerwomen's strike (in which, contrary to Hunter's account and the historical record, we learn that city officials "backed down.") Later, Tuck provides several compelling paragraphs on the 1887 Louisiana sugar strike and its brutal suppression, and to his credit, he briefly mentions the black mine worker organizer Richard Davis. In the following chapter, "Black Leaders Reckon with

49.   Edward Ayers, *The Promise of the New South: Life After Reconstruction* (New York: Oxford University Press, 1992), 284, 431; Leon F. Litwack, *Trouble in Mind: Black Southerners in the Age of Jim Crow* (New York: Alfred A. Knopf, 1998), 166-67; Steven Hahn, *A Nation Under Our Feet: Black Political Struggles in the Rural South from Slavery to the Great Migration* (Cambridge, MA: Harvard University Press, 2003).

Jim Crow, 1893-1916," there are two paragraphs on Booker T. Washington's accomodationist approach and its impact on Birmingham's black workers. And in the chapter on "Great War and Great Migration, 1917-1924," Tuck offers the most extensive treatment of any under consideration here: two-and-a-quarter pages centered on a rare moment in interracial solidarity in Bogalusa, Louisiana, in 1919, with mentions of Chicago's stockyards and biracial unionism in Birmingham and New Orleans.[50]

Two decades ago, I observed that the renaissance of scholarship in African American history in the 1960s and 1970s did little to illuminate the experiences of postbellum black workers outside of the agricultural realm. Those years witnessed the publication of numerous case studies of black communities — mostly in the North — during the decades after the Civil War. And while they paid attention to occupational structures, residential segregation, white racism, party politics, and struggles for civil rights, on whom did they focus? Their cast of characters was drawn overwhelmingly from the ranks of the black elite whose experiences could be more easily reconstructed from the paper trail they left behind. White trade unions were portrayed strictly as agents of discrimination, with black workers as their victims. Although the record of the union movement didn't provide too much evidence to the contrary, their white members, like their black victims, came off as one-dimensional. The real players were black elites.[51] I was once struck by the great historian of the African American experience, August Meier, who concluded in his 1963 classic, *Negro Thought in America*, that "[w]e have no direct evidence on what the [black] masses were thinking" during the late

---

50.   Stephen Tuck, *We Ain't What We Ought to Be: The Black Freedom Strug-gle from Emancipation to Obama* (Cambridge, MA: Belknap Press of Harvard University Press, 2010), 75-77, 88-89, 91, 153-55.

51.   Eric Arnesen, "The African-American Working Class in the Jim Crow Era," *International Labor and Working-Class History*, no. 41 (Spring 1992): 59-75.

nineteenth and early twentieth centuries.[52] That statement, shared by more historians than Meier, suggested to me that if labor history had a race problem, African American history had something of a class or labor problem. As it turned out, within the realm of scholarly monographs, his assertion had a short shelf-life: By the 1980s and certainly the 1990s, historians were disproving Meier's point in case study after case study of various cities (Detroit, Milwaukee, Chicago, New Orleans, Birmingham, Houston, Cleveland, Seattle, San Francisco, among others) and occupations (miners, timber and lumber workers, longshoremen, washerwomen and domestic workers, auto workers, railroaders, Pullman porters, and more). Yet beyond the specialized monographs, the assertion unfortunately has had a longer shelf life. One is hard pressed to discern the voices of black workers — their visions, aspirations, and organizations (at least when they fall outside of the older, conventional models) — in the multiplying classroom textbooks and academic and popular overviews. Those voices remain muffled at best or otherwise inaudible. Few overview works place the multiple studies of black labor activism near the heart of their story or even recognize the basic point, developed by a generation or two of scholarship, that tens of thousands of black labor activists in many southern states also represented a profound "challenge to Jim Crow" or at least to the New South. My point is not that all accounts should revolve around black workers to the exclusion or minimizing of other important themes. Rather, given the importance of race and labor in general and black workers in particular established by a substantial amount of scholarship, the subjects warrant a more prominent place in the narrative of the African American experience than they are currently accorded.

The paucity of coverage to issues of labor — whether of black labor activism or interracial/biracial activism — remains

52. August Meier, *Negro Thought in America 1880-1915* (Ann Arbor: University of Michigan Press, 1963), 208.

perplexing, given the rich scholarly vein available for popularizers to mine. Perhaps the general absence of labor issues can be attributable to the place that labor and labor history holds in our broader culture. The "democratization of the workplace, the solidarity of labor, and the social betterment of American workers once stood far closer to the center of the nation's political and moral consciousness" than they do today, Nelson Lichtenstein once observed.[53] Without proposing too direct a connection, let me suggest that while labor history may be flourishing as a subculture within the academy, the academy isn't exactly showcasing labor history. And as the fortunes of organized labor sink ever lower, it is plausible that labor's visibility in American history grows dimmer as well. Or perhaps the problem comes from a crude if persistent juxtaposing of something American academics call "class" and "race." It's one or the other. Race usually trumps class: The experience of African Americans, it is claimed, can be explained largely by their position within a racial order; their economic position is a reflection of their racial location. In an academic universe that in recent years has made multi-ethnic and multi-cultural (but not economic) diversity its cardinal value, it is not surprising that the subject of labor appears to some as old-fashioned, secondary, or even an afterthought. Since the civil rights revolution of the 1960s, "a transformation in law, custom, and ideology has made a once radical demand for racial and gender equality into an elemental code of conduct," Lichtenstein notes. Simultaneously, the "rights of workers, as workers . . . have moved well into the shadows."[54] Scholars' slighting of the labor dimension of African American history, then, may simply reflect the tenor of our times.

Or perhaps the story itself is too complicated or too messy to fit into the narratives scholars want to construct. Take interracial or biracial unionism, a prominent theme in the

53.   Nelson Lichtenstein, *State of the Unions: A Century of American Labor* (Princeton, NJ: Princeton University Press, 2002), 4.

54.   Lichtenstein, *State of the Unions*, 3.

scholarly literature on race and labor. It was, as I and others have argued, an imperfect vehicle for the pursuit of black workers' goals. In Gilded Age and Progressive Era New Orleans, for instance, the Cotton Men's Executive Council and its successor, the Dock and Cotton Council, advanced a vision of economic equality, at least in some trades. These union federations did not oppose Jim Crow laws; nor did they jointly object to disfranchisement. They specifically steered away from issues of political equality and explicitly rejected social equality. White dock workers may have consented to dividing work equally with their organized black counterparts, but they chafed at the notion of dividing foremen's positions equally with blacks. And the unions they formed were racially distinct; no move toward integration—the word rarely if ever came up—could be observed. Yet even with this imperfect vehicle, black and white dock workers managed to achieve a level of control over the labor process and win wage levels that exceeded those of most other ports. How do we understand this phenomenon and its accomplishments? Was it a challenge to segregation and Jim Crow? Not exactly—or maybe to some extent. Was it a vehicle for advancing black workers' interests? Black workers would have said so. Was there room for improvement? The historical record occasionally records black workers' voices suggesting yes. But the very imperfections embedded in the biracial structure meant that the kinds of celebrations that labor and African American historians like to engage in are harder to pull off. If one contrasts the compromises of the Dock and Cotton Council to the rhetorical purity of the Industrial Workers of the World, the IWW wins, hands down, at least in the historians' popularity polls. Jump ahead to the 1930s and contrast the Communist party's insistence on social equality with the hedged commitments of the Cotton Council (or even the Congress of Industrial Organizations' affiliates). There again, the radicals win, even if what they accomplished in practice, one might argue, pales in comparison to the Cotton Council's achievements.

The attacks on labor history in the 1980s and 1990s by Hill, Roediger, Nelson, and Ignatiev put the field on an unnecessary defensive. Hill was a relentless critic of white trade union practices and of any historian who didn't make condemnation of union racism the centerpiece of her or his arguments.[55] He set up, in my view, a false dichotomy—an accurate (if caricatured) portrait of an inherently flawed racist labor movement verses a false portrait allegedly advanced by new labor historians like Gutman who were ostensibly intent upon whitewashing labor's racist past and concocting a "useable past" based on an imagined, theoretically derived interracial unity. Hill, I have argued elsewhere, invented an opposition, attributing to it motives, arguments, and sensibilities it did not possess. But his invention had considerable staying power.[56] And those who explored interracial interactions that could not always be reduced to white hostility were placed on the defensive, where they largely remained. But Hill's wasn't the only challenge. Whiteness scholars had little patience for nuanced examinations of working-class race relations; white racial identity became whiteness, and whiteness became manifest in most everything white workers pursued. Hill, Nelson, Roediger, and others offered up a strong dose of moral indignation that, I've suggested elsewhere, measured scholarship and evaluated the past according to their own particular politics. That too is an argument I've countered behind podiums and in print. And while I think that I had the better of the arguments—I am, after all, a partisan, so that shouldn't be surprising—the whiteness school raised the level

55.   Herbert Hill, "Myth-Making as Labor History: Herbert Gutman and the United Mine Workers of America," *International Journal of Politics, Culture, and Society* 2, no. 2 (Winter 1988), 132-200; Hill, "The Problem of Race in American Labor History," *Reviews in American History* 24 (1996); Hill, "Lichtenstein's Fictions: Meany, Reuther and the 1964 Civil Rights Act," *New Politics* 7, no. 1, n. s. (Summer 1998); Hill, "Race and the Steelworkers Union: White Privilege and Black Struggle," *New Politics* 8, no. 4 n. s. (Winter 2002): 1-2.

56.   Eric Arnesen, "Passion and Politics: Race and the Writing of Working-Class History," *Journal of the Historical Society* 6, no. 3 (Fall 2006): 323-56.

of skepticism about the significance of the very movements that race and labor scholars were studying.

If one were to judge the health of the field by the number of case studies filling up our bookshelves, my earlier positive assessment of labor history would have to be revised to allow for an even more positive assessment. If labor history once had a race problem, a proposition I have questioned, it certainly doesn't have one today. When I began research for *Waterfront Workers* in 1981, and when my colleagues began their research on coal miners and domestic workers, we did not have a large historiography to build upon. Today, just try keeping up with the outpouring of scholarship. What was once a shortfall is now an embarrassment of riches. But for all of its richness, its sophistication, and its nuance, the field *does* currently have a problem: that of impact. The narratives and conclusions found in the case studies of the many scholars examining race and labor have yet to fundamentally transform, on a larger level, how we understand race and labor in southern or American history. The older narratives remain largely intact: Accomodationist Booker T. Washington vs. the militant W. E. B. Du Bois; the exclusionary practices of the AFL in the Age of Gompers. Yes, a number of new actors are allowed to enter the picture—club women, professionals, soldiers, and artists/writers, to name the most prominent—but their inclusion does little to disturb, much less transform, the older narrative.

The authors of *Stevedore* saw little need to respect the past or draw from actual history to frame their narrative. Because the history of the New Orleans waterfront was too imperfect, too complicated, and too compromised to serve effectively as the backdrop for their political tale, they impressed actual history into political service with considerable literary license. In their hands, the Crescent City's history had to be scrubbed and recast; without the erasure, they would have had a harder time advancing their political program of left-wing interracial unionism. Historians today do not necessarily share Peters's and Sklar's vision, but either consciously or unconsciously they also confront the problem of what to do with historical developments that do not conform to established paradigms. Unlike Peters and Sklar, they tend not to make things up. But when actual history does not quite conform to familiar narratives, they do what historians often do — they choose. Since they cannot do everything, they select the parts of the story that conform to the narratives they want to advance. Too often this involves ignoring or reducing to a passing reference or footnote the very complexity of African American workers' experiences. This, I would argue, does an injustice to the past and the men and women who lived and struggled through it. If the history of black labor is far richer and messier than the overviews would have us believe, our challenge is to insist on the incorporation of the newest and by now not-so-new scholarship that renders the standard narratives problematic and even misleading.

2 La Nouvelle Orléans: Rebuilding a Nascent City from the 1719 Flood to the 1794 Fire

CELINE UGOLINI

By looking at the early history of New Orleans, and particularly the repeated attempts to build and populate a city under extremely difficult conditions, this essay suggests two things. First, it examines the city's location, and particularly its susceptibility to storms and flooding, that have defined New Orleans from the very beginning. What this research finds is that the original founders chose reasonably well. New Orleans was vulnerable to storms and prone to flooding, but so too were the other alternatives, and few locations were as well situated in terms of strategic access to important waterways. The city was destroyed, or nearly destroyed, by weather and fire numerous times, offering its inhabitants and the colonial authorities multiple opportunities to cut and run. Instead, they chose to stay, recognizing the city's economic potential and strategic importance by continuing to invest in the city's future. Following the flood of 1719, supporters of promoting New Orleans to the rank of capital of the colony considered the flood a devastating event, but others, favoring places such as Mobile, Biloxi, or Natchez, saw the flood as an opportunity to abandon the town for good. Discussions about relocating the town to Bayou Manchac or Biloxi emerged, but New Orleans eventually pulled through.[1] The second point, is that the repeated experience with disasters and the resilience it instilled have been a defining feature of New Orleans's

1.   Lawrence N. Powell, *The Accidental City: Improvising New Orleans* (Cambridge, MA: Harvard University Press), 53.

history. Few cities have faced so many disasters during their formative years, an experience that pushed the limits of human and financial capacity, while at the same time making New Orleans the unique city it is today.

In the late 1600s and early 1700s, it was very difficult to get anyone to settle in the new French colony of Louisiana. This led to creative initiatives by colonial authorities. Among other tactics, they forced prisoners, prostitutes, and other convicts to move to Louisiana in order to both build the city and protect it from Spanish and English incursions. The French police were given significant incentives to apprehend citizens and ship them off to the colony.[2] Similarly, on November 16, 1716, Louis XV, King of France, by means of the regent, ordered that all

> commercial tradesmen of the ports of France, who send ships to the French colonies of America and New France in Canada, to board a certain number of volunteers . . . and to order that the said volunteers who know the professions of builder, stone cutter, blacksmith, locksmith, joiner, wet cooper, carpenter . . . and other professions useful in the colonies be sent in large numbers.[3]

As a result, in June 1718, several ships carrying three hundred immigrants and five hundred soldiers and convicts arrived, instantly doubling Louisiana's population. Involuntary Louisianans were usually treated as indentured servants,

2.   Gwendolyn Midlo Hall, "The Formation of Afro-Creole Culture," in *Creole New Orleans: Race and Americanization*, eds. Arnold R. Hirsch and Joseph Logsdon (Baton Rouge: Louisiana University Press, 1992), 62.

3.   All French to English translations done by author. Louis XIV, "Permission au Sieur de La Salle de découvrir la partie occidentale de la Nouvelle France," 12 May 1678, 2, Archives Nationales de France: Archives coloniales, correspondance à l'arrivée en provenance de la Louisiane, Tome I et II, The Historic New Orleans Collection at Williams Research Center, New Orleans. (hereafter cited as ANF)

working for three years before receiving their freedom and a small piece of land.

Authorities not only forced colonists to settle in Louisiana, but worked hard to insure they remained.

> [H]is Majesty, in agreement with the Regent Duke of Orleans, asserted and asserts that, all his subjects of whatever quality or condition they may be, should pay the price of their lives, if leaving the Kingdom without permission from his Majesty and signed by the Governor, Commander or Administrative Official of the said provinces.[4]

Additionally, each captain or ship owner should pay,

> one month after the arrival of their ship to the port of disembarkation, the amount of sixty livres for each volunteer they did not deliver to the said colonies, and for whom they did not bring a valid certificate. . . . And that for the skilled volunteers they did not deliver, they should pay the amount of one hundred and twenty livres.[5]

Despite these efforts, by 1727, New Orleans was still a very small settlement. The father of Ursuline nun Marie-Madeleine Hachard wrote in a letter to his daughter (October 27, 1727) that he had purchased a map of the colony in France that did not even show the city of New Orleans. As Marie-Madeleine Hachard noted, it was "not until 1723 [that] New Orleans beg[a]n to take on the appearance" of a town.[6]

---

4.   "Ordonnace du Roy, Portant Deffenses sous peine de la Vie, à tous Sujets du Roy de sortir du Royaume jusqu'au premier de Janiver prochain, sans Passeport ou Permission," 29 October 1720, 2, Kuntz Collection, Louisiana and Special Collections, Tulane University, New Orleans.

5.   Ibid.

6.   Letters from Marie-Madeleine Hachard Ursuline of New Orleans 1727-

Populating the colony of Louisiana was not the only challenge facing the area. According to a letter dated October 12, 1708, by Jean-Baptiste Le Moyne, Sieur de Bienville, the founder of New Orleans, early settlers faced troubles along the Gulf Coast to such extent that they were forced "to go to the Mississypy [*sic*] to live with the savages" until they could receive help from the mother country.[7] Furthermore, as for the Crescent City itself, "keeping the city dry, or separating the human-made environment from its natural endowment, has been the perpetual battle for New Orleans."[8] Most of the region sat below sea level, in a place surrounded by the lake on one side, the river on the other, and many swamps all over, making it particularly vulnerable to flooding. French colonists had no idea about this when they built New Orleans and other nearby settlements. Adrien de Pauger, for example, believed that the "Island of La Balise of which the land is strong and stable, [was] not subject to flooding, as you may have wrongly heard the contrary" and perfectly suitable for the establishment of a new city at an essential position by the mouth of the river.[9] His beliefs turned out to be inexact; La Balise encountered many devastating hurricanes shortly after its construction as described by Louis François Benjamin Dumont de Montigny, a French military officer, in the following poem:

We feel, during the winter, much cold;
To the contrary, in the summer we endure the heat; (…)
However, almost everyday, we hear the sound of thunder
Which, by its frequent strikes, threatens this land,

1728, Louisiana Historical Center at the Old U.S. Mint, New Orleans. (hereafter cited as LHC).

7.   Bienville, Letter to the Ministre, 12 October 1708, ANF.

8.   Craig Colten, *An Unnatural Metropolis: Wresting New Orleans From Nature* (Baton Rouge: Louisiana State University Press, 2006), 2.

9.   Adrien de Pauger, "Letter to the directors of the Company of the Indies," 29 May 1724, 4, ANF.

And what can be surprising, is, that every seven years,
We feel in this country, vigorous wind blows.
It seems, at that instant, that the world is coming to an
end;
Each person feels this pain, a deep sorrow
Grabs each person's mind. This relentless wind
Knocks over houses (…)
The strongest trees fall on the ground; (…)
Rain falls as a river so that
One cannot leave his house;
One fears to be drowned, rightfully.
Happy is the one who, during this storm,
Is not at sea, in a voyage
He would be much to pity, the one onboard a boat,
Seeing all around him, precipice and gravesite,
Unable to dock, anywhere by the bank,
Being at the mercy of the water and the storm.[10]

La Balise was the first French settlement in the area of the Mississippi River's mouth. Today, it would be located in Plaquemines Parish, at the very southern tip of Louisiana. Ships could, at La Balise, unload and transfer their goods to smaller barges to be delivered to New Orleans.[11] In 1723, Pauger wrote that La Balise "was eaten by hurricanes to the point of being cut and having only a strip of land as peninsula . . . covered with weeds and salt water springs left."[12]

The location of the future city of New Orleans made it a vulnerable place, yet a very strategic one for future

10.   Louis François Benjamin Dumont de Montigny, *Poème en vers touchant l'établissement de la province de la Louisiane, connue sous le nom de Mississipy avec tout ce qui s'est passé de depuis* [sic] *1716, jusqu'à 1742: Le massacre des François au poste des Natchez, les Moeurs des Sauvages, leurs danses, leurs Religions, enfin ce qui concerne le pays en général*, LHC.

11.   Shannon Dawdy, *Building the Devil's Empire: French Colonial New Orleans* (Chicago: University of Chicago Press, 2009), 111.

12.   Adrien de Pauger, "Letter to the commissioners of the Company of the Indies" Ile de la Balise, 23 September 1723, 3, ANF.

transportation and commercial development. Despite its numerous inconveniences and hostile swamps and marshlands, the French almost immediately coveted the sector. They rapidly realized the potential wealth of a city at such a location. Situated near the mouth of a river that had the capacity to be used for transportation all the way to the northern end of Louisiana and towards the Canadian parts of New France, the city had great promise.

According to geographer Richard Campanella, "[t]he proximate cause motivating the foundation of New Orleans was the need for a convenient port . . . [and] the ultimate cause was the French imperial need to defend their Louisiana claim by fortifying its Mississippi River Basin gateway."[13] Despite all the existing challenges of building a city in such an uncertain environment, the plans proceeded. One month into the process, Jean-Baptiste Bénard de La Harpe, a French explorer and military officer observed that

> in March 1718 . . . the building of the city of *La Nouvelle Orléans* started . . . in a uniform and swampy land only proper to rice culture; the water and the river coming to the surface from below the earth and the crawfish being abundant, making all sorts of tobacco and vegetable growing a difficult matter. Fog is a common feature of the region, and as the land is covered with wood and canebrakes, the air becomes feverish and one suffers from an enormous amount of mosquitoes during the summer months.[14]

As Campanella asked, "[s]hould a settlement be built on the safest site, despite its inconvenience? Or should it exploit

13.   Richard Campenella, *Bienville's Dilemma: A Historical Geography of New Orleans* (Lafayette: UL Lafayette Press, 2008), 110.

14.   Marc de Villiers du Terrage, *Histoire de la fondation de la Nouvelle-Orléans 1717-1722*, preface by Gabriel Hanotaux, (Paris: Imprimerie Nationale, 1917), 24.

the most strategic situation, despite its risk?"[15] The fact that, according to Lewis, today "a million people work and make a living on this evil site only emphasizes the excellence of the situation. There is no contradiction. If a city's situation is good enough, its site will be altered to make do."[16] Thus, early in 1718, Bienville reached the area "with six vessels, loaded with provisions . . . thirty workmen, all convicts; six carpenters and four Canadians."[17] The French decided on exploiting a strategic location, despite the risk involved. Pauger saw in the colony of Louisiana an incredible potential from his very arrival. In 1724, he wrote that

> the mouth of the river St Louis[18] . . . in my opinion, . . . [which is located at] such a favorable position, that if a similar situation would happen in France, and that the King would do me the honor of putting me in charge of establishing a post making sure to budget proportional spending according to the size of the post, I would put what is dearest to me on the fact that, in as little as one to two years I would make it a magnificent port.[19]

Disasters

In 1719, the Mississippi River flooded the area, almost completely destroying the nascent city. The flood was seen as indication that the town would not survive, and all building

15.   Campanella, *Bienville's Dilemma*, 15.

16.   Lewis, *New Orleans*, 17.

17.   Shannon Lee Dawdy, *Madame John's Legacy Revisited: A Closer Look at the Archeology of Colonial New Orleans* (University of New Orleans, 1998), 26.

18.   The "River St. Louis" was the name given by the French to the Mississippi River in honor of the patron saint of France, and also as a reminder of Louis IX, nicknamed St. Louis.

19.   Adrien de Pauger, Letter to the directors of the Company of the Indies, 29 May 1724, 2-3, ANF.

work on New Orleans was initially ordered to be stopped.[20] Yet, that same year, five hundred slaves arrived from Africa to further develop the promising colony. Regardless of setbacks, New Orleans was still seen as one of the most valuable places within the colony. Pauger was particularly convinced of the importance of keeping the port city: "New Orleans . . . the mouth of the river, and . . . Mobile . . . [are] the three main posts, or fundamental glue that keeps this colony together." [21]

Indeed, as Richard Campanella notes, the location of New Orleans could not have been better. If the site is prone to flooding, its access to water, and hence transportation, is its very strength.[22] Had New Orleans been built further south or east, it would have encountered flooding, yet lost its strategic location; had it been situated further north, it would have been on higher ground, but too far upriver to take advantage of coastal traffic. In short, the current location for this "impossible but inevitable city" was wisely chosen.[23]

The first hurricane ever recorded in the history of New Orleans took place on September 11, 1722. Since most houses were "of a poor quality, made of wood" they were easily destroyed.[24] Most "were low frame structures, bricked between posts and roofed with cypress shingles . . . *briqueté entre poteaux.*"[25] At the time of the hurricane, many settlers described it in letters sent to the home country as a "great

20.   Powell, *The Accidental City*, 51.

21.   Adrien de Pauger, Letter to the directors of the Company of the Indies, 2, ANF.

22.   Campanella, *Bienville's Dilemma*, 113-14.

23.   Peirce Lewis, *New Orleans: The Making of an Urban Landscape* (Charlottesville, VA: University of Virginia Press, 2003), 17.

24.   Martine Geronimi, *Québec et la Nouvelle-Orléans: Paysages imaginaires français en Amérique du Nord* (Paris: Editions Belin, 2003), 57.

25.   Stanley Clisby Arthur, *Old New Orleans: A History of the Vieux Carré, its Ancient and Historical Buildings* (Harmanson, 1936), 10. This observation was also found in Professor Edward J. Cazayoux's work at the School of Art and Architecture of the University of Louisiana at Lafayette.

wind" that lasted for hours and demolished everything on its path. [26] It was called "one of the most terrible hurricane storms."[27] The hurricane "destroyed at least two-thirds of the houses," many boats on the river were sunk, and residents had "to rebuild the church, the presbyter, [and] the hospital."[28]

While few accounts of the 1722 hurricane exist, one existent source is a poem by Dumont de Montigny, counting how strongly the city was impacted and damaged, and how its residents rebuilt a stronger town following this tragic event:

(…) in September, a horrible storm
And, to explain it better, a terrible hurricane,
Which appeared suddenly, petrified locals,
And knocked over houses. In addition to the wind and dust,
Hail appeared in such way
That it generated everyone's fear, in this despairing moment,
That we will receive our last judgement (…)
Each person was to be pitied in his sorrowful fate.
This wind did not last only for one day;
During three entire days, we suffered from the storm,
And material losses produced many tears
From those affected by this blow.
On the fourth day, the storm ceased,
And the nice weather came back, and filled us with joy.
We started rebuilding,
Encouraging each other like good apostles;
We rebuilt so well, that this establishment
Became suitable to welcome Bienville and his agents.[29]

26.   Le Blond de La Tour, "Sur le houragan arrivé a la Louisiane, Et l'Estat ou il a mis la nouvelle orleans," 1, ANF.

27.   Ibid.

28.   Ibid.

29.   Dumont de Montigny, *Poème Louisiane*, LHC.

According to de La Tour, all the existing buildings in New Orleans at the time of the 1722 storm "were temporary and old,"[30] not a single one was in the alignment of the new town, and they were to have been pulled down."[31] The storm therefore provided an opportunity to flatten the ground and rebuild a stronger town.

Major hurricanes also hit Louisiana in 1732 and 1733. In July 1733, "on the seventeenth of that month at nine o'clock in the morning we saw the beginning of a great wind blow that lasted for about thirty hours."[32] Although it was described as less violent than the one which hit the city the year before, "it caused . . . much damage to tobacco crops . . . cotton crops suffered a lot and corn were ruptured and laid flat on the ground."[33] On top of the hurricane, 1733 brought "very abundant rainfalls that had poured for over forty days beforehand and almost consecutively and which had succeeded a drought of almost two months [at a time when] we had not forgotten about last year's misery yet."[34] Because of recurring disasters many "residents either ask[ed] for their right of passage to France . . . [or] s[old] their homes in order to move up north to the Illinois country."[35]

Edme Gatien Salmon, chief of the police of Louisiana, seemed very concerned by the threat of colonists leaving New Orleans to go up north to higher grounds. He expressed his concerns in a letter asking France what the country had planned "in order for the colony not to be abandoned by its inhabitants" and what kind of financial assistance would

---

30.   The word "old" must have been used in relative terms, maybe in comparison to other settlements nearby, as New Orleans was only four years "old" at the time de La Tour wrote this.

31.   De Villiers, *History of New Orleans*, 236.

32.   Salmon, Lettre au Ministre, 1, ANF.

33.   Ibid., 1-2.

34.   Ibid., 2-3.

35.   Ibid., 3.

be put into place as to avoid this possibility.[36] Salmon, after the 1733 hurricane, and in the face of the city's precarious situation, was forced "not only to take loans on merchandise but also on money in order to help rebuild the houses that were destroyed because of the hurricane."[37]

After the city was finally rebuilt and started to recuperate, a[n] "extraordinary wind blow . . . was . . . violently felt during twenty-four hours" in 1739, and caused much damage to the city and the crops.[38] According to the United States's Agricultural Department Monthly Weather Review and Annual Summary, dated October 1893, there were almost half a dozen hurricanes in the area before the end of the eighteenth century, among which a particularly destructive one hit in late August of 1772.

The validity of building a city in such an unstable environment has always been questioned. Despite the disasters, however, the location for the city could not have been more suitable, considering the possible options in the surrounding areas. Protecting the city became a rightful purpose or even a leitmotiv for New Orleanians over time and each resident was involved in this process. Building and maintaining the levees officially became the responsibility of each inhabitant after the harvest season from 1792.[39] Fines were in place for those who did not maintain their levees. Additionally, the same ordinance forced residents to send their slaves for the repair of levees within the city. Not surprisingly, slave owners did not approve of the measure because it deprived them of their workforce. One was also obliged to inform the government should they not have the capability to maintain their own levees, which resulted in residents having

36.   Ibid.

37.   Ibid., 10-11.

38.   Chevalier De Louboey, Lettre au Ministre, 1, ANF.

39.   Governor Carondelet's Levee Ordinance of 1792, LHC, from the certified copy in the archives of the Louisiana State Museum, New Orleans, donated by the late Miss Kate Minor.

to relinquish their land after the harvest season. This gave landowners considerable incentive to maintain the levees.

In addition to the numerous storms, New Orleans also faced two major fires in the eighteenth century that completely reshaped the city. The fires broke out during the Spanish colonial period and changed the look of the city from a frail French colony to a stronger settlement that was no longer French in appearance, yet not quite Spanish. Both fires gave the Spanish an opportunity to remodel New Orleans and to leave their imprint on the colony. Yet, no Spaniards were among the architects who designed the new city. They were mostly French-Creole, with some local Anglo-Americans. They rebuilt the city using "maritime-French and French-Canadian architectural tradition, enriched with a few elements from the Anglo-American design stream."[40] As a result, the newly built city raised from its ashes as a completely new and innovative architectural style reflecting the melting pot created within the city's population. The city no longer looked entirely French, neither did it look Spanish or American, or entirely Creole or Canadian. The city became singular in its own right. The name French Quarter, however, remained and still does today as a reminder of the French presence and ties to the city. "Spanish ownership failed to make Louisiana or New Orleans Spanish in culture, language, or architecture,"[41] notes Jerah Johnson.

The site of the first fire was at 538 Chartres Street, in a private chapel belonging to Don Vincente José Nunez. It happened "while candles were burning before a shrine, [as] a gust of wind blew the window curtains against the lighted tapers. A few moments later the whole house was ablaze . . . four-fifths of the populated section of the city was reduced to ashes, including the parish church and house, the *Casa Capitular* [today known as the Cabildo, the seat of the Spanish government], and city

40.   Jerah Johnson, "Colonial New Orleans: A Fragment of the Eighteenth-Century French Ethos," in *Creole New Orleans*, eds. Hirsch and Logsdon, 51.

41.   Ibid., 51.

jail."[42] According to one account,

> the fire started approximately at the centre of the city.
> The southern wind, blowing with great violence at
> the time, spread the fire so much that it developed
> immediately in several places . . . the fear generated
> by the explosion of gun powder, that several residents,
> had been incautiously keeping at their home, despite
> the orders of the government, frightened even the
> most intrepid. . . . To relate all the horror of this fire
> and the impossibility to stop its progress, it is enough
> to say that in less than five hours, eight hundred and
> fifty-six buildings were turned into ashes, among
> which were all commercial buildings but three; and
> the small amount of items saved, were taken by
> looters.[43]

The structures right on the river-front were spared, but around
fifty percent of the city vanished.

"What a spectacle it was the next morning! To see in place of a
flourishing town, smoking debris and piles of ruins."[44] Seventy
percent of the city's 4,500 residents became homeless overnight
and Jackson Square, formerly the *Place d'Armes*, became a giant
campsite with tents for the displaced. In an account of the
fire dated March 21, 1788, the unknown author mentions that
"[i[f in such an excessive and general affliction one thing can
diminish our pain, is that not one individual perished in the
confusion and disorder inevitable in such encounters."[45]

Then, according to George Washington Cable:

42.   Arthur, *Old New Orleans*, 120.

43.   "Relation de l'Incendie qu'a éprouvé la ville de la Nouvelle-Orléans, le 21
mars 1788," 1-3, Kuntz Collection.

44.   "Relation de l'Incendie qu'a éprouvé la ville de la Nouvelle-Orléans, le 21
mars 1788," 3, Kuntz Collection.

45.   Ibid.

Six years later, fate made room again for improvement. On the 8th of December, 1794 — the wind was this time from the north-some children, playing in a court in Royale Street, too near an adjoining hay-store, set fire to the hay . . . in three hours — for the houses were mere tinder — again burned out of the heart of the town two hundred and twelve stores and buildings. . . . Only two stores were left standing; the levee and the square again became the camping-ground of hundreds of inhabitants, and the destruction of provisions threatened a famine.[46]

The second fire broke out in 1794, again during the Spanish colonial period; consequently the city's new architectural type became more of a Creole and distinctive style rather than the French it had been before. The second fire destroyed fewer houses than the one of 1788 but its financial damage to the city was greater. Following the fire, having realized the vulnerability of the city not only to natural disasters such as hurricanes, floods, and other storms, but also to the weak nature of the structures that were built, the governor of Louisiana, the Baron de Carondelet "ordained that all homes in the center of the city, built more than one story high, be constructed of brick" and ground oyster shells were used in order to level the streets' pavements and ease pedestrians as well as carriages' paths through the city.[47] As the city was rebuilt, "the tile roof came into general use. As the town's central parts filled up again, it was with better structures, displaying . . . adobe or brick walls, arcades, inner courts, ponderous doors and windows, heavy iron bolts and gratings . . . balconies, portes-cochères, and white and yellow lime-washed stucco. . . . Two-story dwellings took the place of one-story, and the general appearance, as well as

46.   George Washington Cable, "Under Three Flags," in *The World from Jackson Square: A New Orleans Reader* (Clinton, MA: The Colonial Press, Inc., 1948), 56.

47.   Arthur, *Old New Orleans*, 11.

public safety, was enhanced."[48] The two fires had the result of improving the city's defense against future conflagrations. Buildings were more resistant from that point on.

Despite the adversity brought upon the colony, local residents displayed resilience over time and proved that disasters can actually have an overall positive outcome, boost, and possibly brighten a city's fate. The amount of disasters faced by the city over the years is uncountable, routinely raising the question of whether the city should be rebuilt, moved, or better protected. It is the singularity of that experience, of rebuilding and resilience, which characterizes the Crescent City and which is today transpiring once again in the aftermath of Hurricane Katrina.

48.   Washington Cable, "Under Three Flags," 56.

3

Mobility Is Built in the Market: Black Women and Markets in New Orleans Before 1820.[1]

DEMETRI DEBE

In an otherwise typical day in the levee market in mid-April of 1771, a tiff between two chefs brought to light an important aspect of the way that the streets and public markets of New Orleans functioned. That day, Rene Chouteau claimed, in public, to have been told by an unnamed black woman on the levee that Bernardo Shiloc had put poison in his pastries and that they made people ill. Shiloc responded to this accusation by taking Chouteau to court seeking damages.[2] He claimed Chouteau's statement was slanderous and that it had hurt his business. In the trial, the black woman who spoke to Chouteau remains nameless — we do not know who she was, what she was doing in the market — buying, selling, or both — or whether or not she was a free woman. All we know is that she spoke to Chouteau, and two enslaved women, Maniche and Rosa, who worked for Shiloc.[3]

1.   I presented earlier versions of this paper at the New Orleans Labor Studies Conference II at Tulane University in April of 2011 and at the University of Minnesota's Early American History Workshop in October of 2011. My heartfelt thanks goes to the participants of both; this paper (and the author) has gained much from their careful readings, suggestions, and advice.

2.   Shiloc and Chouteau's disagreement may have had an element of ethnic conflict. Since the 1760s, there had been considerable friction between longtime French denizens of New Orleans and the relatively new Spanish arrivals. The conflict reached its zenith in 1768 when the Spanish governor was forced to flee New Orleans by French New Orleanians.

3.   "Criminal Suit for Slander. Bernardo Shiloc vs. René Chouteau Pastry-Cook," 20 April 1771, *Index to Spanish Judicial Records of Louisiana, Louisiana Historical Quarterly* 8, no. 2 (1925), 324–28; It is worth noting that Chouteau, a

This episode helps to illustrate how the work of enslaved black marketing women and domestics was deeply imbricated into the operation of the New Orleans marketplace. This applies to the local public markets and street vending, as well as to owners who relied upon their domestic slaves to function as agents for their owners in everyday matters. Through their often autonomous labor in the local markets, black women also enabled New Orleans to function in the Greater Caribbean and Atlantic markets, both legal and illegal.[4] This meant that enslaved women who conducted business in the city had to have autonomy in order for their owners to make money in a functioning market. In doing this, they moved through and around the city with little, and sometimes no, oversight. Such women had both the opportunity and skills to make their own money and exercise mobility within the slave system.

Colonists in early New Orleans introduced enslaved people, and both took advantage of their existing skills or promoted more specialized training. Slave owners did this not only to have enough labor to make land settlement profitable, but also to lower the wages and take the place of skilled European artisans. This, in turn, helped to increase profitability for planters and business owners in their ventures both in and outside of the law.[5] Having a skill could cut both ways for an enslaved woman. While this skill sometimes allowed her to

---

long time resident of New Orleans, could see a black woman in the market and not know who she was tends to support the idea that there were many black women in the market. The population of New Orleans at the time is estimated at 3,000. John Clark, *New Orleans 1718-1812: An Economic History* (Baton Rouge: Louisiana State University Press, 1970), 251.

4.   In this paper I will use two terms that are roughly analogous. These are "circum-Caribbean" and "Greater Caribbean." In so doing I am supporting a more regional approach to the area, rather than an interpretation that divides the geography according to colonial claims. The circum or Greater Caribbean region stretched from roughly the Carolina and Georgia Low Country, down through Mexico, Central America, and Brazil, and includes the islands in the Caribbean.

5.   Shannon Lee Dawdy, *Building the Devil's Empire: French Colonial New Orleans* (Chicago: University of Chicago Press, 2009), 104–10.

make her own money and save towards the purchase of her freedom, it also made her purchase price higher because she was more valuable as a marketable commodity. This made self-purchase or other roads to freedom more difficult.

Much of the literature on enslaved people being trained as skilled laborers has considered trade workers such as blacksmiths, sailors, horse teamsters, or carpenters. These are almost exclusively male-dominated trades. Work in these trades often required men to be mobile. Women, by contrast, were thought to be confined to the house or the plantation, with little mobility or autonomy. This would have placed them more constantly under the watchful eyes of their owners or slave drivers. This conclusion may lead to an inaccurate picture of slavery, particularly in the towns and cities of the Greater Caribbean.

By expanding the analysis of skilled labor to include black marketing women and domestics, we can gain a more accurate picture of life in early New Orleans. Further, an examination of this group will help to demonstrate that the mobility that black women had in towns and cities was important in establishing networks of connection among blacks in the Greater Caribbean. Any efforts of planters to curb these networks would have meant restricting the labor-based mobility of black women. Attempts to restrict black mobility would have had a real effect upon New Orleans because without black women's work, both the local public markets and the larger staple markets would have seized up. This means that while enslaved men's work was often better paid, enslaved women's work was equally important, if not more fundamental, to the functioning of the colony. This is important to lay out in bold strokes because while historians have argued that a conscious decision was made by settlers in New Orleans to train enslaved black men in order to lower the cost of skilled European labor, it seems that there was no analogous discussion about supplanting European female labor with enslaved female labor. That choice has been naturalized. Seeing it as a *fait accompli* has rendered the decision largely invisible in the literature of early New Orleans.[6] There is another good reason to examine black women's labor. By doing so, we might also be able to break down barriers in the historiography of the practice of slavery in different empires in the Greater Caribbean that have helped lead to both low-country and New Orleans exceptionalism.

What follows then, is a starting point for interpreting the ways in which black women practiced their public roles in the market system in New Orleans. I begin to build a framework to map the idea of market function, mobility, communication, and autonomy onto the economic needs of slave owners and the grounded experiences of women in New Orleans. By way of illuminating these ideas, I will now return to Shiloc's court case versus Chouteau.

In his complaint, Chouteau did not accuse the enslaved women, Maniche, and Rosa, of a crime. Rather, it was Shiloc the baker who was accused of selling his poisoned pastries. Indeed, if Maniche and Rosa had been accused, the criminal case against them would have very likely been more detailed. Because they were not, it is remarkable that Maniche and Rosa appear at all. But their appearance gives us some important details about them both. These particular marketing women sold food not for their owner, but for a food vender who had leased the women from their owner. While Maniche and Rosa barely make an appearance in the colonial archive, it was

---

6.   Daniel H. Usner, *Indians, Settlers, and Slaves in a Frontier Exchange Economy* (Chapel Hill: University of North Carolina Press, 1992), 55; Gwendolyn Midlo Hall, *Africans in Colonial Louisiana: The Development of Afro-Creole Culture in the Eighteenth Century* (Baton Rouge: Louisiana State University Press, 1992), 140–41. Colonial leaders took up the subject of French women in early New Orleans in the context of social reproduction; male settlers needed French women as wives to induce them to settle down and start farming (see, e.g. Jennifer M. Spear, *Race, Sex, and Social Order in Early New Orleans* (Baltimore: Johns Hopkins University Press, 2009), 17-18). French women were also blamed for undermining the social values of the colony with their loose morals. Ibid. 48-50; Dawdy, *Building the Devil's Empire,* 42-48.

women like them who were crucial to the functioning of the markets in New Orleans.

Maniche and Rosa appear in the case records because Chouteau attempted unsuccessfully to claim that he had heard from an unnamed "negress on the levee" that the two slaves who Shiloc used to sell his pastries in the market had sold the tainted food that made people ill. It is only after this testimony that the judges hearing the case thought it necessary to ask the witnesses and defendant if they knew whether the poisoned pastries in question were sold by Maniche and Rosa. While none of the witnesses could identify the sellers for certain, it is this question by the court that allows us to know their names.[7]

It is important to note that in this case, at least two people are profiting from Maniche and Rosa's labor, but both of them are *only* able to do so by allowing the two women freedom to act as agents. The first and most obvious is that they are making money for the baker through their efforts on the levee. They are essentially his representatives in the market. By selling his food, and perhaps even helping him to prepare it, they are working for Shiloc. Further, it does not appear as if Shiloc the baker was always there on the levee, so in order to make more money through his baking, he needed to rely on Maniche and Rosa exercising their judgment in the market. Their autonomy in handling his money and his products allowed him to make a better living.

In this case, the control of the benefits of Maniche and Rosa's labor goes even further, because the baker has leased these two women from a third party and paid their owner for the right to a portion of their work. Finally, there is a possibility that one or both of the women earned extra money through their ability to move about freely in the marketplace. This could have been done with or without the knowledge

---

7.   Shiloc was ultimately exonerated of all accusations of poisoning, and received damages from Chouteau the competing baker, who was found guilty of starting the malicious rumor to ruin Shiloc's business.

and consent of their owner and employer.

The active participation of African and Afro-Creole women in the public markets is well established, if sometimes not so well documented, across West Africa, the Caribbean, and the American South. While scholars and contemporary travelers have noticed this anecdotally, they have often underestimated its importance. This is just as true in New Orleans, though much of the literature on the topic is based on readings of traveler's accounts rather than on evidence grounded in actions of local New Orleanians. In New World European colonies, these spaces often seemed to function as a zone of inversion, where many normal assumptions about free and enslaved, black and white, male and female were turned upside down. From a European perspective, they were unruly and disorderly spaces.

In contrast, many West African women would have seen their occupation of this role as commonplace. Her ability to grow her own food, craft her own wares, then travel to the town's public market or through the streets to trade her surplus, all the while meeting friends and communicating with strangers, was common practice in West Africa and was a skill that was easily transferred to New Orleans as well as other cities, towns, and their hinterlands in the Americas.[8]

For example, in the South Carolina Low Country cities

---

8.   Paul Lovejoy and David Trotman, "Enslaved Africans and Their Expectations of Slave Life in the Americas: Towards a Reconsideration of Models of Creolisation," in *Questioning Creole: Creolisation Discourses in Caribbean Culture*, eds. Verene A. Shepherd and Glen L. Richards (Kingston, Jamaica: Ian Randle Publishers, 2002), 67-91; Paul Lovejoy, *Identity in the Shadow of Slavery* (New York: Continuum, 2009); Robert Olwell, "Loose, Idle, and Disorderly: Slave Women in the Eighteenth-Century Charleston Marketplace," in *More Than Chattel: Black Women and Slavery in the Americas*, eds. David Barry Gaspar and Darlene Clark Hine (Bloomington, IN: Indiana University Press, 1996), 35; Usner, *Indians, Settlers, and Slaves*, 201-203; Richmond F. Brown, ed., introduction to *Coastal Encounters: The Transformation of the Gulf South in the Eighteenth Century* (Lincoln, NE: University of Nebraska Press, 2007), 7-8; Winnifred Brown-Glaude, *Higglers in Kingston: Women's Informal Work in Jamaica* (Nashville: Vanderbilt University Press, 2011), 33.

of Savannah and Charleston, there is strong evidence that black women essentially controlled the public food markets. There are instances where a citizen of the colony of European descent, a white person, would venture into the market and attempt to purchase chickens or some choice vegetables from an enslaved marketing woman only to be told that she was out. A few moments later, when other black woman marketers came by to trade or purchase the same, there would be chickens and vegetables aplenty.[9] A significant element of these exchanges is that often the market women would be selling a combination of their own surplus food from their gardens and selling their owner's produce or meat. Similarly, female slaves, in their role as domestic workers, did much of the market shopping.[10]

This pattern of black women's presence in the public markets was not limited to the North American mainland.[11] It was also present in Jamaica, first in Port Royal and later in Kingston after about 1675. In Jamaica, where the proportion of free to enslaved peoples in the cities was far greater than in New Orleans, it is estimated that people of African descent on the island, overwhelmingly enslaved, controlled upwards of two-thirds of all of the precious metal currency

9. Olwell, "Loose, Idle, and Disorderly," 97-110.

10. Betty Wood, *Women's Work, Men's Work: The Informal Slave Economies of Lowcountry Georgia* (Athens: University of Georgia Press, 1995); Olwell, "Loose, Idle, and Disorderly"; Robert Olwell, *Masters, Slaves, and Subjects: The Culture of Power in the South Carolina Low Country, 1740-1790* (Ithaca, NY: Cornell University Press, 1998).

11. What I am considering here is largely, in Pedro Welch's words, "The urban matrix" in slavery (Bridgetown book). Although female slaves were more common than males in urban areas, for most of the seventeenth and eighteenth centuries, the vast majority of the European and African immigrant populations in the Greater Caribbean lived near a market town. This is particularly true of Caribbean islands, but even the Carolina and Georgia low country was a strip of land about two hundred miles long stretching fifty miles inland from the coast. In areas where no market town was present, Anthony Kaye has explored the ability of fieldworkers to travel to gathering places that were common to many plantations to socialize, meet their families, and exchange goods and food.

in the "black market" economy. The evidence suggests that enslaved women were primarily responsible for food sales in the public markets. Similarly, almost all of the street venders, or higglers, were enslaved women as well.[12]

Le Cap, Havana, and most other port towns in the French and Spanish Antilles also exhibited similar patterns of women's marketing.[13] This was also true of Barbados, an economic and cultural entrepôt to both the British and Spanish Caribbean during much of the seventeenth and eighteenth century. In Bridgetown, Barbados, the market was the commercial hub of the island in a particularly active port of call. Sailors, some of them African or Afro-Creole, were a constant presence in the Bridgetown market for the period in question. Black women often controlled the day-to-day workings of the Bridgetown market, which served as a focal point for mobility, connection, and communication, both within and beyond the island.[14]

As Rosa, Maniche, and the unknown black woman help to demonstrate in the case of Shiloc vs. Chouteau, New Orleans

12.   Sidney W. Mintz, "Caribbean Marketplaces and Caribbean History," *Nova Amricana* 1 (1979): 333-44; Sidney W. Mintz, *Caribbean Transformations* (New York: Columbia University Press, 1989) see especially "The Origins of the Jamaican Market System" and "The Contemporary Jamaican Market System"; Winnifred Brown-Glaude, *Higglers in Kingston: Women's Informal Work in Jamaica* (Nashville: Vanderbilt University Press, 2011), 32-33.

13.   Gaspar and Hine, *More Than Chattel*; Yvonne Fabella, "'An Empire Founded on Libertinage': The Mulatress and Colonial Anxiety in Saint Domingue," in *Gender, Race, and Religion in the Colonization of the Americas*, ed. Nora E. Jaffaray, Women and Gender in the Early Modern World Series (Burlington, VT: Ashgate Publishing, 2007), 113; Bernard Moitt, *Women and Slavery in the French Antilles, 1635-1848* (Bloomington, IN: Indiana University Press, 2001), 54–55.

14.   Hilary Beckles and Karl Watson, "Social Protest and Labour Bargaining: The Changing Nature of Slaves' Responses to Plantation Life in Eighteenth Century Barbados," *Slavery & Abolition* 8, no. 3 (December 1987): 272-93; Hilary Beckles, *White Servitude and Black Slavery in Barbados, 1627-1715* (Knoxville, TN: University of Tennessee Press, 1989); Hilary Beckles, *Centering Woman: Gender Discourses in Caribbean Slave Society* (Kingston, Jamaica: Ian Randle Publishers, 1999); Pedro L.V. Welch, *Slave Society in the City: Bridgetown Barbados 1680-1834* (Kingston, Jamaica: Ian Randle Publishers, 2003).

was part and parcel of this circum-Caribbean practice, albeit with its own local peculiarities. From at least the 1730s, slaves in and near the city cultivated their own grounds and brought surplus into New Orleans for sale.[15] Slaves owned by the Ursuline nuns sometimes produced surplus vegetables and milk that they sold in the city.[16] By the 1790s, when the Cabildo had passed laws in their attempts to regulate commerce and to protect food safety, women did most of the selling along the levee.[17]

Because of their role within the economy, black women in New Orleans were a nexus point of mobility and communication, built in and around the public markets of the colony. African and Afro-Creole women in New Orleans were instrumental in feeding the colony and in providing the services that made the city function. Their work was vital to the economic functioning of the city in the sense that many black women provided the slave and wage labor necessary for the city's planters, businessmen, and artisans. Such people depended on this labor to create the wealth needed to import food and goods for purchase from other parts of the Caribbean basin and greater Atlantic World. But it did not end on the plantations around the city. It was also true in a very direct sense, black women also worked in New Orleans and its hinterlands to grow food for themselves and produce surpluses. Many then traded and sold their extra food in the streets and public markets of the city.[18] Black women's work in the public markets did not end with food, many also earned

---

15.   Usner, *Indians, Settlers, and Slaves*, 201-202; Dawdy, *Building the Devil's Empire*, 104–106.

16.   Emily Clark, *Masterless Mistresses: The New Orleans Ursulines and the Development of a New World Society, 1727-1834* (Chapel Hill: University of North Carolina Press, 2007), 209.

17.   Kimberly S. Hanger, *Bounded Lives, Bounded Places: Free Black Society in Colonial New Orleans, 1769-1803* (Durham, NC: Duke University Press, 1997), 64-65.

18.   Thomas Ashe, *Travels in America*, vol. 3 (London, 1808), 275.

money as laundresses, seamstresses, and even in gathering firewood and selling other goods they made.[19] These work options were likely a feature of New Orleans life from the earliest days of the colony.

Looking at the population data for the city, by 1732 more than a quarter of the population, and nearly one half of the adult population, were enslaved blacks. By expanding the area of examination to account for New Orleans's hinterlands and taking the whole of Lower Louisiana into account, the numbers suggest an even greater reliance on enslaved women's labor in New Orleans, with slaves outnumbering free people by 1727 and by a factor of nearly two to one in the 1730s. Further, African slaves comprised approximately 97 percent of the lower-level workforce by the 1732 Census and, where data exists for New Orleans proper, female slaves outnumbered male slaves.[20] This imbalance is even more pronounced if we include the *libre* population, where women outnumbered men by roughly two to one in the city.[21] The reasons for the gender split are complex, ranging from the desire of white slave owners to have sexual access to and form relationships with black women to traditional European ideas about women in household domestic roles. A significant factor, however, was that European settlers viewed female slaves as less of a threat than males. Because of this, women were allowed more freedom in densely populated areas such as towns and cities as well as access to the private spaces of

19.   Usner, *Indians, Settlers, and Slaves*, 201-202; Jerah Johnson, *Congo Square in New Orleans* (New Orleans: Louisiana Landmarks Society, 1995), 7.

20.   Charles R. Maduell Jr., *The Census Tables for the French Colony of Louisisana from 1699 Through 1732* (Baltimore: Genealogical Publishing Company, INC, 1972); Glen Conrad, *The First Families of Louisiana*, vol. 2 (Baton Rouge: Claitor's Publishing Division, 1970); Hall, *Africans in Colonial Louisiana*, 10; Paul LaChance, "The Growth of Free and Slave Populations of French Colonial Louisiana," in *French Colonial Louisiana and the Atlantic World* (Baton Rouge: Louisiana State University Press, 2005), 204–43; Hanger, *Bounded Lives, Bounded Places*, 23.

21.   Ibid., 21-23.

households.[22]

Travelers' accounts support the demographic evidence from the period. They point to the predominant numbers of African and Afro-Creole women selling food and small dry goods in the public markets and via street vending. John Pintard, writing of his experiences in New Orleans in 1801, attributed almost the entirety of food sales to black marketing women, stating that:

> All is bought by domestics—especially the females—who seem to be the chief buyers and sellers of the place—One meets with wenches with large, flat, baskets containing all kinds of goods with a measure in [*sic*] her hand traversing the streets & country in all directions—they are experts at selling.[23]

At the same time, he was not impressed by the quality of products or market practices with respect to meat:

22.   For an in depth presentation of this evidence, see Rebecca Hall, "Not Killing Me Softly: African American Women, Slave Revolts, and Historical Constructions of Racialized Gender," *Freedom Center Journal* 2, no. 1 (2010): 1-47, Available at SSRN: http://ssrn.com/abstract=1874927; Clark, *New Orleans 1718-1812: An Economic History*, 8–10, 23–25, 149–51, 257.; E.D. Freidrichs, ed., "Alphabetical and Chronological Digest of the Acts and Deliberations of the Cabildo, 1769-1803: A Record of the Spanish Government in New Orleans, WPA Project #665-64-3-112," 1939, New Orleans Public Library; Gilbert C. Din and John E. Harkins, *The New Orleans Cabildo: Colonial Louisiana's First City Government 1769-1803* (Baton Rouge: Louisiana State University Press, 1996) See particularly chapter 8, "Food and Marketing."

23.   Jean-François-Benjamin Dumont de Montigny, *Mémoires Historiques Sur La Louisiane Contenant Ce Qui y Est Arrivé De Plus Memorable Depuis L'année 1687-jusqu'à Present* (Paris, 1753); quoted in Johnson, *Congo Square in New Orleans*, 7; Ashe, *Travels in America*, III: Benjamen Henry Latrobe, *The Journal of Latrobe: Being the Notes and Sketches of an Architect, Naturalist and Traveler in the United States from 1796 to 1820* (New York: D. Appleton and Company, 1905); Jonathan Pintard, "New Orleans, 1801: An account by John Pintard," ed. David Lee Sterling, "Superior Council Records, Louisiana Historical Quarterly," in *Louisiana Historical Quarterly* 34, no. 3 (1951): 217–33.

Mutton I have seen but once, & that was an old ram
executed I suppose for his sins & iniquities, the meat
w[oul]d have disgraced a college dining room—No
other use is made of pork but to be cut up into junks
about 4 inches square for 6d—for stuffing other
dishes—& large quantities are thus daily sold—to
convince me how good it was when I asked the price
of a mulatress [*sic*], she took the piece up & licked it
with her tongue & calmly laid it down again among
the rest—in three minutes it was disposed of . . .[24]

Going beyond white and creole travel accounts is more difficult
because slaves who sold goods in the public markets left few
records behind. This was also the case for higglers, the door-
to-door saleswomen who expanded the markets to the streets,
banquettes, and byways of New Orleans. As we can see with
Maniche and Rosa, even women whose daily presence in the
market was required by their owners, left little record. In some
cases, as with the unnamed woman, they left only a trace of
a trace. For the public markets, there was no need for a stall
owner to draw up a formal contract with a notary to allow a
slave to use their position. In fact, this practice would have
resulted in extra costs and regulations for both parties and
was avoided. Even records of subletting stalls to libre women
are rare, as much of the subcontracting and selling by women
probably took place under the radar.[25]

Similar to marketing women, enslaved women who were
domestic workers left few documents behind, but court
records give some insight into the typical activities of an
enslaved woman named Mannon. The evidence presented in
this case illustrates the mobility and responsibility that was
given to household slaves engaged in domestic work, which

24.   Ibid., 229.

25.   Hanger, *Bounded Lives, Bounded Places*, 63-64. I also wish to thank Sally
Reeves for her discussions and for sharing her research into the records of market
stall contracts and sub-letting practices in the New Orleans Notarial Archives.

often included responsibilities as household manager and personal assistant for their owner.

On March 5, 1775, Mannon was arrested in connection with the theft of a gun stolen from a dry goods store owned by Salomon Mallines in September of 1774. A free man of color named Luis was arrested as well. Besides the gun, some blankets, a mattress, and a wool coat were also taken. In early March of 1775, Mallines had some business with Nicolas, a gunsmith, and visited the man's gun shop. Perhaps Mallines was purchasing a replacement for his missing gun. While in the shop, Mallines recognized one of the guns awaiting repair as his rifle, stolen six months before. The gun in question had a badly damaged stock and a scratched barrel. This damage, perhaps in an attempt to disguise the weapon, was the reason that the gun needed to be brought in to the shop.[26] Mannon was arrested because the gunsmith had told the authorities that she brought the gun in for repair. At the time of her arrest it was not known whether Mannon was an accomplice in the theft or a material witness. However, it seldom took more than a simple accusation of being associated with a crime to have a slave, or even a libre, apprehended and taken to jail. Mannon testified that she had taken the rifle to the shop for her employer Pedro Dutertre, who had purchased the gun from Luis.[27]

Further testimony from Dutertre supported Mannon's story. He also stated that he did not believe she was involved in the theft. Luis was ultimately found guilty of the crime.[28] The importance of this lies not in its outcome, but in what it tells us about Mannon's domestic work for Dutertre. The

26.   "Solomon Mallines seeks judicial inquiry to discover the author and ac-complices in the robbery of his store on the 5th of September the year just past," 5 March 1773, SJR, *LHQ* 9, no. 2 (1926): 324.

27.   Dutertre leased Mannon and she lived and worked in his boarding house.

28.   Luis worked as a cook two leagues out of the city, but lived in Dutertre's house in town when he was in New Orleans. SJR, *LHQ* 9, no. 2 (1926): 325–27. This also shows that Mannon was part of a regional network.

most significant thing about this case is that the repair of the gun was commissioned by a slave woman on behalf of her owner and that this fact, in and of itself, was not remarked upon by any of the parties involved.[29] This speaks to the integral way in which black women were deeply imbricated into the everyday functioning of the city. If Dutertre could trust his female slave with a gun, then what wouldn't he trust her to do in his service. If Mannon did not give a second thought to taking a long arm through the city, what errands would she hesitate to run in Dutertre's service? If Nicolas the gunsmith took Mannon's business on behalf of her owner without batting an eye, how uncommon could it have been for an enslaved woman to bring in a firearm for repair and then pick it up again? Clearly Mannon was a domestic slave, responsible for running the household, and free to run such errands as needed to be accomplished for this purpose around the city. That she was accused of having a part in the theft is immaterial. The suspicion of her guilt did not last beyond Dutertre's testimony.[30]

This episode helps to illustrate the pattern of freedom of mobility for enslaved women involved in domestic work in colonial New Orleans. Running errands, they were commonplace in nearly every part of the city. They were seldom noticed for being out of place, even while carrying firearms through the streets of the city in broad daylight.[31]

---

29.   There are multiple examples of female slaves taking charge of firearms for their owners, though none so detailed as the above. See, e.g. Records of the French Superior Council, 10 April 1747, "Declaration," *Superior Council Records, Louisiana Historical Quarterly*, 18:1 (1935), 177; "Criminal Prosecution of the negroes Clement and Jocobo belonging to Don Pedro Caberet, charged with murder," 30 October 1777, SJR, *LHQ* 12, no. 4 (1929): 690.

30.   "Salomon Mallines," SJR, *LHQ* 9, no. 2 (1926): 325.

31.   I am using the construct of in-place and out of place to connote the idea of belonging and transgressing. To be "in place" is to be doing something normal or acceptable in practice. To be "out of place" is to violate the rules of society and transgress boundaries. Mannon's ability to carry a long arm, a conspicuous piece of hardware, indicates that her actions were not transgressive in nature, but were

Mannon and other domestic enslaved women were a part of, and essential to, the everyday functioning of the city of New Orleans. At the same time, Mannon and other black women's mobility were subject to very different treatment than enslaved black men. Because women were seen as less threatening, they could carry firearms around the streets of New Orleans and were less likely to raise alarm.[32]

The last will and testament of Francisco Muñoz, a powerful office holder, allows further insight into how the markets for the skills of enslaved women worked in New Orleans as well as insight into the fundamental assumptions that the colony's slaveholders held towards their slaves.

In late August of 1784, Muñoz, the long-serving warden of the Royal Prison in New Orleans passed away. Maria had served him for many years by the time of his death. In drawing up his will, Muñoz left provisions for the manumission of his domestic slave, the "seeming to be 28 years old," Maria. He had done what some slave owners did at their death by either freeing their slaves or providing them with what the owner deemed to be a fair path to emancipation. He allowed that when she could raise the sum of 350 pesos she would be granted her manumission without need for appraisal. Further, Maria's owner kept her earnings for her in a "cypress chest" that he willed to her upon his death:

> which contains…130 pesos, more or less, that she has earned in my house, in various ways, with my consent.

accepted. Tim Creswell, *Place: A Short Introduction* (Malden, MA: Blackwell, 2004), 102-104.

32. "Motion of Trial of Rebellious Negro Slave," 12 July 1728, SCR, *LHQ* 4, no. 4 (1921): 491. Enslaved men walking around the city with guns were, however, taken much differently. They were often stopped and detained no matter the circumstance. "Interrogation," 9 January 1742, SCR, *LHQ* 11, no. 2 (1928); "Ordinance of Governor Kerlerec," 1 June 1753, The Cabildo Archives, *LHQ* 3, no.1 (1920): 89-90; It is important to note that male slaves were often permitted or even encouraged by their owners to hunt on plantations. Gwendolyn Midlo Hall, *Africans in Colonial Louisiana*, 143.

It must be well understood that if, at the time the said
chest and money be delivered to her, a sum in excess
of the amount specified above be found, my executor
must extract the surplus, because it is certain she could
not have earned it by means at her disposal.[33]

Leaving aside the limitations that Muñoz placed upon
Maria's earned wealth, he did allow his slave the possibility
of manumission. Instances of such agreements over the price
of freedom between owners and slaves were fairly common,
particularly during the Spanish period.[34]

What is interesting about this case is that even while
allowing for the possibility of Maria's manumission, he limited
the amount that it was possible for Maria to have at the time of
his death to just over one-third of what it would have cost her
to purchase her freedom. Further, Muñoz attempted to set the
upper limit of what Maria could earn at four reales per day —
or one-half of a peso, thus insuring that she remained a slave
for at least another year and a half providing she could earn
the maximum amount over that time and not spend anything
at all. In writing his will, Muñoz assumed that he knew of
every possible marketable skill of his domestic slave Maria.
This included the amount of money she had accumulated and
the ways in which she made every bit of her income. Muñoz
was confident enough of this to make a close estimate of her
assets.

There is little doubt that Maria, together with Sr. Muñoz's
other slave, a fourteen-year-old male, Francisco, "a creole of
this province" whom he willed to his heirs with no mention
of emancipation, ran the older man's domestic life. Maria
may also have been Muñoz's sexual slave. Muñoz was a
three-time widower with an important job that probably left

33.   "Last Will and Testament of Francisco Muñoz," 20 August 1773, SJR,
LHQ 24, no. 3 (1941): 899.

34.   Spear, *Race, Sex, and Social Order*, 101. See particularly chapter 4, "Slavery and Freedom in Spanish New Orleans."

him little time for the details of the day-to-day operation of a household. The scope of Maria's duties probably increased when Muñoz grew old and suffered from the illness that led to his death. He probably received treatment from a doctor or surgeon, but his daily care was most likely left to his slaves. During this time he was bedridden, and his ability to oversee most, much less all, of their actions was all but impossible. Maria and Francisco were likely responsible for every detail of the functioning home. Muñoz's will indicates that for Maria, this certainly included the pursuit of work for income and travel around New Orleans as she, like Mannon, Rosa, and Maniche, went to the shops and markets. There are clearly limits on what is knowable about Maria from Muñoz's will, but because Maria's owner allowed her to keep income earned and presented her with a clear path to self-manumission, it is fair to infer that Maria had both some degree of trust and a large degree of responsibility in Muñoz's household.

It is important to note that sometimes the very thing that allowed slaves to earn money for self-purchase was also the thing that made such an act more difficult. The skills that allowed a slave to earn more money—as a cook, washerwoman, market trader, domestic worker—all made the slave more valuable. A good domestic worker or cook was often valued at a considerably higher rate than slaves without such skills which, in turn, made it more difficult for her to purchase her freedom.[35] That it worked this way is an important reminder that even in the Spanish period, where the numbers of libre women increased significantly, the legal and economic systems in place were constructed to protect and reify the institution of slavery.[36]

While there were many cases where slaves, particularly enslaved women such as Maria, were able to earn money to

35.   Joseph Tort v. The Succession of Roberto Scaire, 10 May 1790, Spanish Judicial Records of Louisiana, Louisiana Historical Center at the Old U.S. Mint, New Orleans.

36.   Spear, *Race, Sex, and Social Order*, 103.

purchase their freedom, there were also cases that illustrate how narrow the margin between slavery and freedom could be for New Orleans's marketing women. Jeannette's story helps to show that even when an enslaved woman gained her freedom and went into business for herself, her new status as free woman was not necessarily a permanent one. For blacks in early New Orleans freedom was precarious. Something as simple as going into debt could change a status from free to re-enslaved.

On April 8, 1747, Jeannette, a libre woman became a slave once again.[37] Some years before, Jeannette had begun working for herself. She may have done this on her own, but perhaps worked in partnership with her sister, Marguerite Coustilhas. Whether together or separate, the evidence seems to suggest that both were selling food for part of their income. It is unclear from the evidence whether the two sisters sold in the *Place des Nègres* or in the more integrated public market on the levee. They probably spent at least some time selling from door to door and to individuals they would meet in the streets of the city. It is likely that they worked all of these modes in some combination, as was perhaps most usual for women selling foodstuffs in New Orleans.

It is speculative, though quite likely, that both Jeannette and Marguerite, in working for themselves as free people, were using skills that they had come by as enslaved women. Perhaps they were domestic slaves, with multiple skills in cleaning, cooking, washing, ironing, and, of course, doing such errands as market shopping and vegetable gardening to keep food flowing into their owner's household. As slaves, their abilities earned each of them some capital, whether social or monetary, because they were each able to gain their freedom, either by saving up and purchasing it through their own labor

---

37.   "Order of Council to sell a Free Negress into Slavery to pay debts contracted by her," 8 April 1747, SCR, *LHQ* 18, no. 1 (1935): 168; "Order of Council to sell a Free Negress into Slavery to pay debts contracted by her," 8 April 1747, SCR, *LHQ* 18, no. 1 (1935): 168.

or through the good will of their owner they earned in their years as chattel. It is also something to note that each was able to earn freedom at an age where they could still work for themselves.

In 1745, in order to stay afloat, Marguerite was forced to borrow thirty-five pesos from Sr. St. Martin Jauregibery, a New Orleans trader and businessman. She may have had an ongoing business relationship with St. Martin, buying items on account or borrowing revolving sums of money. When Marguerite died suddenly in mid-1746, she left a small inheritance to her sister Jeanette.[38]

Jeannette was probably already in debt at the time of her sister's death. Perhaps she had suffered an injury that required a doctor's treatment or had some other piece of bad luck. It is conceivable that she used the small proceeds from this inheritance in order to keep herself afloat. This was in vain, as by April of 1747, the court declared her a refractory debtor and ordered Jeannette to be sold back into slavery to settle her debts.

It was not enough that Jeannette was forced to use the sale of her person to settle with her own creditors, she also had to settle with one of her sister's creditors. Sr. St. Martin petitioned the courts, alleging that Marguerite's estate was given to her sister with the understanding that it be managed in such a way as to settle her decedent's debts. He further alleged that Jeannette had acted irresponsibly, even criminally, and spent the proceeds from her sister's estate as if it were her own rather than earmarked to pay off debts. As a remedy, he asked the council to award him thirty-five pesos from Jeannette's re-enslavement auction.[39] For blacks in colonial New Orleans, it was often a thin line between scraping by and losing one's freedom. This was particularly true for free people of color. Unlike their European and white creole counterparts, libres could lose their legal personhood and become chattel. There

---

38.   "Petition," 27 April 1747, SCR, *LHQ* 18, no. 1 (1935): 168.

39.   Ibid.

is no question that while Jeannette's status may have changed, the skills she had learned made her a more valuable purchase. Her sale price at auction of 1,900 livres is consonant with the price paid for a skilled domestic or marketing woman at the time.[40]

By examining this small sample of cases of the marketing and marketability of women's skills in early New Orleans, I suggest the importance of the ways in which black women functioned in the market places of New Orleans. Black women used their skills as domestic workers, gardeners, and market workers to gain mobility, autonomy, and opportunity. That this happened also suggests that the structures of New Orleans relied on black women's labor to function. Black marketing women were ubiquitous in the public spaces where the daily business of the city and of the colony occurred, in fact the city's daily business could not have occurred without them. It was possible for a long-standing member of the community to say he heard a rumor from an unknown black woman on the levee market in a town of three thousand and it was possible for another black woman to travel the streets of the town with a long arm in view without being stopped or questioned. These episodes, along with the value placed on Jeannette's skills as a market woman when she was re-enslaved at auction, help to illustrate the importance of black marketing women. These markets relied on the skills, mobility, and autonomy of black women to function.

40.   Gwendolyn Midlo Hall, "Afro-Louisiana History and Genealogy 1719-1820," http://www.ibiblio.org/laslave/index.html; Gwendolyn Midlo Hall, *Slavery and African Ethnicities in The Americas: Restoring the Links* (Chapel Hill: University of North Carolina Press, 2005), 173-79.

4 | Interracial Unionism Meets the Open Shop Drive: African American Membership in the Carmen's Union, 1918-1926

Michael Mizell-Nelson

One of the most curious episodes involving race relations in New Orleans labor history is found in the 1918 decision of white streetcar union officers to include African American street railway and gas works company employees as full members of their traditional American Federation of Labor (AFL) local, Division 194. During World War I, federal intervention provided the organized labor movement its strongest period of growth in twenty years. In New Orleans, wartime prosperity and the National War Labor Board (NWLB) brought skilled and unskilled black and white workers into new and existing unions.[1] Rather than following the typical pattern of biracial unionism and creating a colored subdivision, the New Orleans branch of the Amalgamated Association of Street and Electric Railway Employees of America admitted African American employees directly into their local. From 1918 through 1922, white conductors and motormen knew the large number of unskilled and semi-skilled black and white laborers brought into Division 194, at least nominally, as union brothers. This rare experiment in interracial unionism and the early adoption of industrial unionism by an AFL local proved to be contentious; white union officials pursued a grievance with the NWLB after it approved substantial wage gains for blacks and a black union member filed suit against those same

---

1.   Eric Arnesen, *Waterfront Workers of New Orleans: Race, Class and Politics 1863-1923* (New York: Oxford University Press, 1991), 228-30.

officers. Despite such litigation, white officers of the local acted several times to improve working conditions for the black members. A movement among some white union members first forced African Americans into a colored subdivision in 1922 and eventually led to their disfranchisement four years later. Black members fought every move to strip them of their rights as union members, both within the local and through appeals to international officers.

Few primary sources survive from the period, except the union local records and newspaper articles.[2] These documents provide insight into the generally unstudied world of black street railway and other public utility workers in the early 1900s and a window into an exceptional period in the history of a traditional AFL local.

Over the last twenty years, labor historians have produced local studies from the Appalachian coalfields to the Gulf Coast docks that collectively have demolished the long-held view of southern workers as hopelessly divided by race during the Jim Crow era. Scholars are finding examples of biracial union cooperation and "mixed locals" or interracial unions throughout the region.[3] Biracial union organizations and white

2.   All railway company records burned in a suspicious fire during the company's 1919-21 receivership, and scarcely any local newspaper accounts of Division 194 mention black membership during this period. One scholar treats the topic tangentially. See Joseph A. McCartin's *Labor's Great War: the Struggle for Industrial Democracy and the Origins of Modern American Labor Relations, 1912-1921* (Chapel Hill: University of North Carolina Press, 1997): 116-17, 155.

3.   For the most recent and comprehensive historiographical treatments of biracial unionism in New Orleans and other port cities, see Eric Arnesen's "Race and Labour in a Southern U.S. Port: New Orleans, 1860-1930," in vol. 1 of *Dock Workers: International Explorations in Comparative Labour History, 1790-1970*, eds. Sam Davies et al. (Aldershot, UK: Ashgate Publishing, 2000): 38-56; and Arnesen's "Biracial Waterfront Unionism in the Age of Segregation," in *Waterfront Workers: New Perspectives on Race and Class*, ed. Calvin Winslow (Urbana: University of Illinois Press, 1998), 19-61. Also see Rick Halpern's "Organized labour, black workers and the twentieth century South: the emerging revision," *Social History* 19, no. 3 (1994): 359-83. Important monographic studies concerning biracial and interracial unionism during the early 1900s include Daniel Letwin's

unions with colored subdivisions typified New Orleans's waterfront labor movement during the early 1900s. Most simply expressed, the biracial union structure rested upon segregated unions whose officers cooperated across racial lines when negotiating contracts with employers or considering the need to strike.[4] For New Orleans's dock workers and other workers pursuing biracial organization, pragmatism underlay the cooperation. Losing economic ground to their employers when negotiating as separate racial blocs convinced white and black union leaders that a form of racial alliance best suited every worker's interests. Eric Arnesen, a leading scholar of New Orleans as well as United States labor history, describes biracial unionism as "an imperfect but unprecedented strategy that reflected the strength of the white South's racial ideologies and practices while simultaneously violating many of its racial expectations and norms."[5] Arnesen's assessment also applies to the carmen's union during this period.

A question that one cannot fully answer is why did white officers of a traditional AFL local choose to break from the pattern of using a colored subdivision? For more than a decade, Division 194 had already worked with a sub-division that represented white workers employed by a street railway serving Algiers, a neighborhood of New Orleans located on the West Bank of the Mississippi River. Many references to the "committee representing sub-local Division 194" appear in the union records. During the summer of 1918, union officers examined the colored subdivision model favored

---

The Challenge of Interracial Unionism: Alabama Coalminers, 1878-1921 (Chapel Hill: University of North Carolina Press, 1998) and McCartin's *Labor's Great War*. For a comparative view of African American railroad workers, see Eric Arnesen's *Brotherhoods of Color: Black Railroad Workers and the Struggle for Equality*, (Cambridge, MA: Harvard University Press, 2001).

4.   See Arnesen, *Waterfront Workers*, 120-21, 154-55, 195-96, 199-201, and 254-55, et al. for background regarding the role of biracial unions in the New Orleans labor movement.

5.   Arnesen, "Biracial Waterfront Unionism," 47-48.

by New Orleans's dock workers. The carmen consulted the agreement between New Orleans's steamship agents and the Screwmen's Benevolent Association (SBA) Local No. 412 (ILA) and the SBA No. 237 (ILA colored). The SBA representative's letter stated that he "hop[ed the] same will be advantageous to you and your honorable body, and will be instrumental and beneficial in bring [*sic*] about an amicable [*sic*] adjustment in your present controversy between yourselves and your employers." After some consideration the carmen decided not to follow the biracial subdivision model.

The carmen pursued an even more exceptional course that hinged upon racial cooperation *within* a union local that had previously adhered to the AFL tradition of excluding black as well as unskilled workers. The carmen's case most resembles not the waterfront workers, but other short-lived radical examples of interracial or "mixed locals" in the South found in the Knights of Labor in the late 1800s and the Brotherhood of Timberworkers in the early 1910s. Arnesen has described the carmen's decision to allow integrated membership or interracial unionism as "highly unusual."[6]

Anticipating a particularly difficult period of negotiations with their employers, the carmen decided to bring back one of their previous leaders, John Stadler. Little is known about this founding member of Division 194, whose official union histories had celebrated his early leadership role. Stadler had served as Division 194 president in 1906, 1907, 1909, and 1910 before leaving to take a political job; he worked as superintendent of the city's Sanitary Department of the Board of Health immediately before assuming his final term as president in 1918. Many members of Division 194, anticipating a particularly difficult period of negotiation with the company, had requested that Stadler return to the position.[7]

6.   Eric Arnesen, e-mail message to author, January 15, 2001.

7.   "President John Stadler," *The Motorman and Conductor* 25, no. 2 (January 1918): 12; "Greet Returning President," *The Motorman and Conductor* 26, no. 10 (September 1918): 20.

Stadler's earlier record as a staunch AFL man makes the decision to allow black members into the carmen's union even more interesting. During the 1907 waterfront workers general strike, he and another member of the Central Trades and Labor Council instigated a libel suit against one of their left-wing critics: Socialist writer and radical labor organizer Oscar Ameringer. The *Labor World* newspaper, edited and published by Ameringer, had printed acerbic remarks regarding one of Stadler's AFL colleagues. Inglorious assessments of Stadler as a typical AFL union official opposed to industrial unionism appear in the memoirs of both Ameringer and Covington Hall, another radical labor organizer in the same period.[8] Despite Stadler's conventional record, he led his local to accept both industrial unionism and integrated membership only one decade later.

Contract negotiations between the railway company and the union in June 1918 revealed great opposition to the union's call for including utility employees in the new contract. After the second set of negotiations had broken off, Stadler responded to a reporter's questions about why the carmen sought to organize the utility company employees.

You know that the New Orleans Railway and Light Company owns or controls the various street railway companies of this city, the gas company and the electric light and power companies. Well, the union wants to control the gas company employees for the same reason. Whatever reasons the company has for controlling all its subsidiary corporations those are our reasons for wanting to control the gas company employees. I wish you'd make that point clear.[9]

---

8.   Oscar Ameringer, *If You Don't Weaken: The Autobiography of Oscar Ameringer* (New York: Henry Holt, 1940); Dave Roediger, ed., *Covington Hall's Labor Struggles in the Deep South* (Chicago: Charles H. Kerr Publishing Company, 1999), 85.

9.   "City Heads Will Use Authority to Force Car Operation Here," *New Orleans Times-Picayune*, June 20, 1918, 5.

Transit company officials and Mayor Martin Behrman had both contacted the carmen's international president, William Mahon, seeking intervention from above, but Stadler maintained that Mahon had already ruled favorably on the carmen's request to organize utility company workers.[10]

In late June of 1918, the new contract included New Orleans Railway Company and New Orleans Gas Light Company support workers, both black and white, as members of the carmen's division; however, their inclusion rested on the question of their eligibility, given their status as unskilled workers. In the meantime, the new agreement covered the utility workers while both sides waited for the NWLB to rule on the question of wage rates. Local trade unions proved willing to concede jurisdiction over these unskilled workers to the carmen's union, and a constitutional amendment at the next national convention of the carmen's union allowed Division 194 to officially enroll them.[11]

A survey of African American membership revealed that 421 black members belonged to Division 194 in 1923, when the entire union contained about 2,900 members.[12] Most black workers were spread throughout the various departments, where they worked on railway track crews, as porters and in other less desirable jobs. The gas company contained the most sizable presence, yet whites still outnumbered blacks. Since most of the union men, primarily conductors and motormen, did not work directly with African Americans, they possibly tolerated the idea of admitting blacks to the union as part of the mass of unskilled laborers on the periphery of the carmen's

10.   Ibid.

11.   "Street Car Men Ratify Contract Without Dissent," *New Orleans Times-Picayune*, June 28, 1918, 1, 15; Joseph Finnegan to John Stadler, 15 July 1918, box 2, correspondence, New Orleans Street Railway Union records, 1902-1948, Louisiana Research Collection, Tulane University, New Orleans. (hereafter cited as Union records).

12.   Gus Bievenu to James Rodgers, 1 October 1923; Gus Bienvenu to William Mahon, 14 July 1925; both in box 3, Union records.

workplace. Despite the racial division, all of the men brought into the union in 1918 were united by their classification as largely unskilled workers. Motormen, conductors, and the specialized workers of the car barns had always worked in some isolation from the black and white unskilled workers who did the dirtiest work associated with street railways and public utilities: digging trenches for gas and electrical lines, laying and servicing railway beds, and cleaning the cars and car barns. Their unskilled nature as well as the significant presence of black workers likely had allowed the union's international officers to eventually support the efforts of Division 194 to organize these men. The new groupings of unskilled workers brought into Division 194 during the 1918 organizing campaign consisted of blacks and whites working in relatively integrated environments.

The railway company's willingness to allow for the expansion of union representation may have stemmed from several crises involving the company during the negotiation period. In June, the assistant for Frederick Ballard, a utility company consultant, arrived to begin work appraising the company in preparation for a proposed city takeover. In the same month, 1,400 members of the carmen's union signed resignations effective July 1 if the railway refused to sign the new contract.[13] Also in June, two breakdowns in the company's central Market Street power plant had interrupted electrical service and streetcar operations for several hours each time, arousing even more public criticism for a company already in terrible financial condition.[14] Finally, the company's greater concern involved the wage rate question, which was to be decided by the War Labor Board. The company gave in on

13.   "Appraiser Here Today to Begin Railway Work," *New Orleans Times-Picayune*, June 18, 1918, 1; Arthur R. Pearce, "The Rise and Decline of Labor in New Orleans," (master's thesis, Tulane University, 1938), 72.

14.   "Power Plant Wreck Ties up Streetcar Service for Hours," *New Orleans Times-Picayune*, June 11, 1918, 1; "Another Breakdown in Power Plant Cuts Service on Car Line," *New Orleans Times-Picayune*, June 17, 1918, 1.

the question of allowing the enrollment of several hundred unskilled laborers, both black and white, perhaps hoping to stand firm on the wage question.

The railway company had proposed fare increases in previous years as a route towards financial solvency, and, when their overtures failed, the War Finance Committee had loaned the company one million dollars. The cash-strapped company perhaps saw a wage increase as an opportunity to succeed at raising fares. When the National War Labor Board decided to establish a compromise wage scale, the company immediately asked the city commission council for a fare increase, from five cents to seven. Citizens and representatives of organized labor held mass meetings and wrote angry letters to the editor decrying the request. Public demands for receivership intensified. The 1918 wage agreement that seemed to expand union strength led directly to the 1919-1922 receivership period. Conditions set in the 1918 contract later led to the 1920 and 1929 strikes and the demise of the carmen's union. The high wage set by the NWLB allowed the railway company to slip "from precarious solvency into bankruptcy." Arthur O'Keefe, the court-appointed receiver and a former Railway Board member, provided Division 194 with its first anti-union employer in more than fifteen years. O'Keefe encouraged company supervisors to harass workers and initiated an open shop campaign.[15]

The 1918 agreement covered many workers outright, but

---

15.   Adam Fairclough, "The Public Utilities Industry in New Orleans: A Case Study in Capital, Labor, and Government, 1894-1929," *Louisiana History* 22, no. 2 (1981): 50-53; Pearce, "Rise and Decline," 72-73; "Street Railway Employees Will be Paid in Full," *New Orleans Times-Picayune*, August 21, 1918, 1; Michael Mizell-Nelson, "Challenging and Reinforcing White Control of Public Space: Race Relations on New Orleans Streetcars, 1861-1965," (PhD diss., Tulane University, 2001); Michael Mizell-Nelson and Matthew J. Martinez, *Streetcar Stories*, University of California Extension Center for Media and Independent Learning, 1997; Charles G. Carpenter, "The New Orleans Street Railway Strike of 1929-1930," (master's thesis, Tulane University, 1970), 138; 1918 contract, box 26, Union records.

the jurisdiction of many tradesmen working in the Gas House plants remained to be negotiated. For example, the recording secretary of the International Brotherhood of Stationary Firemen contacted the carmen's union to see whether the latter intended to claim the firemen, oilers, and water tenders working at the Market Street Power Station. Once again, the long extant tradition of African American members belonging to a colored sub-division was brought to the attention of the carmen.[16]

The advent of the integrated union seemed as quiet as it was peculiar. The black worker presence in the union received little attention. Newspaper accounts include details of the contract and mention the inclusion of Gas House workers but do not note the significance of the change. An April 1919 letter from the carmen's legal representative, William H. Byrnes Jr., indicates his surprise at finding a black man claiming membership in the Street Carmen's Union. Byrnes assumes that the man must belong to a colored subdivision, and asks if any such organization exists. Given the protracted 1918 contract negotiations, this question seems especially odd. Byrnes referred to a court case, *Wilkens* v. *the Street Carmen's Union*, which involved Joseph Wilkens, a member of the carmen's union and the secretary treasurer of the People's Benevolent Insurance Company of Louisiana, a black-owned business.[17]

The National War Labor Board, citing the higher costs of

16.　William Finigan to John Stadler, 9 July 1918, box 2, correspondence, Union records.

17.　William H. Byrnes Jr. to Gus Bienvenu, 1 April 1919, box 2, correspondence, Union records; New Orleans City Directory, 1917. Attempts to locate any Orleans Parish Civil Court records of this case were unsuccessful, as were several digital searches within America's Historical Newspaper and LexisNexis Academic (Federal and State Cases combined) databases. Searches were performed using information about the case as well as names of principal individuals. Consultation with Loyola and Tulane University Law Librarians (including conventional searches performed by these experts) also did not uncover any additional information.

living associated with the war, had first established a forty-two-cents minimum wage for all New Orleans railway and utility workers in their August 1 ruling. Skilled white mechanics and others objected to the idea of unskilled blacks earning hourly wages very close to their own. New Orleans politicians and white unionists objected to the tripling of black workers' earnings and successfully pursued a revision of the NWLB decision. Reducing the minimum wage to thirty-eight cents in this case satisfied white workers and set precedent for future discriminatory treatment of black workers by the board.[18] The board's October 24 ruling lowered the raises for mechanics and other utility company employees from its 71.5 percent increase; they now set a ten cents per hour raise across the board for those not operating the cars. "The [original] award required the company to pay negro and other common labor $4.20 per day, while the city and other large employers of such labor paid $3.50 per day," according to the railway company.[19] Joseph McCartin emphasizes that these wage reductions affected black workers, but these integrated workspaces included even more white workers in the same positions. Two notices of threatened strikes by the men operating the gas and power generating stations are mentioned by New Orleans news coverage. Refiguring wage rates for mechanics, unskilled, and black workers along with the threatened, unsanctioned work stoppage dominated the newspaper coverage. No mention of a colored subdivision or how exactly these workers would fit into the union was made as the railway company sought to avoid bankruptcy while keeping the local war economy on track.[20]

Outsiders paid little notice to the presence of African Americans, but internal politics were affected soon afterwards. In late July of 1919, a member of the local protested a union

18.   McCartin, 116-17, 155.

19.   "War Board Raise Postpones Strike At Powerhouse Crisis," *New Orleans Times-Picayune*, October 25, 1918, 10.

20.   Ibid.

election, charging that election commissioners had helped the black members vote "a great number of the ballots." A member of the local's executive board responded that these commissioners had merely assisted those black members who did not know how to read or write and had no experience in voting. He also stated that two commissioners helped each voter while closely following the rules and laws of the Australian ballot. A union trial later found the man who reported the alleged impropriety guilty of falsifying a protest.[21]

In several instances, the white officers attempted to represent the interests of their black union brothers. Responding to a request for his legal opinion, union counsel Byrnes concluded that "a foreman in charge of a gang of laborers lending them money at a usurious rate of interest" could not be prosecuted criminally. That white officers even investigated the possibility of litigation is noteworthy. The penultimate version of the 1920 contract contained a line intended to prevent railway managers from discriminating against black track gang members. "It is further agreed that colored trackmen shall be paid on Friday, or no discrimination on day of payment," according to the last line of a section defining the payment schedule. This sentence disappeared from the final version of the contract. Even more significantly, the black members remained in the new contract though the railway company had sought to remove all "track and other labor, largely colored, meter readers, and employees of the New Orleans Gas Light Company who, as heretofore stated, were for the first time included in the 1918 contract."[22]

The long tradition of foremen on the waterfront extorting money from non-union workers, particularly black ones, is

---

21.   Philip Engelbracht to William D. Mahon, 1 August 1919, box 2, correspondence, Union records.

22.   "Learn the Truth, Receiver J.D. O'Keefe's Proposal to the Amalgamated Association of Electric and Street Railway Employes [*sic*]," advertisement, *New Orleans Times-Picayune,* June 27, 1920.

well documented.[23] A similar sort of tyrannical hold on labor "gangs" existed in the street railway industry. In completing their applications for union membership, many black laborers identified their employer using the surname of their foreman rather than the railway company. Unionization provided at least a few attempts to end the worst abuses. Several months later, the superintendent of Way and Structures circulated a warning meant to protect track gang laborers from foremen who solicited or accepted money from their workers. Any employee, whether foreman or a laborer, would be discharged for violating company policy.[24] Division 194's grievance procedure likely played a role in management's decision to circulate the warning. Numerous examples of grievances filed by black as well as white employees and pursued by the local's leadership are found in the street railway union collection.[25]

Beginning in January 1921, carmen locals throughout the nation began to accept drastic wage reductions following the generous wage concessions established by the National War Labor Board. The First International vice president reported: "it is regrettable that reductions are before us, yet it is a situation that we have no control over and our organization is passing through it very good under the terrible circumstances." In New Orleans, the railway company succeeded in winning steep wage reductions in May 1921. While motormen and conductors suffered wage reductions ranging from four to five cents per hour, depending upon seniority, wages for

23.   Arnesen, *Waterfront Workers*, 61, 254.

24.   William H. Byrnes Jr. to Gus Bienvenu, n.d., box 2, correspondence, Union records; Contracts, 1920, box 13, Union records; G.C. Estill, Supt. of Way and Structures, to all employees, leaflet, 1 March 1921, box 14, NOPS 1920-25 folder, Union records.

25.   Boxes 2-5, Union records. From 1920 through 1929, several periods characterized by an especially high number of grievances filed by employees and pursued by Division 194's Executive Board members reflect the combative nature of union and company negotiations that began during the 1919 receivership and ended with the destruction of the union in 1929.

track laborers fell from forty-three cents to thirty cents per hour, and many other positions experienced similarly steep reductions.[26]

Black and white groundsmen, groundsmen helpers, and truck drivers, all of whom assisted linemen employed by the New Orleans Gas Light Company, experienced a five-cent wage reduction. Following the tradition of craft unionism, the linesmen remained in the International Brotherhood of Electrical Workers (IBEW), Local 4. In June 1921, IBEW Local 4 asked Division 194 to release the groundsmen, chauffeurs, and undergroundsmen to the former union, noting that they wanted "white only." This request led to a minor dispute over jurisdiction. International President William Mahon noted that in 1918 the Electrical Workers had said that they could not accept these unskilled men because of their union's laws, yet now that these same workers had been organized, the IBEW wanted to claim the same white workers. Mahon explained in his letter to Division 194 officers that since no proper petition had been prepared, the request could be ignored on procedural grounds.[27]

Secretary Gus Bienvenu's correspondence with the carmen's international president explained the recent history. After first checking with the IBEW leadership in 1918, Division 194 had proceeded to organize all of the groundsmen and other workers who assisted the linesmen. IBEW officers had even assisted in the recruiting process.

> Now Brother Fitzgerald Local 4 does not want to take in the Stockroom keepers and helpers, and they draw the color line, and we have a great many colored

26.   William B. Fitzgerald to Gus Bienvenu, 11 May 1921; Wage Rate Report, Conference Committee to General membership of 194; both in box 2, correspondence, Union records.

27.   H.J. Lagarde to Gus Bienvenu, 13 June 1921; William B. Mahon to Gus Bienvenu, 7 June 1921; Gus Bienvenu to William B. Mahon, 1 July 1921; all found in box 2, Union records.

members working in the underground department, in other words Brother Fitzgerald Local 4 wants to pick the men they want, and what is left can remain in Local 194. [28]

Division 194 did not want to lose workers that they had only recently organized, and the officers certainly did not want to be left with only the black workers. In the same period, the prospect of losing white members inspired a movement to force the black members to accept a separate charter. While white members outnumbered black by more than two to one, union officers seemed to act to prevent any further weakening of the white voting bloc. Division 194 President Edwin Peyroux introduced a resolution at their July 1921 monthly meeting.

Whereas, much dissatisfaction has from time to time arisen because of the inclusion of the negro employment of the New Orleans Railway and Light Company in Local 194, and, Whereas, many members have expressed their opinion that it would further the best interest of both Local 194 and of the Negro members themselves, that if a separate charter in the A.A. of S. and E.R.E. of A. should be obtained for the benefit of the Negro employees of the New Orleans Railways and Light Company, a vote should be taken to find out whether a separate charter for black members should be sought at the upcoming International convention. [29]

In rejecting the subdivision model once again, white union officials now insisted that the black members must form an entirely separate union. When Peyroux introduced the resolution, "about 8 to 12 colored members at the very most" attended the meeting. The August 1 election, wrote Secretary Bienvenu, resulted in "810 for and 340 against, which shows

28.   Gus Bienvenu to William B. Fitzgerald, 5 July 1921, box 2, Union records.

29.   Gus Bienvenu to William B. Mahon, 10 August 1921, box 2, Union records.

that the colored members are against resolution." He described the event to the international president in a personal letter that seeks his advice and intimated that

> [separating the black members] has been Brother Peyroux['s] attitude since last Convention, if you can remember the conversation he claims he had with you on that subject.
>
> Now Brother Mahon I don't want you to think that I am overstepping my duty, by informing you of this situation, but I am doing it solely as a true Trade Unionist. I don't know how some of the members might take this, not being authorized by Local to communicate same to you. But if I have done wrong kindly advise me, I am always ready and willing to take advise from you.[30]

In a personal response, Mahon assured Bienvenu he had done nothing wrong by informing him of the matter. Mahon stated that the International could not grant a charter to the black workers separately because "the question of jurisdiction would be raised against us and they would be out of membership." If Peyroux decided to continue toward that goal and the convention approves the resolution, "it will mean that these members will lose their membership in the Association," according to Mahon, who promised to explain the situation to Peyroux at the convention.[31] The international officers held this position throughout most of the controversy over black membership.

Mahon also commented upon the strained efforts to recruit the black members in 1918. "Your division appealed urgently to take in these men who were really not eligible to membership in our organization. It precipitated quite a fight with the employing company but we finally succeeded

30.   Ibid.

31.   William B. Mahon to Gus Bienvenu, 13 August 1921, box 2, Union records.

in holding them," Mahon argued. A few days later, Mahon fielded a letter from George Mosley, a representative of the African American union members who served on the local's executive board. According to Mosley's account, Peyroux surprised everyone at the July 27 meeting by producing the resolution, and a vote later that night favored passage. Since the black members were "dissatisfied with the result of the election," Mosley had advised them to attend the next regular meeting, which was held on August 10. About one hundred of the colored members were present.

> When the minutes of the previous meeting, held on July 27th, 1921, were read, I made a motion that the minutes be adopted as read except the resolution pertaining to a separate charter for the colored employees be referred to the heading of new business. The Chair accepted my motion and it was carried. After disposing of the regular order of business, the secretary called up the resolution under the head of new business. I then made a motion that the resolution be non-concurred in, or, in other words, stricken out from the minutes of the previous meeting. The President ruled that this motion was out of order, statement stating that a referendum vote had been previously taken and the resolution had to be carried out.[32]

Mosley had considered appealing the decision; instead, he decided to seek Mahon's advice. The letter ends by explaining that the black members never "tried to direct the affairs of 194. We were always satisfied and pleased to have a white man as our leader and we do not understand why President Peyroux

32.   George Mosley to William B. Mahon, 15 August 1921, box 2, Union records. Little information survives regarding Mosley. A death notice published in the January 17, 1937, *New Orleans Times-Picayune* indicates membership in the Public Service Benevolent Association. The company union then, to some extent, included African American members.

wishes to separate us at this time." If the move succeeded, Mosely predicted that "it will only be a short while before the colored employees of the Railways Company return to where they were in 1918 'unorganized.'"[33]

Mosley used suppliant language to depict the African Americans as satisfied members of a union dominated by its majority white membership. Mosley apparently believed that the best chance for support would be found among the international leadership. Since the international president forwarded Mosley's letter to the local, one can surmise that he was more concerned with helping the local's white officers weather a rough spot than in helping the African American members. Meanwhile, only days earlier a petition had been submitted by the white groundsmen and other linemen assistants requesting their release from 194 "as we are positive we can better our conditions" by joining the IBEW.[34]

At the September convention, the resolution committee deferred the matter to the general executive board.[35] Early in 1922, in response to recurring questions about black members of Division 194, the First International vice president advised the local officers to separate its black membership by creating a colored sub-division for "the colored membership of Division 194 employed as Trachmen [*sic*], Gas Makers, Porters, and all other colored employes [*sic*] of the New Orleans Railway and Light Company, also the New Orleans Gas and Light Company." All meetings of the subdivision were to be held separately from the "parent body," and a chairman of the subdivision would represent the black workers at Division 194 Executive Board meetings.[36]

33.   Ibid.

34.   Linemen helpers et al. to Division 194, petition, 8 August 1921, box 2, Union records.

35.   "Conference Proceedings," *The Motorman and Conductor* 29, no. 11 (October 1921): 75, 112.

36.   William B. Fitzgerald to the Officers and Members of Division 194, 12 March 1922, box 2, correspondence, Union records.

Only the effort of the international officers to block the separate charter resolution forced Division 194 officers to accept this compromise position. While many white members appeared eager to remove all black members, Division 194 fought to hold onto the white members lost to the IBEW. At least four former 194 workers recruited by the IBEW Local 104 paid dues to 194 in February 1922, "under protest," while awaiting the final decision regarding a jurisdictional dispute.[37]

In preparation for another attempt to force the black membership to accept a separate charter, Divsion 194 officials sent "petitions gotten up at the various barns in regards to the separate charter" to delegates preparing to attend the 1923 international conference. Once again, Secretary Gus Bienvenu expressed misgivings about the process and privately asked another union member whether he thought that the procedure was wrong.

> I could not see or learn what [the petitions] read. Don't you think the entire membership should have had the chance to vote for or against same, on this question. The remark as told me by some of the members is that, those in charge of the lists said that it was a resolution adopted by the association and that the association wanted to get such information.[38]

Division 194 President James Rodgers, temporarily located in Oregon, requested a complete accounting of Division 194's black membership. Bienvenu responded: "Jim, I am giving you the dada [sic] as you requested, but don't forget the fact that if the Negro is placed in the Maintenance and Ways Union, it will take all our pavers, paver helpers, druck [sic] drivers and construction carmen away from us." The 421 African American sub-division members represented about

---

37.   IBEW Local 4, letters, box 2. No further information regarding this dispute exists in the union records.

38.   Gus Bievenu to Joe, 6, 7 September, 1923, box 3, Union records.

15 percent of the union's 2,900 members.[39] The gas company employed 59 black and 102 white members; "offroad" employed 31 black and 667 white workers; and the majority of black workers, 330, were listed as working under the "others" category, which included 190 white workers.[40]

Once the efforts to purge black members began, union officers regularly blamed former Division President John Stadler for opening membership to all railway company and gas company employees and thus creating what the union now defined as the problem of black membership. Efforts to force African Americans out of 194's subdivision and into a separately chartered union continued throughout 1923 and 1924. International President Mahon once again reminded Division 194 that their desire to remove blacks from the union was thwarted by their local's special efforts in 1918 to enroll them. Mahon now argued, "these men have their property rights in your Division and if they will not voluntarily go into a separate division there is no power that can force them to do it." Mahon feared a federal court order prohibiting the international from "barring them as members or transferring them to another Division."[41] Two questions needed to be answered before Division 194 could proceed to push the black members out. First, the majority of the membership had to favor the black members giving up their membership in the union over the compromise subdivision arrangement. The more difficult question centered upon the black members. "Are the colored men willing and will they make application for a separate charter and withdraw their membership from your Division and affiliate with a new Division under a new charter name?" Mahon asked.[42]

From 1924-1926, the black members must have answered

39.   Gus Bienvenu to William B. Mahon, 14 July 1925; Gus Bievenu to James Rodgers, 1 October 1923; both in box 3, Union records.

40.   Gus Bievenu to James Rodgers, 1 October 1923, ibid.

41.   William B. Mahon to Gus Bienvenu, 7 January 1924, box 3, Union records.

42.   Ibid.

"no" to the second question. A gap of more than two years exists in the union record regarding the status of 194's black workers, who remained in a subdivision when the issue of establishing a separate charter reemerged in April 1926. This time an African American executive board member brought the idea forward. After he "became insulted at a remark made by one of our white Board Members," the representative of black members stood up at the regular Executive Board meeting and discussed his resentment of such remarks. The black union leader later told the Division 194 president that "he intended to apply for a separate Charter" and would start the petition process. The president responded: "go to it." The black board member then circulated a petition signed by "a number of the colored members" requesting a special meeting to discuss the separate charter issue.[43]

At the next meeting of the white union members, the Division 194 president noted that the matter seemed to be "out of our jurisdiction," since the international president had already passed on the question. After the black members requested a special meeting, the Local 194 president said, "I will explain to them that it is up to them to get enough colored members to decide if they want a separate charter," and then refer the matter to the international president.[44]

In the same letter, President Veillon argues, "I think this thing has been worked up by some of the same members who have been trying to get the colored men out of #194." The president's comment implies that a significant number of union men did not wish to remove the African Americans. Veillon probably correctly assessed the feelings of most white members, but the ultimate source of this effort likely came from outside Division 194. Veillon also mentions that "on several occasions the general manager of the Railway Company told me that he will not sign a contract for the colored members with us, and I beleive [sic] he is determined to stand by

43.   Ed Veillon to William B. Mahon, 22 April 1926, box 3, Union records.
44.   Ibid.

what he says."[45] This final and ultimately successful effort to disenfranchise black members may have been steered by managers of the railway company who sought to undermine the union by keeping the workers battling with one another.

First International Vice President Fitzgerald responded in lieu of Mahon, recommending that Veillon "keep going along in the way you have." He expressed some regret at the circumstances, "for in the end it means the men on the road who are working for wages are going to be the losers but I am of the opinion that things will change materially and to the best interest of our people."[46] The meeting called to discuss the separate charter instead handled the company's sudden reduction in the pay table for black workers, for which no notification had been provided. At the close of a regularly scheduled meeting only days later, "a Resolution was passed, instructing the President to do all in his power to help the Colored men to obtain a separate Charter." This meeting was much better attended than most because of the continual feuding among the elected officers of the union and a group of former officers. The union had rented the auditorium of the Labor Temple to accommodate the crowd. The vote on the resolution suggests that a great number of the white membership agreed with plans to remove the black members; these actions were not likely the maneuvering of a small number of union men. The Division 194 president said that he was willing to do as ordered, but he sought advice regarding exactly what action to take in the matter.[47]

Following the meeting, President Veillon reported once again that the railway company manager had told him "he would not sign a contract covering the Negro men," and old members of the union were daily being asked to visit the Railway Company office, where they were told that the company did not intend to sign a contract with 194 that

45.   Ibid.

46.   William B. Fitzgerald to Ed Veillon, 28 April 1926, box 3, Union records.

47.   Ed Veillon to William B. Mahon, 4 May 1926, box 3, Union records.

would compel new men to join the union. Disturbed by the developments, Veillon urgently sought President Mahon's advice.[48] First International Vice President Fitzgerald responded that the union should ignore any reports from the company and proceed as usual toward the beginning of the contract negotiation process.[49]

A special meeting of the colored subdivision convened to discuss the possibility of establishing a separate charter. Management proved to be "very active" in attempting to orchestrate a vote favoring a separate charter. "[T]he track foremans [*sic*] of the various gangs has warned their men to go down to said meeting, and for them to vote for a separate charter," Veillon reported to Mahon. Only about sixty black members of Division 194's colored subdivision attended the meeting, and "some were afraid to vote and the majority of those who were not present, did not come on account of being afraid to vote against a separate charter," according to the Division 194 president. Following a long period of discussion, the separate charter proposal failed, with nine votes in favor and forty-three opposed. The president also reported that one of the leaders of the rival group was holding "clandestine meetings around the various barns."[50]

> Every one of our meetings are packed with this bunch, they can get off whenever there is a meeting and I am informed, paid to attend these meetings and the members who are loyal to their Organization [c]annot get off, and those that do attend these meetings are afraid to express their opinion on any question, because the Rys Co. knows exactly what transpires and who voted for or against any question that might come up

48.   Ibid.

49.   William B. Fitzgerald to Ed Veillon, 10 May 1926, box 3, Union records.

50.   Ed Veillon to William B. Mahon, 14 May 1926, box 3, Union records.

before the meeting adjourns [*sic*].[51]

This rival group of union men, soon to establish a company union named the Progressive Benevolent Association, used the long extant controversy involving the presence of black union members to generate animosity toward the union leadership. The local president interpreted the actions of the railway company in the context of its larger efforts to dismantle the union. The president still considered the black members to be part of the union, and he closed with a brief reference to having recently begun work on the new proposed contract. The contract in place was due to expire at the end of June.

Only two weeks later, the division leadership worked to remove the black members completely from union representation. Division 194 President Veillon sought the advice of International Vice President Fitzgerald in handling the refusal of the colored subdivision members to request a separate charter for black members. Fitzgerald advised the local's executive board to continue to behave as if the black members would still be covered in the new contract. "[L]et that Division go along and ask for conditions just as if nothing had occurred and when we arrive where we are going to meet the danger points, we will meet the whole situation at the one time," Fitzgerald recommended.

Division President Veillon responded, "I am very much worried that the action of our A.M. meeting of May 26th, in regards to our negotiating a new contract for the white members only and attempt [*sic*] to get one for the negros under a separate Charter may cause us a law suit." Veillon acknowledged that the majority of white members favored forcing the black members out and the railway company managers "have already told me they were not going to sign up for the colored men any more." At two subsequent meetings, the black members continued to refuse to apply for a separate charter. During the second meeting, the black members voted

51.   Ibid.

eleven in favor and eighteen against.[52] Despite the tenacious resistance of the black members, their tenure with the union was coming to an end.

Division 194's letter to General Manager A.B. Patterson initiating contract negotiations began by stating that the carmen sought the same conditions as in the 1924 agreement, "in so far as the white men are concerned." The president's letter closed with, "in conference we will be pleased to talk on the colored members of this Association."[53]

As promised, railway managers did not sign an agreement that covered black workers. Unlike previous contracts, the new working agreement that resulted from these negotiations listed specific job titles in departments as "white." Thus, in the streetcar maintenance barns, the contract excluded black night watchmen. In the Maintenance of Ways and Structures Department, commonly known as the Track Department, the contract covered only white truck drivers and night watchmen. In the Gas Department, the local now represented only white night watchmen, caulkers, service layers, truck drivers, syphon pumpers, and shopmen.[54]

The Railway Company soon used this 1926 innovation in conjunction with its most powerful concession from the 1920 contract: the right to fire workers "for any reason whatsoever," other than belonging to a union.[55] Several weeks into the new contract period, the company laid off the union's white paver helpers, "and ha[d] replaced them with negrow [sic] helpers,

52.   William B. Fitzgerald to Ed Veillon, 18 May 1926; Ed Veillon to President William D. Mahon, 14, 28 May and 8 June 1926; all found in box 3, correspondence, Union records.

53.   Ed Veillon to A.B. Patterson, 11 June 1926, box 3, Union records.

54.   1926 Contract, box 13, Union records.

55.   Carpenter, "New Orleans Street Railway Strike," 19-20; for a concise interpretation of the role of public utilities in New Orleans economic and political life, see Adam Fairclough, "The Public Utilities Industry in New Orleans: A Study in Capital, Labor and Government, 1894-1929," *Louisiana History* 22, no. 1 (Winter 1981): 45-65.

which we have no jurisdiction over and in my opinion is a strict violation of the Contract," complained President Veillon to the international vice president.[56] The railway managers double-crossed the white union leaders, pretending during contract negotiations to favor them, only to dump them for cheaper, unorganized black workers.

In late December, several black members complained to International President Mahon about the exclusion of blacks from representation under the latest contract. After stating that the black members had been "solicited and forced to become members" of the union in 1918, the letter writers allowed that "[i]n the past, up to a recent date, we have been given a little protection according to working agreements" negotiated on behalf of white and black union members.

> There is an agreement between 194 and the subdivision. The agreement is that the subdivision is entitled to representatives on the conference board and the question of wages and hours. The contract that was signed August 12, 1926, would not allow us representation nor would not allow us colored, to vote on any question. We further state that the present contract was signed for a "closed shop" which specifically specifies "white" only, and none of the colored members were included in said working agreement or contract as signed by said officials of said Public Service Company. We further state that colored members that are employed by the Public Service Co., of them, some twenty years or more, are not allowed to join Local 194.[57]

The aggrieved black union members also complained that they had not been allowed to participate in the recent strike

56. Ed Veillon to William B. Fitzgerald, 23 September 1926, box 3, Union records.

57. (Colored) members of Division 194 to International President William D. Mahon, 19 December 1926, box 3, correspondence, Union records.

vote. The local president explained to the African American members that Division 194 would not accept any more black members, and "those who were in would not have the protection of the working agreement other than the endowment and Sick benefit."[58] It is possible that an attorney supplied by New Orleans Public Service, Inc., (NOPSI) aided the black members in writing their complaint letter. The union later noted that the company union incorporated in 1927 with the assistance of one of NOPSI's attorneys and the carefully chosen legal language and relative absence of grammatical mistakes found in the protest letter submitted by the black workers contrasts markedly with the style of writing that characterized letters penned by Division 194 officials.[59]

Mahon sent a December 31, 1926, letter to Division 194's officers requesting their position on the issue, but no record of their response survives. In 1926 and subsequent years, union leaders were confronted with larger issues concerning the survival of the union. The threat from rival union members who first confronted the elected officers expanded in 1927 when they formed a company union supported by NOPSI. One resolution submitted during the Louisiana State Federation convention of 1927 urged the merger or consolidation of the PBA with 194 and observed that 1918 had been 194's strongest year. However, after organizing "all other crafts working for the railway company," the 194 had witnessed the stripping away of its membership by craft unions. Simultaneously, the New Orleans Steam Ship Association was purging workers and trade unionists of both races from the docks.[60] Cooperating with the leaders of the company union was impossible.

58.   Ibid.

59.   The attorney, Benjamin W. Kernan, had worked almost exclusively for New Orleans Railway and Light and New Orleans Public Service. Carpenter, "The New Orleans Street Railway Strike," 141.

60.   Letter, 4 April 1927, box 4, Union records; Edith Ambrose, "A Revolution of Hope: New Orleans workers and their Unions, 1923-1939," (PhD diss., Tulane University, 1998) 46-50.

The 1926 contract that originally seemed to
union officers' race problem hastened the cor
management that caused Division 194's demis
strike. Railway managers had skillfully exploited ᴜᴛᴇ ₊₋
in their battle to establish the open shop. This rare experiment
with both interracial unionism and industrial unionism
within a traditionally conservative AFL local underscores the
ongoing reevaluation of the meaning of segregated unions
for African Americans. In taking in track gang workers, gas
company laborers, and other groups previously excluded
from organized labor, Division 194 had broken new ground
for pragmatic reasons that temporarily served to strengthen
their union. Mosely and the men he represented were forced
to rely on local and international white leadership, which,
despite some efforts to represent black interests and provide
higher wages, could never be trusted.

Division 194 leadership exploited the unprecedented
intervention of the federal government into the wartime
economy in a fashion unlike most other union locals. They
sought to extend control over the vast network of transit
and utility company employees while simultaneously filling
their coffers with dues paid by newly organized black and
white workers. Some of these workers, according to AFL
regulations, belonged in other craft unions, but most were
unskilled and deemed unworthy of union membership; as a
whole, they must have appeared to Division 194 officers as
relatively easy to control. In one of the earliest documented
instances, an AFL local employed both interracial and
industrial organizing tactics that most traditional American
workplaces would not experience in tandem until twenty
years later when the Committee of Industrial Organization
(CIO) took advantage of the next widespread extension of
federal power in the workplace. More documentation would
help in understanding why Division 194 took aberrant action,
but none may ever emerge. The anomaly provides insight
into how one AFL local seized an opportunity to better their

ircumstances while also improving workplace conditions and wages for some of the most exploited and least respected workers in the transit and utility industries.

Examining the intricate calculations of this particular local in the early 1900s reveals an undercurrent of resistance against some Jim Crow strictures in the workplace. Ironically, this move was taken by the men charged with enforcing race segregation in one of the most visible and crowded public spaces in any city: streetcar platforms. White passengers regularly complained that the carmen too often neglected to "do their job" and opted to ignore the race segregation aspect of their work. New Orleans's troubled heritage of interracial and biracial cooperation among dock workers provided a counter-narrative to that of the city's white business elites that the carmen officials negotiated contracts with. John Stadler's shift from union local to city politics and back to the local in 1918 brought a seasoned negotiator intent on taking full advantage of federal intervention into the war economy.

McCartin ends his treatment of New Orleans's transit workers following news of the wage reduction, which he acknowledges still left them better off financially as organized workers. His study also notes the antipathy skilled northern union organizers displayed towards black workers as well as the violent reaction of many white workers against the arrival of African American workers in northern cities. The more contentious and dramatic efforts to organize black and white steelworkers in Alabama serve as McCartin's leading narrative for race in WWI.[61] While the Birmingham campaign failed, owing to ferocious, racist opposition, the subtler expressions of bigotry among New Orleans street railway organizers deserve more attention. Despite McCartin's focus on race — as well as the references made by company and union officials in arguing for the readjustment — the positions affected by the wage reduction included white as well as black workers. Union representation for unskilled workers

61.   McCartin, 149-56, 49.

the carmen's international officers considered unworthy of membership remained intact. The integrated powerhouse workers, union members for all of a couple of months, twice threatened a wildcat strike in response to the new NWLB ruling; the carmen leaders mostly kept them in check, but about 120 powerhouse workers walked out for ten days.[62] In addition to unsanctioned actions taken by black and white workers, many black union members were empowered to file grievances against racist track crew bosses and to report problems with local leaders to the international officers in Detroit. Within the first few months of the landmark contract, at least one member participated in a lawsuit against his union local regarding insurance benefits.

The long extant interest of labor historians in streetcar strikes characterized by days of hyper-masculine violence and destruction of company property must be complemented by increased attention to the complex stories found in locals. Recent street railway industry scholarship influenced by the rising interest in working-class studies may help to reveal more of the nuances of transit union politics.[63]

62. "Official Award to Railway Men Reaches Orleans; Dissatisfaction on Part of Gas and Powerhouse Employees Reported," *New Orleans Times-Picayune*, October 31, 1918, 13; "Interpreters Uphold Railway Company; Appeal of Head of Carmen's Union Fails to Effect Change," *New Orleans Times-Picayune*, November 16, 1918, 2.

63. Organization of American History/National Council on Public History, 2012 Annual Meeting, April 18-22, 2012, Program, Session: "Race and Class on the Roads and Rails: New Approaches to a Working-Class History of Mass Transportation," 85; "Black Workers in Jim Crow Workspace: Transit Workers and Teachers in Mid-Twentieth Century New Orleans," Mizell-Nelson, panel organizer, presenter, Social Science History Association, November 2005; unpublished paper: "'Still Working for Jim Crow': Streetcar Track Maintenance Workers in 1970s New Orleans."

5 "Brother, I guess this is a world of money": Centrality of Economics and Employment to New Orleans Voodoo during the Great Depression

KODI ROBERTS

In the late 1930s, while gathering information and interviews with known Voodoo practitioners in and around New Orleans, researchers with the Louisiana Writers' Project (LWP) sought out Lala Hopkins, a woman referred to them and identified by other practitioners in the city as a well-known Voodoo Queen. LWP researchers painted a rather unflattering picture of Mrs. Hopkins, a brown complexioned woman who at approximately fifty-three years of age was described as "small in stature" and "thin," with "decaying teeth" and "matted hair." Despite her appearance Lala apparently had quite a reputation among Voodoo practitioners. This reputation was bolstered by her claim to a rather impressive spiritual lineage. She identified her mentor as a queen called Marie Comtesse. Comtesse was, according to her protégé, a powerful practitioner in her own right. What was most impressive about this education in Voodoo was that Lala claimed that Comtesse had learned her trade from the infamous nineteenth-century Voodoo Queen Marie Laveau. Like many other workers, a term used to denote professional practitioners of Voodoo, Lala viewed Laveau as the indirect source of her power and ritual expertise.

While these claims demonstrate how Voodoo practitioners in New Orleans looked to the past, it is crucial to remember that they were also influenced by the historical moment in which they lived. The hold on tradition undoubtedly bolstered Lala's claim that she was the best worker in town. Lala boasted about her spiritual-professional lineage, telling interviewers that because she trained with Comtesse, and Comtesse trained with Laveau, she knew what Marie Laveau knew. Lala maintained that anything she didn't know wasn't to be known. In praise of her teacher, Lala proudly admitted that she learned everything she knew from Comtesse, and she told the interviewer that it was only natural that she would use her teacher's techniques. Despite her pride in the Voodoo of Laveau and Comtesse however, Lala did admit that the rites she performed were not identical to those of her predecessors. She told interviewers that she altered and "streamlined" the Voodoo she had learned in order to better serve her clientele, explaining, "Ya know ya got to fix dis bisness lak de people wants it. Dis makes it different."[1] This act of recreating ritual was at the heart of the practice of Voodoo in early twentieth-century New Orleans. The dynamism and adaptation of workers in giving "de people" the "bisness" they wanted during times of economic hardship, often centered on providing for their economic needs, specifically their need for employment. If it wasn't already, this catering to employment needs pushed the spiritual practices that characterized Voodoo in New Orleans firmly into the realm of market relations.

For Lala, like her mentors before her, Voodoo was a business. One of the monikers most frequently used to describe professional practitioners, "worker," and references to their professional religious and magical services as "the work" implied the centrality of the economic exchange for professional practitioners of Voodoo. The myths and history about the iconic Voodoo Queen Marie Laveau are deeply indebted to the nineteenth century for the culture that characterized both Laveau and accounts of her spiritual practices. Similarly, the tracing of her professional lineage back to Laveau, positioned Lala within a cultural and historical context specific to the

---

1.   "Marie Comtesse," Robert Tallant Collection, reel 8, 803, 805-807, Manuscripts Collection, Louisiana Division, New Orleans Public Library.

social and economic milieu that characterized New Orleans at the beginning of the twentieth century. In addition, many of the formula, practices, and services conducted by Lala and other workers in this period were heavily influenced by the socio-economic circumstances under which they were performed. As Lala so eloquently explained, professional practitioners had to ascertain the needs of local clientele and then adapt their services to meet those needs, thereby making innovation as much a part of their profession as tradition. Most salient, especially by the 1930s, was the shift of workers to meet the economic needs of clients who, like a large segment of the U.S. population at the time, were suffering in the grips of the Great Depression.

Employment and money were scarce during the 1930s and professional practitioners spent a great deal of their effort attempting to improve clients' economic circumstances in general and, more specifically, obtaining jobs for the unemployed. In addition to the influence exerted by clients, workers also had to reshape their rites so that they could practice within the constrictions put into place by city ordinances and local law enforcement. Rather than deal with the complications that might result from prosecuting Voodoo practitioners for their religious practices, authorities specifically targeted the economic aspects of their spiritual practices as various types of fraud. Further, the push of consumerism and the triumph of a cash-based economy that began at the end of the nineteenth century and continued in the early twentieth century led practitioners in New Orleans, as well as most Americans, to begin to understand U.S. currency as powerful in its own right. [2] Practitioners in New Orleans often translated this as an understanding that currency actually held metaphysical power, including money as components in magical rites. Rather than simply offering food or alcohol to the saints and spirits they entreated for

---

2.   William Leach, *Land of Desire: Merchants, Power, and the Rise of a New American Culture* (New York: Pantheon Books, 1993), xiii, 3,7-9.

assistance, they often began to pay the spirits in cash, as well. All these influences on workers point to the extraordinary impact of money on Voodoo in early twentieth-century New Orleans.

The dynamic adjustments to the needs of customers, the constrictions of law, and the rise of consumerism demonstrate the fluidity and malleability of Voodoo in early twentieth-century New Orleans. The ways in which practitioners bent and shaped the work illuminates the importance of indigenous American cultural exchanges, the social and economic vagaries of life in New Orleans, and the centrality of economics, specifically employment, to determining the character of Voodoo in the Crescent City.

At a ceremony to mourn the passing of spiritualist and Voodoo practitioner Mother Kate Francis, Mother Louise Bowers was interviewed by researchers from the Works Progress Administration's Louisiana Writers' Project. She offered her services to the interviewer who had come to speak to her about Mother Kate. She told him, "Fo' a quarter, I could stimulate yo' luck with her blessings direct." Even in the wake of her mentor's death Mother Bowers was hard at work. She then, in no uncertain terms, let the interviewer know that she required compensation for her services. To make her position clear she asked rhetorically, "What could I do fo' nothing? Nothing." Even in the midst of honoring her co-worker, a term used by spiritualists to denote fellow practitioners often trained in the same church, Mother Louise had not forgotten the bottom line. [3] Bowers explained that "What the people don't know is that the saints want money too. Brother, I guess this is a world of money."[4]

In her statement Mother Louise hit on two key points: first, that she lived in a "world of money" or a society preoccupied with the pecuniary value of goods and services; second, her

3.   The term *worker* is not to be confused with the term *co-worker* used by spiritualists, though they are probably not unrelated terms either.

4.   "Mother Kate Francis" Federal Writers Project, folder 39.

statement that the "saints want money too" displayed an understanding of the connection between the material and spiritual realms engaged by practitioners of Voodoo in which the spiritual realm was not exempt from this consuming concern with money. In the early twentieth century many workers had managed to monetize and often institutionalize their spiritual practices. Those practices ran parallel to changes underway throughout the United States around the turn of the century.

Between 1880 and 1930 American society was transformed by corporate business. The new reigning culture was preoccupied with consumption, comfort, and bodily well being, and the predominant measure of all values in society became economic. Establishment of a relatively stable currency-based economy in the second half of the nineteenth century led to a new standard by the beginning of the twentieth in which pecuniary or market values became the base measure for all other values, including beauty, friendship, and in this case, spirituality. The value of anything was determined by what price it could fetch on the market. Voodoo practitioners, as privy to these changes as most Americans, embraced them in order to meet the needs of their clientele that was, by the twentieth century, overwhelmingly economic.[5] The story of Mother Kate and Mother Bowers is a reflection of the complex dynamic that saw the embracing of the values of consumer culture in workers' garnering of profits for themselves and their clients. The ubiquity of those values is implied by workers' use of spiritual power to improve the economic situation of clients. The services most frequently requested of workers dealt with relieving the financial burdens on those who came to them for help. In exchange, both workers and the saints they enlisted for aid often demanded monetary compensation for that aid.

By the early twentieth century, establishing a model of practice that would allow them to turn a profit and earn a

5.   Leach, *Land of Desire*, xiii, 3,7-9.

living was apparently common among Voodoo practitioners in New Orleans. Reports of Voodoo related gatherings or ceremonies in the nineteenth century suggest that rather than finding legal ways to operate, practitioners simply performed rites clandestinely. If this was the case, it would have severely limited the activities of nineteenth century practitioners and effectively made the practice of Voodoo unsustainable. By the end of the turn of the century however, workers began to come up with methods for operating within the constrictions of the law in order to make a profit practicing Voodoo. Similarly, the extreme privation coinciding with economic downturns in the late nineteenth and early twentieth centuries also made economic well-being an overwhelming concern of workers' clientele. I argue here that workers internalized larger American ideological trends and priorities concerning currency, spending, and employment, and that those were in turn reflected in their rituals.

Economic downturns in the 1890s, 1920s, and again throughout the 1930s increased the attractiveness of Voodoo, despite the racialized stigma attached to the religion. Amateur ethnographer Harry Middleton Hyatt defined *hoodoo*, a more common term among his informants than *voodoo*, as the eruption of modern commercialism in the field of magic.[6] Workers in this period, consistent with a dire need due to the financial hardships that accompanied the aforementioned economic downturns, focused their services on the rites that could be marketed both for their own economic gain as well as that of their clients. Hyatt believed that there was a direct correlation between his ability to find an abundance of good informants, many of whom came to him seeking employment, and the economic privation of the people in any given locale.[7] Despite the stories of enormous wealth being earned

6.   Harry Middleton Hyatt, 1970. *Hoodoo-Conjuration-Witchcraft-Rootwork: Beliefs accepted by many Negroes and white persons, these being orally recorded among Blacks and whites* (Hannibal, Mo.: Western Publishing, Inc., 1970), 4: I.

7.   Hyatt, *Hoodoo*, 3: 1,903.

by workers, stories told both by outsiders and by workers themselves, interviews with some of these professional practitioners of Voodoo seemed to indicate that they were in a precarious economic state. This might imply that their services as workers were supplementing other relatively meager sources of income, rather than making them wealthy.

In this economic climate workers were most commonly solicited to improve the material conditions of their clients by aiding in businesses or job searches, helping clients in acquiring and maintaining living space, and increasing their chances in gambling. By detailing the variety of rites consistently aimed at creating or increasing profits for their clients, this essay establishes the centrality of economics for these clients and the professional practitioners of Voodoo that served them.

Perhaps the most common aid sought by workers' clients was for luck in finding employment or prosperity in business. Most workers had rites they used to influence employers to hire or keep on employees that varied widely in form. The number and diversity of these rites implies a preoccupation among the clients of workers with supporting themselves that aligns with the economic difficulties throughout the country during the 1930s, when many of these men and women were interviewed about their work as practitioners of Voodoo. The difficulty many Americans had finding employment during this same period suggests that Voodoo practitioners were reacting to the employment market to better serve their clients. They did so, again, by focusing or re-focusing a large number of the rites they used on finding or sustaining employment.

In the early stages of the Great Depression Louisiana's unemployed population was concentrated in New Orleans. In 1930, the U.S. Department of Commerce and the Bureau of the Census collected detailed figures on unemployment in the state. The census reported 2,101,593 individuals living in the state, 1,622,868 of whom they classified as gainful workers, or those older than ten years of age and able to work—the employable. The cutoff of this category being ten years tells us about the necessity of work for all members of the household in Depression-era Louisiana as well as the preponderance of agricultural labor in the state. That being noted, of the more than one and a half million employable people in the state, some 39,396 were unemployed or receiving no income in 1930. Of the over two million people in the state, 1,268,061 were classified as living in rural territories. Of the 833,532 living in urban areas, 535,417 lived in one of the state's two largest cities, Shreveport (76,655) and New Orleans (458,762). Of the state's 39,396 unemployed workers, only 2,121 lived in Shreveport with a full 19,782 concentrated in the city of New Orleans. This meant that with 9.6 percent of the employable population of New Orleans having no income, the city's unemployed population made up nearly 70 percent of the unemployed population of the state.[8] This is undoubtedly why employment rites became so important to New Orleans's professional Voodoo practitioners and their clients during this period.

One indication of the importance of employment to the clients of professional Voodoo practitioners may be evidence that suggests the use of pre-existing rites, formerly used for purposes other than finding or maintaining employment. A worker who claimed to be from Havana, Cuba, used a rite that required his client to wear his underclothes inside out and bathe his feet in sugar and cinnamon bark, after which, he would go seeking employment without wearing socks. The instructions for inside-out underwear are very similar to rites used by other workers to get clients accused of crimes acquitted in court cases. Here, however, presuming that obtaining and maintaining employment was a more common need among his clients than dealing with the courts, the worker that ethnographer Harry Hyatt called "Havana Man" enlisted this formula to help his clients get or keep their jobs. Similarly, a

---

8.   Fifteenth Census of the United States: 1930 Unemployment Bulletin, Louisiana, Unemployment Returns by Classes, 1-22.

different worker described a ritual used simply to "make one man favor another." Rather than changing the use of the ritual, he suggested that if used on an employer, then this same rite was good for getting a job.[9] If these rituals were initially used for purposes other than gaining employment but adjusted to get work for clients due to demand for employment, this shift says a great deal about how important employment was to those seeking the aid of professional Voodoo practitioners.

Candle rites were often used to exert control over lovers or harm someone in conflict with a worker's client, but by the Depression these ceremonies were also performed to control employers for the benefit of the clients of Voodoo practitioners. One candle rite described in the 1930s was supposed to be effective even if an employer had already turned a worker's client down when he or she was seeking a job. If conducted properly, the candle rite was supposed to ensure that the client would be rehired eight days after its completion.[10] One worker even claimed he could use a candle rite to influence not only employment, but the pay his clients would get when they got hired at a job.[11]

In addition to candle rites, workers also had a formula to "sweeten" the disposition of employers to their clients. To get an employer to select a worker's client from a group of potential applicants for a job, one worker suggested reading the 27th Psalm of David, a common prescription among workers, and rubbing "pecone [pecan] oil" on one's hands, which would draw the employer to the client. Another worker suggested shaking a honeycomb toward oneself to achieve a similar result.[12] Madam Lindsey, a worker from

9.   Hyatt, *Hoodoo*, 3: 2,295

10.   Hyatt, *Hoodoo*, 1: 805-808. Most often candles are burned by workers in order to call upon the aid and power of the saints but they were also a method for influencing individuals, usually by burning the candle over a piece of paper with the intended object of the rite's name.

11.   Ibid., 1,787, 832.

12.   Hyatt, *Hoodoo*, 2: 1,072, 1143

Algiers, a neighborhood of New Orleans on the West Bank of the Mississippi River, had one of the more interesting prescriptions for swaying an employer. It required a client to drink water sweetened with a particular sugar, then spit it onto the ground and walk across it just before seeing an employer about a job. Finally, the client would bite into a "wishing bean" while talking to the interviewer, who would then hire him.[13] The hope here was obviously to curry favor with someone who might provide a job by using something sweet to attract him, a formulation common among workers that dealt in romantic relationships.

What this wide variety of formulas suggests is an extraordinary need to secure employment among those seeking out Voodoo practitioners. Finding and holding a job when unemployment soared throughout the nation, reaching an estimated 25 percent at points in the 1930s, was the most urgent concern of a great many Americans during the Depression when both Harry Middleton Hyatt and members of the Louisiana Writers' Project interviewed Voodoo practitioners in New Orleans. These rites aimed at aiding laborers were common. Perhaps just as common, if not more so, were rites to help clients who were attempting to earn a living as entrepreneurs.

Workers listed dozens of formulas for "scrubs"—liquid mixtures—peddled to entrepreneurs to improve the state of their businesses. It is not certain from testimony whether this is because workers were sought out by a larger number of business owners during this period or because workers, often in business for themselves, had a bias toward entrepreneurs. It is also possible that the difficulty in getting jobs inspired individuals to strike out on their own in hopes of supporting themselves. Whatever the case may have been, the most common prescription for business owners were scrubs used to clean or bathe a place of business. The scrubs contained cinnamon, honey, white and brown sugar, filé, soured

13.   Ibid., 1,508

smartweed, parsley, green onions, John the Conqueror powder or root, syrup, milk, rosewater, garlic, fish, ants, perfume, rainwater, and numerous other components in various combinations and permutations.[14] The thinking behind some of the combinations was obviously to combine pleasant tasting or smelling spices and other substances in hopes of "sweetening" one's business and or customers. Others used less pleasant components with a less obvious logic. Nonetheless, all manner of scrubs were suggested by workers for everything from temporary ventures common during this period like house parties and fish fries, to permanent establishments and underground economic ventures of questionable legal status, like bootlegging and gambling houses. Scrubs used for most businesses were designed to attract large numbers of customers and even make those customers amiable.

Those formulas used to help businesses tied to underground economies were often aimed at keeping law enforcement away from the establishments in question. An informant who admitted to working as a bootlegger before the end of prohibition said he had managed to keep the law away from his business by simply sprinkling holy water from a Catholic church on his floor under the advice of a local worker. Another professional Voodoo practitioner suggested keeping the law or other enemies away by keeping a Bible opened to the 35th Psalm next to a glass of water sweetened with white or brown sugar. One of the most interesting rites required the placing of a beef tongue, nails, and a number of other components at the entrance to a bootlegging business. The client was to invite in a law officer who would pass over the charm and afterward not only refrain from taking action against the bootlegger, but

---

14.   Hyatt, *Hoodoo*, vol. 2-3, 2,121, 2,127, 2,296, 1,062, 1,143, 1,231, 1,369, 1,402, 1,467, 1,505, 1,656, 1,769, 1,782, 1,382. John the Conqueror was one of the most common ingredients in Voodoo related rites. It is difficult to identify the root with any one plant, as different suppliers may have used different plants calling them all John the Conqueror. See Carolyn Long, *Spiritual Merchants*, chapter 8.

protect him from his competition in the same illicit business.[15] Beef tongue rites were often used to silence an individual who might speak against a worker's client, especially opposing witnesses in court cases. Here however, co-opting the power of law enforcement seems a great deal more proactive, and again we see an example of a rite with another purpose being co-opted to aid in economic advancement. However they went about it, all these rites described by workers point to their concern with helping the economic enterprises of their clients. The legal status of those enterprises seemed to be of little or no consequence. The power of the workers was aimed at increasing the profits of entrepreneurs.

By contrast, improving business or gaining employment for clients were not the only ways workers worked on work. A particularly invidious method of harming the enemies of clients was to assault their livelihoods. The custodian of a spiritualist shrine said she could use a concoction of mustard, wine, and a number of other components mixed in a glass jar in conjunction with a reading of the 109th Psalm of David to get someone fired.[16] Another method this same practitioner prescribed for getting someone fired involved putting their bosses name and the victim's name on a piece of paper and feeding them to a frog, which was subsequently released.[17] The custodian in this case did not specify whether this was a spell employed out of malice for the victim or perhaps to commandeer the job of the fired individual. Nahnee, a practitioner who called herself the "Boss of Algiers," was from the section of New Orleans on the West Bank of the Mississippi River so famous for its workers it was often referred to as "Hoodoo Town." Nahnee described another rite that consisted of simply blowing "disturbance," "confusement," and "get-

15.   Hyatt, *Hoodoo*, vol. 1-3, 878, 2,297, 1,682, 1,368-89.

16.   Hyatt, *Hoodoo*, 2: 1,141, 1,146.

17.   Ibid.

away" powders into someone's place of business.[18] Another practitioner used a rite that required a person's photo and a lock of their hair. She promised to not only run the victim crazy, a common assault by workers on subjects, she also claimed that the rite would induce general poverty, perhaps resulting from the insanity.[19] Other workers who sought to "run" someone crazy implied that this was an end unto itself. Here the worker may have only adjusted how the rite was marketed rather than changing the actual formula but there remains the leaning toward employment as a key concern. In an era when unemployment was rampant, there were few things worse than losing one's livelihood. Anyone looking to hurt their enemies or a worker attempting to market their services to such an individual could not do much better than depriving a subject of their ability to bring in adequate income. Despite the innumerable rites available to workers to kill, maim, or otherwise harm subjects; the use of rites that specifically targeted jobs demonstrated the preoccupation of workers and their clients with economic matters.

Outside of these rites, the way workers used saints to aid with their businesses or jobs also demonstrates the centrality of monetary concerns. Nearly every saint commonly used by workers—St. Anthony, St. Expedite, St. Peter, St. Raymond, the Mother of Perpetual Help, and the Sacred Heart of Jesus— were all enlisted by workers for help with employment.[20] The implication is that with a few exceptions, no matter what a saint was traditionally considered patron of, most of them were called on to help with money or jobs.

In order to serve the needs of a clientele overwhelmingly preoccupied with earning a living, workers provided numerous rites intended to improve the chances of securing a living wage for everyone from unemployed laborers to small business owners and bootleggers. In order to do so

18. Ibid., 1,381.
19. Ibid., 3: 2,226
20. Hyatt, *Hoodoo*, vol. 1-2: 862-864, 869, 873, 878, 949, 1,374, 1,820

they used scrubs they invented for that purpose and other rites specially adapted to help with finding work. They also called to almost every saint commonly used by workers. By offering these services, workers could attract any of the 25 percent of Americans out of work or the business owners suffering because these and others could not frequent their establishments. Workers thus created a broad base to which they could appeal in a time of rampant unemployment by making their clients' overwhelming concern with making a living their own.

Housing rites were among the most telling categories of Voodoo performed by workers, demonstrating the diversity of their clientele. Economic difficulty that precluded an individual from covering the cost of their housing had an adverse effect both on their ability to secure living space and their landlord's ability to turn a profit. In turn, that may have affected a landlord's ability to pay his or her bills depending on what segment of his income was tied to rental property. Therefore, the rites performed by workers in connection with housing costs point to an economic diversity among the clientele that sought the aid of workers, including both tenants and landlords. This in turn suggests that workers' priorities were with making a profit by aiding anyone with economic needs they felt unable to meet on their own. For tenants, workers performed rites to stop their landlords from evicting them from their homes. If they had already been evicted, or were seeking a place to live, they might also come to workers to move someone out of a house or to stop that space from being rented or occupied by a new tenant. Landlords also came to workers to move people out, presumably undesirable tenants, of their own buildings and for help finding tenants for rental properties that they owned. In the case of housing, professional practitioners worked both sides of the class divide. They could do so because the widespread effect of the Depression created a sense of powerlessness and a concomitant preoccupation with money among both renters and landlords.

Even at rates as low as three dollars a week, it was often difficult for tenants during the Depression to make rent. In most cases, workers dealt with this scenario by performing rites aimed at influencing or controlling landlords. Many of these rites involved scribbling your landlord's name down and burning a candle on it, or sweetening it with cinnamon or syrup to gain his favor or control over him. Some of the rites were less directly aimed at the landlord. An Algiers worker interviewed in New Orleans had one of the more interesting rites for resolving renting issues:

> If yo' have a notice tuh move an' yo' jes' cannot pay yore rent an' if yo' kin git chew a crawfish. Git chew a live crawfish an' wrap him all ovah three safety matches. Take an' tie him, jes' tie him enough so he cain't back up, backwards an' fo'wards, an' turn him loose into yore house. Yo' understan', yo' see, an' dat crawfish goin' all roun' an' he kin not git out, he cain't git in no hole or crack. An' if yo' keep dat crawfish in dere until dat crawfish dies, yo'll stay right wit dat landlord. He cain't move yo'. . . . take dem matches an' tie 'em undahneat' his belly — wrap 'em, don' tie 'em.[21]

This is a rite predicated on a relatively common principle in Voodoo, where the animal involved became a surrogate for the person the worker or his client intended to affect. In this case, the presence of the crawfish in the house until his death is representative of the client who wanted to remain in the home indefinitely. Therefore, the landlord seems affected indirectly as he would not be able to change tenants, but the primary purpose was for the client to gain power over his or her own living situation — control over the landlord via his property was collateral in this instance. Further, the use of a rite with an indefinite ending might imply a perpetual rather

21.   Hyatt, *Hoodoo*, 2: 1,770

than a momentary concern with paying rent.

Control over a landlord could be more direct and often extended to attempting to make his property un-rentable. The implication was often that the client or the worker targeting the landlord was aiming to settle a vendetta after being evicted by making certain the landlord could not turn a profit from the rental. A worker named Ida went as far as suggesting the burning of oil of lodestone and sulfur in a house to stop it from being rented for six months. In that case, the resulting odor might accomplish this particular goal, even absent any metaphysical power.[22] Like the cases of attacks on the livelihood of laborers, along with the sense that the punishment here fit the crime of evicting a tenant, attacks on the ability of the landlord to rent his or her property may suggest a preoccupation with money by workers and their clients.

In addition to stopping a house from being rented, workers also claimed to be able to move someone out of a home. The reasons clients commissioned these rites were varied and often ambiguous in descriptions of the ceremonies. They could be used to harm the landlord by cutting off income or to make the home available for the worker's client to rent. If the presumption is that there is a shortage of desirable rental properties, the intended victim might also be the tenant. In one instance a worker called Madam Murray specified that a spell to move someone out of their house was more difficult if they actually owned the property. In this case, the sole motivation seems to be to get rid of the person in the house and not to acquire the space for the client's own use.[23] There is also at least one instance cited by a worker of a rite used specifically by a landlord to move one of his own tenants out, presumably not to lower his own income, but to replace an undesirable tenant with a better one. [24]

22.   Ibid., 1,666-67

23.   Hyatt, *Hoodoo*, 2: 1,277, 1,628

24.   Hyatt, *Hoodoo*, 1: 814

There were also rites used to rent a house, suggesting the use of workers' power to aid landlords that we would normally view as dominant in relation to tenants. Frequently, the scrubs used to improve businesses and draw customers were also used by landlords to attract renters to a property. Workers suggested scrubbing homes with cinnamon, sugar, and sweet milk and burning candles. Some even gave specific time limits promising the property would be rented by a specific date or that candles burned to St. Peter or the Virgin Mary would make certain that tenants paid their rent on time.[25] Here it is not the rites that are new but their use in the service of the landlords that were perceivably the dominant power in relation to renters. In the end, the rites provided to interviewers in this period suggested that workers were working both sides of the class divide. By serving the interests of the renter they worked counter to the interests of the landlord. In contrast, by aiding the landlords in securing tenants and even timely payment of rents, workers also served their interests.

Both landlords and renters sought out the aid of workers to improve situations they felt powerless to alter on their own. If a tenant could not produce enough income to cover rent, they were at the mercy of their landlords. Conversely, presuming that tenants were not simply withholding rent but could not afford to pay, there was little a landlord could do to extract payment. Eviction would not make up for lost rent, and in a period when funds were difficult to come by, there was a significant chance that the next tenant might not be any more financially stable than the last. These financial obstacles could seem insurmountable. When renters had no money and landlords couldn't keep renters, the vagaries of the economy could be an oppressive adversary against whom individuals of any social class might have felt powerless. Arraying their power and that of the saints against such forces was a specialty of New Orleans workers. Therefore the rites workers performed concerning housing demonstrate

25. Hyatt, *Hoodoo*, vol. 1-2: 1,666-67, 874, 1,652 (St. Peter).

both the preoccupation with economic concerns and the tendency of workers to keep a wide client base by serving diverse and even seemingly contradictory groups of clients. By internalizing, manipulating, and invariably profiting from what was a national culture of privation brought on by the Great Depression, professional practitioners of Voodoo were demonstrating their ability to adjust to the socio-economic milieu in which they operated their businesses. In turn, their spiritual practices were marked by this economic culture based in want and need in a way that was unique to the circumstances in the nation in general and New Orleans in particular.

In addition to securing employment and living space, clients frequently sought out workers to augment their luck in gambling. The most frequent prescription workers gave to gamblers was the creation and use of a "hand" or charm, to increase their probability of winning these games of chance. These hands varied greatly in composition. The active ingredients in a lot of the charms were components of various small animals. The creation and use of gambling hands illuminates several important concepts of cost and accumulation that characterized the practice of Voodoo in the twentieth century, namely the centrality of economic concerns to practitioners, the intertwining of the realms of spiritual power and monetary gain, and the exchange of life for profit.

One of the more unique formulations was to create a hand to stop anyone from cheating you while shooting dice. It required one to leave a frog to be eaten by ants in order to extract a particular bone from its leg. The bone in turn was then kept in one's pocket with the dice. Another hand required the use of a live frog which the worker would cut and subsequently sew a mixture of salt, pepper, and other components into, at which point the live, but perceivably anguished animal, would bring luck in gambling. Other hands included use of rabbits' feet, a hog's hoof, or a bat's heart as well as various lodestones, steel dust, and other ingredients commonly used by workers aimed at attracting or drawing luck.[26] Here, life and suffering of the animal are indirectly exchanged for economic gain. Unlike the cases of employment and housing rites, the point here does not seem to be securing just what is a necessity for the worker's client, but to aid in the accumulation of wealth. Abstractions like pain and death gain a pecuniary value through their involvement with games of chance in these instances; the equating of these intrinsically negative states with accumulation demonstrates the ambiguous feelings of Voodoo practitioners about accumulation in the era of rising consumerism in the early twentieth century.[27]

Used in many rites, including those for luck and gambling, the black cat bone was one of the most well known ingredients used by workers. However, there was often some moral ambiguity expressed by workers about the use of the bone because of the suffering of the animal from which it was extracted. Madam Lindsey said she could use the black cat bone to make a charm infallible for gambling that was also good for "general success." The problem was that to obtain the bone the worker would have had to gruesomely dispatch the cat itself, dropping it alive into a kettle of boiling water until its flesh boiled away from his bones. After extracting the specific u-shaped bone, the worker would have to combine it with other more common ingredients available at Voodoo drug stores and sewn into a bag. The charm, according to Lindsey, would bring success in anything, but she maintained that this was not a rite she performed because of the suffering involved for the animal.[28] By asserting that they would not

26.　　Hyatt, *Hoodoo,* 3; 2,276, 1,772, 1,680,

27.　　Jackson Lears, *Fables of Abundance: A Cultural History of Advertising in America* (New York: Basic Books 1994), 44-45. There is a long tradition of protestant denunciations of gambling in the United States, and the resemblance between stock market speculation and gambling was a major theme in the late nineteenth-century critiques of capitalism in general.

28.　　Hyatt, *Hoodoo*, 2: 1,506. Similarly, an informant identified as the Black Cat Lucky Bone Maker said that this making of a black cat bone required the worker to have someone else kill the animal due to the negative spiritual conse-

work with or extract the black cat bone themselves, workers made the choice that the resulting material gain was not worth causing the suffering of the animal. In Madam Lindsey's case this value judgment is clear cut in that she refused to work with the black cat bone at all. The certainty that those negative consequences exist, however, is a clear demonstration of a moral ambiguity surrounding the exchange of the animal's life, and perhaps more importantly in this case, the animal's suffering, to gain material benefit for oneself.

The implication was that, in general, the black cat bone was used in what practitioners classified as evil work. An informant identified as the Black Cat Lucky Bone Maker stated that in addition to other uses the bone was good for thieves specializing in breaking and entering. In this case however, he claimed that wearing the black cat bone amounted to selling oneself to the devil.[29] Workers believed that great or even unlimited power was available to those who performed this kind of magic.[30] The cost for that power and the accumulation of wealth that might follow has been raised in this case. Rather than exchanging the life and suffering of animals, the benefactor is bartering with his own soul. The implication was that material gain could result in a loss of what is in Judeo-Christian thinking the most precious commodity a man has. This Faustian bargain points to a distinct value judgment of accumulation in a growing culture of consumption. While workers seem generally invested in improving both their own and their clients' material condition, the extreme cost they attached to these rites seemed to place a limit on how far they were willing to go while simultaneously expanding the things they believed could be exchanged for material wealth

quences that might result from performing the rite oneself. The Black Cat Lucky Bone Maker thus implied that he would profit or help a client profit by using the bone but he was unwilling to incur the negative spiritual consequences of extracting the bone.

29.   Hyatt, 3: 2,265.

30.   Hyatt, 3: 1,909.

to include even an individual's soul.

These kinds of exchanges may be a result of the creation and recreation of Voodoo in the American context, which combined both the Judeo-Christian conception of the soul as a kind of contested moral commodity, a possession of the individual coveted by both God and the Devil, and what Arjun Appadurai classified as a highly commoditized society, a society in which many or most things in a society sometimes meet these criteria. What is intriguing about this case, is that while Appadurai is generally speaking about the commoditization of goods and services, objects and labor, the "diversion" of a philosophical abstraction like the human soul into what he calls a "commodity situation" seems to further accentuate the high level of commoditization in this national context. In Appadurai's estimation even human beings have passed into and out of this commodity situation at various points in history via the institution of various forms of slavery.[31] But in this case it is not the person as an object or as labor passing into the commodity situation, but a moral-philosophical construct like the "soul" that becomes commoditized.

An informant recounted to Harry Hyatt what may be an even clearer example of commoditization of the soul in the service of consumerism. The account is of a similar rite:

> Well, she tole me dat dere wus a woman by de name of Marie Baptiste. She had two daughters an' she liked fo' her daughters tuh outdress de girls down in de 7th ward. . . . An' she sol' herself to de devil at twelve a'clock at night wit de fire of furnace—a furnace fire, yo' know at de fo'k of de road in the woods . . . an' she sol' herself to him dat she could git anything she wanted so she could go in de sto's an' anything she

---

31.   Arjun Appadurai, ed., *The Social Life of Things: Commodities in Cultural Perspective* (Cambridge: Cambridge University Press, 1988).

take dey couldn't see her.[32]

This account demonstrates a moral ambiguity about accumulation that associates this kind of consumerism with stealing and the Devil. The exchange of the soul to acquire consumer products also suggests a concern about the intangible costs of accumulation. The significance of the woman in the story out-dressing the girls in the Seventh Ward is tied to the perception of New Orleans's Seventh Ward as an enclave of success or privilege among middle-class African Americans.[33] The Seventh Ward had long been known as home to a significant portion of the city's Afro-Creole population. The perception of that population as business and property owners also led to an association between the Seventh Ward and economic success. With the expansion of the consumer economy the number and appeal of products multiplied and many retailers and advertisers targeted women.[34] Fashion in particular was integral to the rise of consumer culture in the United States. The fashion industry sought to lift women in particular into a world of pseudo-luxury beyond the drudgery of obligations (like bills) by offering them "release through purchase." In the process, however, "this often led to anxiety and restlessness in a world where people feared not being able to afford things other people had."[35] The implication that the affluence embodied by the Seventh Ward in the public imagination could only be maintained in the privation of the 1930s by selling one's soul is a powerful statement of both the moral ambiguity of material accumulation and the pull of

32.   Hyatt, *Hoodoo*, 1: 794-95.

33.   Arnold Hirsch, "Simply a Matter of Black and White: The Transformation of Race and Politics in Twentieth-Century New Orleans," in *Creole New Orleans: Race and Americanization*, Arnold R. Hirsch and Joseph Logsdon (Baton Rouge: LSU Press, 1992).

34.   Viviana A. Zelizer, "The Social Meaning of Money: 'Special Monies,'" *The American Journal of Sociology* 95, no. 2 (September 1989): 359.

35.   Leach, *Land of Desire,* 6.

consumerism.

There are also instances where the cost of material gain might also extend from one's own soul to the lives of family members. A number of informants believed that whether it was St. Peter, St. Expedite, or St. Roc, praying to some saints for favors could carry a high cost outside of monetary compensation to workers. One informant claimed that if clients did not give St. Peter the promised offering for services he provided, their worldly possessions would be consumed in a fire. Another claimed that the penalty extracted by St. Expedite for not providing the promised offering of flowers would be the death of a family member.[36] Similarly, Nahnee claimed that St. Roc was a vengeful saint called upon to maim victims. In exchange, St. Roc always took the life of a family member of the person who called on him.[37] Thus in the economy of Voodoo, even the lives of family members could be used as a form of currency to purchase power. Further, the inclusion of Catholic saints popular in New Orleans as well as sites like the Seventh Ward demonstrates the dependence of Voodoo practitioners on the cultural milieu in which they constructed this economy.

These exchanges again imply a moral judgment that equated malice with material gain. Here again, workers seemed to believe that almost anything might have a pecuniary value, but maintained a discomfort with making such exchanges. These rites may demonstrate what Margaret Radin terms a "crystallization" of concerns about inappropriate commodification that she associates with the use of market rhetoric, especially when applied to ideals like love or human beings, considered properly inalienable in a market economy.[38] This concern may have been best stated

36.   Hyatt, *Hoodoo* 1: 876; Ibid., 2: 957.

37.   Ibid., 2: 1,374, 1,652.

38.   Margaret Jane Radin, *Contested Commodities: The Trouble with Trade in Sex, Children, Body Parts, and Other Things* (Cambridge, MA: Harvard University Press, 2001), 6.

by a worker describing a rite that would kill a victim when he said, "It's a very hard task to go through, it's very cruel to do such of those things; but when we gets paid for it, why we does it."[39] Workers who were willing to involve themselves in the more morally ambiguous rites were functioning very much like brokers, a class expanding exponentially in the twentieth century.

As intermediaries, brokers were required to repress their own convictions in favor of forging profitable relationships. It has been posited that the vast expansion of this class in corporate business helped to inject a new amoral attitude conducive to the inflation of desire that drove consumerism forward.[40] Like the gambling hands that included parts of animals, the implication here is that accumulation had a cost, and that such accumulation at another's expense did not come without a parallel cost to the benefactor. However, the willingness of some workers to provide these services despite that cost demonstrates an amoral attitude among that segment of the community of Voodoo practitioners about this kind of accumulation in comparison to the employment and housing rites that seemed to be more widely accepted.

Some rites performed by workers demonstrated an increase in cost that was not vertical, as in the increase in price from animal to human to family lives, but horizontal, calling for not just rising, but continuous payment. Gambling hands were often not a onetime investment, as many required "feeding" to renew their power.[41] Perhaps the most common substance used to feed a gambling hand was whiskey. An informant Hyatt identified as the Hoodoo Book Man described a gambling hand made with lodestone, steel dust, garlic, and a dime, wrapped in a flannel bag that was kept in one's pocket. In order to ensure the bag's effectiveness the user had to make certain that he poured whiskey onto it while he

---

39.   Hyatt, *Hoodoo*, 2: 1,684.

40.   Leach, *Land of Desire*, 6.

41.   Hyatt, *Hoodoo*, 2: 1,655.

was gambling.[42] Paying for the alcohol to continuously feed a gambling hand required a continuing investment.

In some cases money was not only exchanged for power, but was also used to generate it in a way even more direct than paying for magical services. The charge for gambling hands varied greatly, ranging from about twenty five to fifty dollars. The ability of a worker to charge a substantial fee for a hand depended on the supposition that the initial fee would be returned in gambling profits. Often, the fee charged for the hand was not the only currency necessary to make them effective, however. As demonstrated by the two above examples, U.S. currency, in those cases a dime, was often an ingredient in making a hand. In these instances, the buying power of currency is understood as the metaphysical power to create more wealth. In fact, the Hoodoo Book Man described the creation of a hand that came in both a large and small size, the larger being more expensive and requiring a larger denomination of currency but supposedly achieving better results: "Dey use de same thin' in both size, but de biggah pieces dey make mo' powah…you put a quartah; if you gon'a make a small one, you put a dime. It got to be silvah money."[43] In this instance, more money quite literally translates into more power. [44]

Outside of gambling, a number of other rites included currency as components. One of the most frequent uses of currency in rites was to cure ailments, natural or otherwise.

---

42.   Hyatt, *Hoodoo*, 2: 1,755, 1,825, 1,635-38. A similar hand was made with John the Conqueror root, devil's shoe string (another root employed by workers), lodestone, and a silver dime, but rather than whiskey, it was fed by soaking it in the chamber lye, or urine, of the client's wife.

43.   Ibid., 1,755

44.   Hyatt, *Hoodoo*, 2: 1,769. There is also at least one instance where neglecting the use of almost any other components, money in and of itself generates luck for gambling and thus, more money: "If yo' wants tuh be lucky an' if yo' wants tuh gamble, git chew a piece of white lodestone an; git chew three silvah dimes. An' don't let chure wife or none of yore friends put dere han's on it, an' don' shoot dat fo' no money, don' fo'git an' spend it, but keep it wit chure silvah money."

Again, the denomination of the coin seemed to take on some significance. Often workers would grind or shave pieces of a coin and have someone drink or eat it in a solution to cure them of poison or to get rid of an animal, namely a frog or snake, magically put into their bodies to harm them, probably by another worker. While these rites usually specified what coin was to be used, none of the rites that required filing or grinding the silver from coins required filing or grinding of the entire coin. If using the coin as a source of silver was the point, and the denomination of the coin was irrelevant, it would never make sense to spend more money by extracting silver from a quarter or half dollar, instead of a dime. Therefore, workers specifying what coin was to be used implied that the value of the coin had some bearing on the rite and the currency itself (not just the metal used to create it) held some metaphysical significance.[45] Just as in the prior instance of a gambling hand in which both the power of the charm and its cost increased due to the inclusion of a quarter rather than a dime, the value of the currency was often a factor in the potency of the rite, again suggesting an understanding that more money equated to more spiritual power.

Other formulations also suggested that currency itself held power. Some rites allowed workers to use a coin to attack the person attempting to harm their client rather than simply curing the client.[46] Other workers used shavings of silver coins to put harmful creatures into the stomach of a victim rather than extract them. There is even an instance where what the worker seemed to describe was "wishing" on a silver dollar rather than using it in a specific formula with additional components. Even rites with other major components, for example animal parts, also required inclusion of currency. The implication seemed to be that U.S. currency held power

---

45.   Hyatt, *Hoodoo*, 3: 1,912, 1,073, 1,377.

46.   One practitioner claimed by praying to St. Raymond on the thirteenth of the month and later heating a penny and scratching the word "one" from the penny, a worker could "destroy" the person trying to harm their client.

like the other spiritual accoutrements used in these rites. The use of currency in so many different instances may speak to the confidence or overwhelming belief in the power of U.S. currency by workers, not necessarily in a world market as we might think of today, but rather in their own lives. It suggests that the importance of money had been imbibed so fully by workers in New Orleans that money took on metaphysical characteristics in their rites.

Others have long speculated about the power of money in society and the concomitant effect of culture on money. The quantification of quality that Viviana Zelizer labels a "morally dangerous alchemy" is a quality of all money that allows it to reduce all qualitative distinctions between objects to a system of numbers. Further, she argues that "money turned even intangible objects devoid of utility — such as conscience or honor — into ordinary commodities." At the same time Zelizer argues that while money is corrupting values into numbers, values "reciprocally corrupt money by investing it with moral, social, and religious meaning."[47] In this sense, the money used in these rites attained a quality that made it a source of spiritual or magical power.

As workers understood it, even the saints and spirits required payment for their help. Saints and spirits were given offerings of flowers, spices, alcohol, cigars, and all manner of material goods. Often though, they were simply paid in U.S. currency. What may be unique about payment of the saints, however, is that there is no perception that the saints need money or want to accumulate wealth. Workers often left dimes or other currency on graves for spirits when collecting graveyard dirt. However, one worker specified that it was only necessary to pay the spirit to do something negative — positive work with grave dirt was apparently free.[48] One formulation for burning a candle to St. Raymond to get bread for your children specified that it had to be burned in church

47. Zelizer, "The Social Meaning of Money," 346-47.
48. Ibid., 1,063.

where one would pay twenty-five cents. It is unclear what happened to the money in this case as some formulations that required money to be left for a saint, required it to be left there indefinitely. Madam Lindsey of Algiers specified that when asking St. Anthony for help with a job, one had to leave bread for the poor in a church.[49] Similarly, another informant reported that he had been instructed to pay St. Expedite to give someone else bad luck by putting a quarter in a box at a Catholic church when burning a candle to the saint.[50] The custodian of a shrine in Algiers described a similar phenomenon in her use of "St. Rosalie":

> She's de money Queen. . . . She's a saint dat she had so much money she didn't know whut tuh do wit it. . . . Yo' always make'em leave a penny or a Nickel . . . an' tell'em dat's fo St. Rosalie an' don't nevah spend dat money . . . jis' give it to de sick an' de blind. . . . Dey goin' Pay yo' fo' whut chew doin' fo' dem separate but dat penny is fo' de poah.[51]

While this hagiography for St. Rosalie is probably peculiar to Voodoo, this idea of paying for the favor of the saint with an act of charity is not. It does, however present an interesting contrast to the profit motive often expressed by workers. Even though the saints have been drawn into the world of monetary exchange, there is no notion that the saints need the money. Instead the payments seem to benefit others who need help. Unlike money given to the spirits in some other African-descended New World religions though, the money here became sacrosanct, at least for the practitioner. To give it to a fellow practitioner, even after it has served its ritual purpose, apparently did not adequately qualify as a sacrifice

49.   Hyatt, *Hoodoo*, 2: 1,503-1,504.

50.   Hyatt, *Hoodoo*, 1: 865, 867. These boxes are generally for donations to the church or collections for charitable causes.

51.   Hyatt, *Hoodoo*, 2: 1,140, 1,155.

to the saints. This conception may also represent a value judgment of the money in rites that involved "bad work" by making it singular and nonfungible.[52] Unlike monetary sacrifices provided to the spirits in some of the Afro-Diasporic religions throughout the Americas that are collected and redistributed to members of the community, whether this money is given to the poor via a Catholic donation box, left near a statue of a saint or grave of the deceased, the money passes out of the hands of the practitioner. There is an effort not to pragmatically move the money to other practitioners in an effort to sustain them and perhaps ritualize the practice, but to rather "sacrifice" the money in the most literal sense of giving it up.[53]

Together the rites that include currency suggest a wide faith in the power of money in the occult economy of Voodoo. The use of currency in gambling hands differed from its inclusion in curative rites, the counter spell formulas, or the notion of paying saints. The ubiquity of the idea of monetary cost in these exchanges seemed to demonstrate the importance of currency, a preoccupation with tangible, material needs, and an understanding of value, even the value of spiritual power, in monetary terms. Workers suggested that pecuniary payments to the saints could result in a great deal of help in meeting material needs. This suggested that practitioners assigned a monetary value not only to the power of workers, but also to the power of the saints. While workers' association of soul bartering and loss of goods and life with excessive accumulation suggested a moral ambiguity about the material success that would seem to be the end goal of much of the

52.   Zelizer, "The Social Meaning of Money," 351.

53.   Brian Brazeal, "Blood, Money and Fame: Nago Magic in the Bahian Backlands," (PhD diss., University of Chicago, 2007); Beatriz Gois Dantas, *Nago Grandma and White Papa: Candomble and the Creation of Afro-Brazilian Identity* (Chapel Hill: University of North Carolina Press, 2009); Karen McCarthy Brown, *Mama Lola: A Vodou Priestess in Brooklyn* (Berkeley: University of California Press, 2001).

work performed by Voodoo practitioners, in general spiritual power was used to influence luck, health, and even the saints for the material benefit of both workers and their clients.

The adjustments made to create a business model for practicing Voodoo that both internalized rising consumer culture and demonstrated the importance of both local predecessors, corporeal and spiritual, and national economic culture, demonstrates the centrality of indigenous American cultural influences on the practice of Voodoo in New Orleans. The ways in which practitioners bent and shaped rituals illuminates both the centrality of economics and employment to the practice of Voodoo, and the importance of New Orleans as a site where ritual was being constantly and dynamically shifted to determine the character of Voodoo.

The economic culture of the United States in general and New Orleans in particular provided salient influences on Voodoo. Both clients and workers needed money to survive. Professional practitioners molded their services to meet the needs of a market filled with clients who needed jobs, housing, and luck. For those engaged in underground economies like bootlegging or gambling, Voodoo practitioners also offered aid that could increase profits. As economic concerns became increasingly central to practice, the understanding of both material and metaphysical realities began to reflect the importance of these concerns for workers.

Understanding the focus on economics and employment in the thinking of professional Voodoo practitioners for meeting the immediate material needs of their clients represents a step in a process that saw many economic successes achieved by workers and their associates who were able to monetize their practices, giving them the means to build economic and religious institutions around their work and in turn legitimize their practices and allow them to accumulate wealth and property without the fear of legal persecution. In this formulation, the focus on jobs and money financed an institutionalization that allowed for the accumulation of more money. This institutionalization created safe spaces for these practices, their continuation, and even their proliferation.[54]

---

54.   This essay is part of a larger book project forthcoming from LSU press tentatively entitled *Vooodoo and the Promise of Power: The Racial, Economic and Gender Politics of Religion in New Orleans 1881-1940.* These issues of institutionalization, legitimacy, and racialized and gendered notions inherent in early twentieth-century Voodoo are discussed in depth in that project.

6

"Cream With Our Coffee":
Preservation Hall, Organized Labor,
and New Orleans's Musical Color Line,
1957-1969

ELIZABETH MANLEY

In January of 1957 a group of New Orleans musicians were arrested at a French Quarter venue for purportedly "disturbing the peace." According to art dealer and improptu venue proprietor Larry (E. Lorenz) Borenstein, the judge who set their bail "managed to combine the juridical dignity of a kangaroo court and the philosophy of lynch law with the humor of Milton Berle."[1] Addressing the group of white and black musicians, Judge Edwin A. Babylon took issue with "Kid" Thomas Valentine, whom he professed to know as a "good yard boy" in his neighborhood of Algiers. He told the assembled group that in New Orleans people did not take kindly to "mixing cream with our coffee." Musician Charlie Devore noted that the assembled group included himself, Punch Miller, Eddie Morris, Joel Salter, and Donnie Berg and that while the judge was concerned with "baggy pants Northerners" like Devore coming south with their ideas, it was

---

1.   The account of the bail hearing appears in several oral histories, although nearly all are from Borenstein's perspective. See Noel Rockmore and Larry Bo-renstein, *Preservation Hall Portraits* (Baton Rouge: Louisiana State University Press, 1968), 1-6; See also William Carter, *Preservation Hall: Music from the Heart* (New York: W.W. Norton, 1991), 112-16; Tad Jones, "'Separate but Equal': The Laws of Segregation and their Effect on New Orleans' Black Musicians, 1950-1964," *Living Blues Magazine* 77 (December 1987), 24-28; Bruce Boyd Raeburn, *New Orleans Style and the Writing of American Jazz History* (Ann Arbor: University of Michigan Press, 2009), 255; and Thomas Sancton, *Song for My Fathers: a New Orleans Story in Black and White* (New York: Other Press, 2006), 107.

Valentine he really laid in to. After a thirty-minute lecture, he warned Valentine that he would let him off if he remembered "his place in the future" and promised "not to get uppity."

The location of the arrest was 726 St. Peter Street, a venue informally known as Mr. Larry's Art Store that was soon to become Preservation Hall. "Mr. Larry" Borenstein hosted informal—and often bi-racial—jam sessions in the evenings at his gallery in the mid- to late 1950s, a time in which such integration was strictly prohibited by both the culture of Jim Crow and official New Orleans segregation ordinances. While there was public resistance to these informal sessions— orchestrated primarily by Kid Thomas and Punch Miller— there are also indications in Borenstein's remembrances that small fissures in the musical color line were beginning to open. As he noted of the 1957 arrests and others, "it was simpler to charge them with 'disturbing the peace' than with breaking down segregation barriers."[2] In other words, while some public opinion may have inveighed against the gatherings, participants were more than willing to deal with the nuisances of working and playing across the color line.

The 1960s in New Orleans was a decade filled with intensely waged battles over entrenched racial lines created by Jim Crow and the ifs, hows, and whens of the city's social restructuring. Working musicians, club owners, and their clientele lived, worked, and played at the center of this storm that often seemed like it might erupt into a full-fledged hurricane. Yet the story of the integration of one of the city's most beloved cultural forms and its purveyors complicates the story of both race and labor within the larger narrative of the 1960s United States. On the one hand, while musicians by no means inhabited some kind of racial utopia, their world certainly exhibited clear cracks in the walls erected by Jim Crow. On the other, the unions that represented them—despite being part of a larger structure that professed racial solidarity—mirrored many of the problems exhibited by a society struggling to come to

2.   Rockmore and Borenstein, *Preservation Hall Portraits*, 6.

terms with centuries-old racial hatred and misunderstanding. In this essay I argue that the merger of the white and black musicians' unions in New Orleans during the second half of the 1960s — and the context within which it happened — demonstrates some of the most important complications of both the civil rights movement and labor organizing in the late twentieth-century United States. While New Orleans exhibited some of the ways in which a more fluid set of racial lines and greater inter-racial personal relations facilitated a smoother transition out of Jim Crow, the example of music and the color line could still — within the context of organized labor — foster a racially separatist ideology that resulted in a forced and resented process of desegregation. At the center of this story is the irony that while many musicians worked together at the same ends of art and entertainment, it was the well meaning yet poorly organized efforts at integration that served to drive them further apart.

This essay also highlights the role of Preservation Hall and venues like it in supporting an integrated music scene during a period in which first segregation and then desegregation ruled the day. Running parallel to the growth of Preservation Hall is the story of the nationally mandated merger of New Orleans's two musicians unions, Locals 174 and 496. Between 1960 and 1970, a uniquely collaborative music scene grew and evolved, all while local union officials across the color line bickered over the fiscal and administrative terms of a desegregated union. Ultimately, the joining of white and African American musicians under one organizational umbrella happened in spite of an existing understanding of racial collaboration in the artistic endeavor of New Orleans's music scene. As Eric Arnesen argues, race and labor are "invariably intertwined" yet only in the past few decades have scholars begun to comprehensively look at them together. This study of music, labor, and desegregation contributes to recent efforts to "chart the tensions between the labor movement's ideals of solidarity and inclusion and its all-too-common failure to live up to those ideals."[3] Yet even more ironic, historiographically speaking, is the absence of any significant study of the role of music in the process of desegregation in New Orleans, a city which has, since at least the 1950s, depended on the commodification of its culture for economic survival.[4] Stitching together the intertwined histories of New Orleans's musicians' unions, the protracted battles of the civil rights era, and the artists, proprietors, and clients that existed in the middle of it all ultimately provides not just a more comprehensive vision of the city and its workers, but also complicates the New Orleans narrative of integration that often takes for granted its cultural producers.

Race and Music in New Orleans, 1955-1965

From the mid-1950s through the 1960s, a significant number of individuals in the music business chose deliberately to ignore the dictates of Jim Crow. Mac Rebennack (more popularly known as Dr. John), one of the most flagrant defiers of racial segregation laws, recalls discussion of a "white session": "I asked them [union officials], 'What's a white session?'; they couldn't answer that one. They were pissed because I would hire guys for their playing ability, which always ended up in

---

3.   Eric Arnesen, introduction to *The Black Worker: Race, Labor, and Civil Rights Since Emancipation* (Urbana: University of Illinois Press, 2007), 6. See also his *Waterfront Workers of New Orleans: Race, Class, and Politics, 1863-1923* (New York: Oxford University Press, 1991) and his contribution to this volume.

4.   For the civil rights movement in New Orleans see Kim Lacy Rogers, *Righteous Lives Narratives of the New Orleans Civil Rights Movement* (New York: New York University Press, 1993); Adam Fairclough, *Race & Democracy: The Civil Rights Struggle in Louisiana, 1915-1972* (Athens: University of Georgia Press, 1995); and Arnold R. Hirsch and Joseph Logsdon, eds., *Creole New Orleans: Race and Americanization* (Baton Rouge: Louisiana State University Press, 1992). On New Orleans's development as a major tourism center, see particularly Jonathan Mark Souther, *New Orleans on Parade: Tourism and the Transformation of the Crescent City* (Baton Rouge: Louisiana State University Press, 2006).

racially mixed sessions."[5]

According to fellow musician Eddie Hynes, to Rebennack, "there was no such thing as segregation. He didn't bother what color you were; he was going to talk to you in front of everyone."[6] For many individuals within the New Orleans music scene, the lines separating races seemed far less important than the skill a person could bring to the set or the economic imperative to secure a given gig. Tad Jones notes that "black and white musicians seemed generally unaffected by legal codes or artificial standards" as they maintained, historically, "a strong affinity for one another based on mutual respect, and one's musical ability."[7] While this might be a slight over-simplification, it is clear that significant social and economic ties and solidarities existed between white and black musicians in multiple arenas.

Similarly, many patrons and owners of local venues failed to abide by the dictates of a segregated club. As Jones argues, the laws of segregation had a lesser effect on musicians because owners particularly "felt no personal allegiance to the law" and often sought the widest possible audiences for their acts.[8] The Dew Drop Inn and Café, an African American music venue on LaSalle Street, booked some of the most famous R & B acts of the day, and owner Frank Painia patently refused to recognize the city rules regarding socialization between blacks and whites.[9] By the 1950s, the club was

5.   Dr. John (Mac Rebennack) and Jack Rummel, *Under a Hoodoo Moon: The Life of Dr. John the Night Tripper* (New York: St. Martin's Press, 1994), 89.

6.   Jason Berry, Jonathan Foose, and Tad Jones, *Up from the Cradle of Jazz: New Orleans Music Since World War II* (Athens: University of Georgia Press, 1986), 182.

7.   Tad Jones, "'Separate but Equal,'" 24.

8.   Ibid., 25.

9.   The nightclub grew from a sandwich and beer stand to a full-fledged venue in 1942. Desiring a club atmosphere, he hired white French Quarter artist Johnny Donnels to paint murals in the interior. In dealing with police harassment, owner Frank Painia would simply tell the officers that he and his friends were the "interior decorators" for the real artists who had stuck around to see the show. Berry,

attracting white patrons and high-level music executives. In 1952 Painia was arrested along with Hollywood star Zachary Scott and several others for "violating the city ordinance regarding segregation."[10] Laura Jackson, Painia's daughter, recalls that her father "decided to make a stand and went to jail. Whites had always come in to the Dew Drop—in fact a lot of policemen visited the place." Judge Babylon—apparently embarrassed at the arrest of Scott—decided that the star and his guests must have been "ignorant of Louisiana law." He chided them gently, suggesting that if they were again in the South, "if you do go into those places, just go as spectators and don't drink."[11] While many referred to the Dew Drop as a "subculture within a subculture," owner Frank Painia felt strongly that it should be open to whomever wanted to experience it.[12] Music writer Jeff Hannusch argues that Painia was a "highly respected man in the black community" and a "pioneer in the civil rights movement in New Orleans."[13] Painia would soon become one of the city's biggest agitators in seeking to break down segregation codes. As his daughter remembers, after the Scott incident he "continually lobbied city council to eliminate segregation laws."[14] In 1960 he helped form the Tavern Owners of Greater New Orleans, Inc., the goals of which included combating "problems of police infringement," promoting protective legislation, and attacking

---

Foose, and Jones, *Up from the Cradle of Jazz,* 54. See also, Mary Beth Hamilton, "Sexual Politics and African-American Music; or, Placing Little Richard in History," *History Workshop Journal,* 1998 (46), 161-76.

10.   *Louisiana Weekly,* December 22, 1952, 1.

11.   Ibid.

12.   Berry, Foose, and Jones, *Up from the Cradle of Jazz*, 54. His was not the only African American establishment frequented by young white musicians seeking to learn more about the city's musical traditions. Tom Sancton and Don Marquis both recall similar scenes at Buster Holmes Restaurant preceding and following second-line parades.

13.   Hannusch, *The Soul of New Orleans*, 131.

14.   Ibid.

"discrimination in employment."[15] Painia eventually sued the city to allow white patrons to frequent and consume at his bar.[16]

In addition, it was not any one type of music that encouraged collaboration across the color line. In their history of rhythm and blues in New Orleans, Jason Berry, Jonathan Foose, and Tad Jones argue that while "the popularity of jazz had long been a force of moderation between the races in New Orleans," R & B continued and even expanded upon that tendency. Using Fats Domino as an example, they argue that "people of both races loved his music because it spoke straight to them."[17] Given the rising popularity of the genre, it is not surprising that people faced segregation-related obstacles in radio programming and recording. At Cosimo Matassa's studio in the French Quarter, harassment was frequent. Matassa and regular collaborator Allen Tousaint cared little as to the race of their session musicians, something that union officials did not take kindly to at the time. As Matassa notes, "a lot of my experience with the union was as adversary. They were antagonists."[18] Musician Earl King actually directly blamed the black local (496) for the failure of the recording business in New Orleans:

> The black local was responsible. We never had any problems with the white local. They (the black union) was nothin' but crooks and swindlers. They were so busy stealin' and what have you, they gave the musicians a hard way to go. It's one of the primary reasons New Orleans [recording business] crumbled.

15.   Advertisement, *Louisiana Weekly,* December 3, 1960, 115.

16.   Painia, along with his lawyer Dutch Morial, sued the city in 1964 over ordinance 828, declaring it unconstitutional. Tad Jones, "'Separate but Equal,'" 27. Ironically, it would be the end to segregation laws, along with chronic illness, that would be the death of both the Dew Drop and its much-lauded owner.

17.   Berry, Foose, and Jones, *Up from the Cradle of Jazz*, 95.

18.   Ibid., 132.

They made it difficult to record in New Orleans and the major companies got tired of this and went elsewhere to record.[19]

Rebannack, a member of the white local (178) who started recording with Matassa in 1960, expressed similar frustrations with the situation, and he frequently ignored rules, played many integrated sessions and gigs, and was constantly called to account with his union representatives.[20] More than one member viewed the unions as antithetical to the goal of creating great music.

While Grunewald's music school maintained a segregated program (African Americans upstairs/whites downstairs) it was here that many musicians made their first contacts across color lines.[21] According to Earl Palmer, the school was "another point of integration." Despite being taught upstairs, Palmer recalled many of the musicians downstairs. "That was also an opportunity for us, where musicians could meet without the threat of going to jail. To perform together and enjoy the music and learn from each other . . . And so it became very much accepted that we could get together."[22]

Located at 829 Camp Street, the school may not have

19.   Ibid.

20.   His problems with union rules in 1963 and 1964 resulted in fines of at least $1,100 for illegal session work, including "playing with non-union members and committing minor infractions." Ibid., 184.

21.   Doc Paulin enrolled after serving in World War II. See Michael G. White, "Dr. Michael White: The Doc Paulin Years, 1975-1979," *The Jazz Archivist* 23 (2010); 2-20. Al Beletto also attended Grunewald's (downstairs) as did Richie Payne (upstairs). See Charles Suhor, "Modern Jazz Pioneers in New Orleans: A Symposium, Loyola University, New Orleans, April 22, 1998," in *Jazz in New Orleans: The Postwar Years through 1970* (Newark, N.J.: Rutgers University Press, 2001), 267-90. David Lastie recalls attending while in high school (1948) and "falling in love." See Berry, Foose, and Jones, *Up from the Cradle of Jazz*, 46. Earl Palmer enrolled in 1946 on the G.I. Bill. See Raeburn, *New Orleans Style and the Writing of American Jazz History*, 242.

22.   Suhor, "Modern Jazz Pioneers," 286.

been accepted by higher education institutions, but it had an excellent reputation and expert teachers. In addition, many African American war veterans used their G.I. Bill benefits there. The *Louisiana Weekly* advertised Grunewald's as "the only school where an entire curriculum is devoted to music in the modern idiom . . . every member of the faculty is an approved instructor as well as a successful professional in his own right." While the economic incentive for Grunewald's to accept African American musicians because of their G.I. Bill benefits was high, musicians themselves recall the racial solidarity it engendered. Journalist Charles Suhor argues that it has been remembered as "a gathering place for dedicated musicians" who spoke "of the camaraderie of the black and white musicians at Grunewald's, despite formal segregation."[23] Like a number of other venues, Grunewald's elided the racial constructs of the day to provide for a more integrated artistic atmosphere.

The precedence for the jam sessions held at the music school reaches as far back as the mid-1940s when interracial jam sessions took place in the French Quarter. According to Earl Palmer and Al Beletto, such sessions were frequent at Benny Clement's house in the Quarter, and their sheer visibility often brought arrests. As Suhor tells it, the arrests only "amounted to tweaks of harassment in laissez faire New Orleans," while at the same time they illustrated "the framework of legal oppression in Louisiana that had far more serious consequences."[24] During the same period, the New Orleans Jazz Club, a collective of white jazz afficianados,

23.   Suhor, *Jazz in New Orleans,* 233. See also Berry, Foose, and Jones, *Up from the Cradle of Jazz*, 46.

24.   Suhor, *Jazz in New Orleans,* 205, 270. Beletto and Palmer also account being arrested frequently at the Texas Lounge, and the cops saying, "Why you guys keep doing this?" Similarly, Mac Rebennack reports being regularly harassed by police at Leroy's Steakhouse, a restaurant next to the Dew Drop. After awhile they began leaving him alone, he imagined, because "they figured I must have been completely psychotic, showing up there no matter how much heat they laid down on me." John and Rummel, *Under a HooDoo Moon*, 49.

managed to plan a number of events "employing black and white jazz musicians on a fairly regular basis," including a 1949 "Battle of the Bands" between Papa Celestin and Phil Zito.[25] They also hosted integrated sessions at their regular meetings beginning in 1954. As producer Al Rose explains, while there was apprehension given the reigning social codes, once the music began no one seemed to notice.[26] That being said, many of the clubs in the Quarter only hired white musicians, while a number of others hired black musicians and maintained a "back door" policy. At a few strip clubs—among the few venues for jazz at the time—black musicians would be hired but forced to perform behind a sheet, apparently shielding dancers from the stares of African American men. Gradually, social pressures would force these policies to change. One venue that played a crucial role in breaking down racial barriers in music was the soon-to-be named Preservation Hall.

In early 1961, a young couple from Philadelphia stopped in New Orleans on their way back from their honeymoon in Mexico. The city made a profound impression on Sandra and Allan Jaffe, and they returned shortly thereafter for good. They quickly fell into the company of Larry Borenstein, the gallery owner in the French Quarter involved with the Kid Thomas arrest. Borenstein, legend has it, had grown tired of having to work during the evening when traditional jazz performances dotted the city's social scene and had decided to host jam sessions in his gallery beginning in 1956.[27] The

25.   Raeburn, *New Orleans Style,* 243.

26.   Ibid., 249.

27.   A number of scholars and journalists have documented the founding of Preservation Hall and argued for its significance in a number or arenas, including Shannon Brinkman, *Preservation Hall* (Baton Rouge: Louisiana State University Press, 2011); Carter, *Preservation Hall: Music from the Heart*; Raeburn, *New Orleans Style*; and Souther, *New Orleans on Parade*. Charles Suhor spent much of the early 1960s reporting for *Downbeat* magazine and much of his work—in the magazine and elsewhere—has detailed much of the early history of the Hall. See, for example, Suhor, "Preservation Hall: New Orleans Rebirth," in *Jazz in*

concept took off, and the Jaffes took over management of the place in 1961. It was originally called, among other things, the "Slow Drag" Hangout, and Ken Mills and Barbara Reid had briefly run the place before the Jaffes assumed control. By then dubbed Preservation Hall, it became a center for the renewal of the careers of many African American traditional jazz musicians, as well as for the rejuvination of what William Carter refers to as "America's only original art form."[28]

Preservation Hall has become nationally known for its importance to the New Orleans music scene, and accounts of its role in reviving and maintaining the traditional style of jazz in New Orleans are not lacking, yet this is only a part of its history. Scholars, musicians, and fans alike have lauded the Jaffes and their incredible efforts to support multiple generations of African American musicians and the city's deep musical roots.[29] Many scholars contend that Preservation Hall is inextricably linked to the slow revival of traditional jazz that began in the 1940s yet had been slowly overshadowed by trendier and more modern styles in the 1950s and 60s. Suhor argues that "Preservation Hall did not follow the 1950s formula viz., fame and fortune for young white jazzmen playing post-twenties Dixieland. Rather, the music was traditional New Orleans jazz and the artists were almost exclusively little-known African American musicians who were active in the early 1960s." Suhor goes on to heap praise on the role of Preservation Hall in the rebirth of the 1960s, noting that no earlier efforts had so successfully caught the attention of the press and city officials, nor had they had

New Orleans, 179-81.

28.   William Carter, "Thanks, Allan," *The Jazz Archivist* 2, no. 2 (November 1987): 1-3.

29.   Charles Suhor defines the genre they celebrated, traditional jazz, as "the range of early jazz styles that evolved in the first two decades of the twentieth century. . . . In the 1960s this style was most strongly represented by the bands that played at Preservation Hall." "Jazz in New Orleans in the 1960s" *The Jazz Archivist* 10, no. 1-2 (May-December 1995), 1-23.

a transformative effect on tourism and the city's image "as a still-thriving jazz mecca" the way that Preservation Hall did. William Carter refers to Allan and Sandra Jaffe's solid management of the place — and the musicians that formed its core — with a praise that is echoed by many other researchers. Referring to "good jobs, under decent conditions" Carter indirectly references the dearth of quality opportunities for African American musicians during the decade of civil rights. The success of Preservation Hall lay not only in the Jaffes' fostering of older generations of African American musicians with deep roots in New Orleans traditional jazz, but also the growth of a tourism industry that pushed the authenticity of local culture. However, what the Jaffes also exemplified in this same era in which the city's musicians' locals were forcefully integrated by national leadership, is that there were some spaces within this New Orleans culture that not only allowed but encouraged the sharing of musical cultural traditions across the racial lines of the South.

When Allan Jaffe, born in Pottsville, Pennsylvania, of Russian-Jewish descent, began playing at the Hall's nightly "kitty" gigs, he was openly flaunting the city's existing Jim Crow legislation.[30] Just as white and black musicians belonged to separate union locals, so too were performances to be segregated according to the city's municipal codes. Yet he was not the only musician to ignore such racial lines and his example drew many young white musicians to the Hall to learn from the talents of the city's forgotten repositories of

30.   The "kitty" being the basket passed during the set to collect donations in lieu of an admission charge. According to an editorial in the New Orleans Jazz Club's newsletter, *Second Line,* there had been some initial resistance to the format from both locals, but that the issue disappeared, presumably because the kitty began to collect sufficient funds to pay musicians at full scale. *Second Line,* (September-October 1961): 19-22. The *Des-Moines Register* reported in 1966 that Jaffe was only able to pay the musicians $13.50 a night initially, but that the figure had risen to $30 a night for leaders and $20.50 for sidemen. *Des-Moines Register*, December 20, 1966, 16; Sandra and Allan Jaffe, clipping in vertical files, Hogan Jazz Archives, Tulane University, New Orleans. (hereafter cited as HJA).

the old style. Young men like Tom Sancton and Don Marquis learned to play with the band members at Preservation Hall and confess to finding a true community among the genre's oldest practitioners.[31] Other scholars and musicians reference the "jazz pilgrims," young men and women that came from across the country and across the world to learn from the African American masters.

Yet on a larger scale, racial discord wracked the city as national desegregation mandates precipitated entrenched battles in the courts, schoolyards, lunch counters, and City Hall. Since the *Brown* v. *Board of Education* decision in 1954, many cities in the South, including New Orleans, witnessed the aggressive actions of a white segregationist cohort intent on maintaining the de facto and de jure firmaments of Jim Crow. Known as the "massive resistance," this effort in New Orleans was facilitated by the office of Mayor DeLesseps "Chep" Morrison who, while courting the black vote, also did little to block arch-segregationists like Leander Perez.[32] After the Louisiana state legislature issued a string of hate ordinances in 1956, similar laws appeared on the books in New Orleans city code.[33] For example, Ordinance 828 made it illegal for whites and blacks to patronize the same clubs and venues, and similar legislation prevented the appearance of mixed bands at any given musical location.

31.   Donald M. Marquis, "My Life in Jazz," *The Jazz Archivist* 23 (2010), 21-29; and Sancton, *Song for My Fathers*.

32.   Arnold R. Hirsch, "Simply a Matter of Black and White: The Transformation of Race and Politics in Twentieth Century New Orleans," in *Creole New Orleans: Race and Americanization*, eds. Arnold R. Hirsch and Joseph Logsdon (Baton Rouge: Louisiana State University Press, 1992), 262-319. More detail on Leander Perez as the ring-leader of the segregationists can be found in Fairclough, *Race & Democracy*.

33.   Jones, "'Separate but Equal," 24. Jones cites LA resolution 4:451 which prohibited "the sponsoring, arranging, participating in, or permitting on the premises any social functions, entertainment, athletic training games, and other activities involving social and personal contacts in which participants are members of the white and negro races."

Fueled by the White Citizens' Councils that had appeared all over the South and were active in New Orleans, the city repeatedly resisted nearly every effort at integration until the cataclysmic public school desegregation in 1960 and 1961. Despite having been hamstrung by legal actions against the NAACP, the black and creole community had continued to press for change through the second half of the 1950s. While certainly not entirely united, groups like A. L. Davis's Interdenominational Ministerial Alliance and the Orleans Parish Progressive Voters Action League, efforts from lawyers like A. P. Tureaud and his protégé Ernest "Dutch" Morial, and the activism of individuals like Arthur Chapital and Rosa Keller all worked to challenge the Jim Crow legislation.[34] Moreover, while not central to the battle, the city's entertainers were clearly engaged when, for example, in 1957 the United Clubs—comprised of four Social Aid and Pleasure Clubs and the black musicians union—called for a boycott of Mardi Gras. They would repeat the strike several more times in the early 1960s, hoping, as they argued, to "curb the spending of money with local merchants who refuse to give negroes employment or opportunities."[35]

The New Orleans school desegregation crisis of 1960-1961 proved to be a pivotal and pitched battle in the struggle to end Jim Crow legislation in Louisiana. In a series of complicated maneuvers between the Orleans Parish School Board, the state legislature in Baton Rouge, and a local federal judge, two public schools were grudgingly desegregated, only to have their entire white student population withdraw over the course of the school year.[36] White Citizen Council housewives not only picketed the schools daily, but taunted and harassed the young girls that had been hand selected by the school board to attend them. As historian Lawrence Powell notes,

34.   Ibid., 278-83; Rogers, *Righteous Lives*.

35.   "35 Clubs Support Social Blackout," *Louisiana Weekly*, November 23, 1963; Carnival / Mardi Gras, 1960-1969, clipping in vertical files, HJA.

36.   Fairclough, *Race & Democracy*, 234-64.

"by May 1961 the city was a tinderbox of racial unrest."[37]

The combination of the school crisis and a change in mayoral leadership—the arrival of former City Council president Vic Schiro—brought a renewed push in civil rights activism. As Arnold Hirsch argues, it was particularly Schiro's lack of interest in his predecessor's style of negotiation that brought African American, creole, and white community leaders "into closer and more direct contact."[38] Several groups coalesced around an invigorated agenda of desegregation and equal access, including a revived Citizen's Committee, CORE, and the NAACP Youth Council. Joining the older guard of activists in what Lolis Elie refered to as a "tenuous" coalition, small victories were achieved in desegregation, including the desegregation of lunch counters on Canal Street, city promises to end discriminatory hiring practices, and a purported end to New Orleans Recreation Department (NORD) segregation.[39] Even the *Louisiana Weekly* lauded the "numerous breakthroughs" which, they argued, had "been accepted by the general public without protest."[40]

The 1964 Civil Rights Act and the subsequent Voting Rights Act significantly changed the realities for activists in the city. In addition to drastically increasing the percentage of eligible black voters, the national legislation served, Hirsch argues, "as a social force" that "stimulated the opportunistic creation of a new range of black organizations."[41] Both acts served as fodder for judges and attorneys seeking to strike down segregationist

---

37.   Lawrence N. Powell, "When Hate Came to Town: New Orleans' Jews and George Lincoln Rockwell," *American Jewish History* 85, no. 4 (1997): 399.

38.   Hirsch, "Simply a Matter of Black and White," 284. Rogers also argues it was the crisis years between 1959 and 1961 that created a new bi-racial working coalition. Rogers, *Righteous Lives,* 49.

39.   Cited in Ibid., 285. However, it is worth noting that while the New Orleans Recreation Department ostensibly integrated, it failed to open any public pools for the next several sweltering summers, claiming budget concerns.

40.   Cited in Ibid., 286; *Louisiana Weekly,* July 27, 1963.

41.   Ibid., 288-89.

policy and as a serious impediment to the efforts of arch-segregationists like Perez. Finally, it encouraged moderate groups on the fence about integration to get motivated to alter existing policies rather than face public admonition or, worse still, a civil suit. One of those organizations was the American Federation of Musicians (AFM).

During the pitched racial battles of the 1960s, two separate American Federation of Musicians locals operated in the Greater New Orleans area. One (Local 174) functioned for the benefit of white members of the music community, while the other (Local 496) accepted the area's African American artists. While they came together on occasion to settle disputes between members, or intervene in cases of fraudulent owners or bookers, they stood in opposition to each other for the entirety of the decade.[42] By the beginning of the 1960s, the international American Federation of Musicians faced a difficult challenge. New Orleans was not unique in its divided musicians' locals, and activists in labor organizing and the nation at large were pushing aggressively toward integration. While little was done from the top until Lyndon Johnson signed the Civil Rights Act in 1964, once legal action became a real threat, AFM leadership mobilized to forcefully merge the many dual locals in the nation's major urban centers.

Pressure to integrate mounted across the union organization from the end of World War II until the legal actions of the mid-1960s, although the American Federation

42.   While New Orleans was ostensibly a closed shop, a number of musicians felt the union had nothing to offer them and refused to join, causing not an insignificant amount of friction at meetings. One example is Doc Paulin, who Michael White argues "became infamous among musicians as one of the last non-union band leaders." As White reports him saying, "What do I want to join dat union for? You gotta pay dem people dues and all kinds of money every time you play a job. Dey don't get you any work. Dey don't do anything for the musician but take his money. I can't do dat. I got thirteen churin to feed. Ain't dat right." White, "Dr. Michael White," 5. While Dr. John was a member—if a delinquent one—of Local 174, he argues that "both unions were trying to keep black and white musicians apart" and frequently engaged in turf wars "because we was mixing races in our sessions." John and Rummel, *Under a HooDoo Moon,* 57, 89.

of Musicians was particularly "behind the times" in its failure to encourage mergers. To historian Clark Halker, much blame was to be placed at the top levels of leadership.[43] While he praises AFM President James Petrillo for his work in improving relations between dual locals during his tenure in Chicago (beginning in 1922), Halker argues that once Petrillo became international president in 1940, he "reacted slowly but deliberately. . . . Aware of black discontent, he cautioned patience and made overtures towards black members. He balked at ending Jim Crow locals, however, until black members, with aid from white members, demanded equal treatment." At once proclaiming "the AFM's commitment to civil rights for blacks," Halker argues that Petrillo "took few substantive measures" toward integration during the 1940s and 1950s.[44]

With the assumption of the presidency by Herman Kenin in 1957 and mounting pressures to desegregate, the AFM began to take steps toward slowly prodding locals to integrate. Much of this might have been the result of a directive from the AFL-CIO in 1960 to end all segregation within their unions, as Halker argues, yet it is perhaps just as likely that pressure came more from internal AFM decisions and perceived pressures.[45] Between 1957 and 1963, only Los Angeles, Denver, San Francisco, and Cleveland locals had merged.[46] At the international level, the AFL-CIO struggled internally to push forward any specific legislation that would force improvements in racial relations within the unions, as the notorious debate between A. Philip Randolph and the organization over labor equity attests. While they had helped pass national civil rights legislation in the mid-1960s, the

43. Clark Halker, "A History of Local 208 and the Struggle for Racial Equality in the American Federation of Musicians," *Black Music Research Journal* 8, no. 2 (1988): 207-22.

44. Ibid., 215-16.

45. Ibid., 217.

46. Ibid., 217-18. Halker notes that New York had always been integrated.

AFL-CIO wrestled with on-the-ground enforcement of Title VII, which prohibited workplace discrimination because it limited local members' rights and could have potentially lowered negotiated wages for both white and black workers.[47] However, following passage of the 1964 Civil Rights Act, AFM leadership under Kenin became more vocal, and the number of merged locals began to steadily increase, including in a few key urban centers like Chicago. Presumably the AFM and its top leadership feared bad press and litigation, and as a result pushed harder after 1964 to force locals to integrate. Many members would come to resent this top-down approach.

Merging the Locals and Seeking "Bi-Racial Teamwork"

By 1965, the word "merger" began appearing in the minutes of the 174's board meetings, but not without a large dose of trepidation.[48] On April 20, board president David Winstein read aloud a missive from AFM President Kenin "regarding the Civil Rights Act of 1964" to fellow board members. A few months later, he repeated the information to the entire membership. The secretary recorded the carefully worded message as the local announced the directive to integrate:

> The President then gave a lengthy explanation of the advice of the American Federation of Musicians relative to the possible merger of Locals 174 and 496. He explained that nothing has been proposed at this time, the first meeting of the two boards [was] scheduled for July 21. Many, many questions were asked and had to

47.   Herbert Hill, "Black Workers, Organized Labor, and Title VII of the 1964 Civil Rights Act: Legislative History and Litigation Record," in Herbert Hill and James E. Jones, *Race in America: The Struggle for Equality* (Madison: University of Wisconsin Press, 1993), 263-341.

48.   Materials from both the 174 and 496 of the American Federation of Musicians, including limited runs of each of their newsletters, are held at the Hogan Jazz Archive, Tulane University, New Orleans, Louisiana. (hereafter cited as AFM-HJA).

be answered theoretically. Many proposals and ideas were offered to the Board as suggestions during the negotiations. The membership was notified that many meetings, of necessity, would have to be held and they would continually be notified of the progress of these negotiations. The President told the meeting that the terms of the agreement would be ratified by a general or special meeting.[49]

In the meantime, Winstein responded to pressure from the international, travelling to Louisville with board secretary John Scheuermann to meet with the Civil Rights Department of the AFM and members of the Kentucky locals. Both former AFM president Petrillo and current president Kenin were in attendance, as were the top brass from Local 496.[50] Winstein reported briefly to the board on the meeting and drafted a letter to Local 496 inviting them to the merger meeting on July 21, 1965. Such meetings would continue for the next four years.

Discussions of integration had begun in Local 496 several years earlier and while members clearly expressed anxiety over the prospect of a merger, their concerns were of a slightly different bent. Responding to merger negotiations in Chicago, the board began correspondence with Local 208. Apparently, given the turmoil, many members of that local had begun to join the white union. President Louis Cottrell considered the news significant enough to read aloud to the general membership and composed a response in his next board meeting in April 1963.[51] Moreover, despite promises that Local 496 representative E.V. Lewis would be able to attend the Southern Conference of the American Federation of Musicians held at the Roosevelt Hotel in November 1963,

49.   Minutes, 1965, Board Minutes (Local 174), 1944-1966, AFM-HJA.

50.   Ibid.

51.   *Jazz Bulletin*, July 1963, Local 496, AFM-HJA. Unfortunately, the contents of both letters were omitted from the bulletin.

the member was unceremoniously escorted out of the hotel before being served his meal because of, he was told, "a city ordinance stating where food and drinks are served negroes and whites are not allowed to mix."[52] He was assured he could attend the sessions the next day but was advised not to show up.[53] Facing the real prospect of a merger by July 1965 under less than ideal conditions, members of the 496 worked to shore up their own membership and the benefits they could afford their own brothers as it remained highly unlikely that they would face equal treatment even when a merger eventually came to pass.[54] The Local 496 also moved quickly to consult a corporate lawyer.

Evidence of dissent is rife in the minutes of board meetings, regular membership meetings, and even newsletters during the second half of 1965 within both Locals 174 and 496. Responding to early grumbling in the 174, President Winstein submitted a short piece on the front page of the local's newsletter *Prelude* in July 1965.[55] Titled "What D'Ya Hear About a Merger. . ?????," the editorial nearly begged members to remain calm and act in a democratic nature, and it took up the entire front page of the publication. In the face of mounting "rumors, gossip, lies, and deliberate misinformation," Winstein argued it was imperative that members "calm down and analyze facts." At hand was a legal situation seeking to end labor discrimination with which his

52.   The incident spurred discussion within the Southern Conference, but little indignation or swift action. While Winstein had been the one at a previous conference to suggest inviting members of African American locals to attend "as guests," the group moved to appeal the motion. It was not until 1968 that they moved to officially revise their by-laws to incorporate African American locals. See Box 1/2, Southern Conference of Locals (1954-1982) and International Executive Board (1966-1981) "Meeting Minutes," AFM-HJA.

53.   *Jazz Bulletin*, January 1964, Local 496, AFM-HJA.

54.   *Jazz Bulletin*, July 1965, Local 496, AFM-HJA. Ironically or perhaps not, it was at the special membership meeting informing members of the merger meeting in Louisville on June 13, 1965, that Allan Jaffe was sworn in to the 496.

55.   *Prelude,* July 1965, Local 174, AFM-HJA.

local was "vitally interested." To Weinstein, the segregationist argument was moot:

> Your President makes the blunt statement that anyone, repeat, "anyone," who tries to tell the members of this or any other labor organization that he has a "solution" to this situation and attempts to capitalize on it or foment agitation, is just not telling the truth. The persons making this claim are in the same group that had the "solution" to halt the desegregation of schools, buses, stores, etc. Did they succeed? NO!! But they *did* inject hatred into the situation. Many of these people make a nice living out of being professional "antis."[56]

Moving beyond the potential "antis," Winstein addressed what seemed to have been the bigger concern surrounding the merger: the local's assets. Winstein assured members that the best way to affect an "equitable and honorable plan" was to work slowly, calmly, and democratically. As he noted, the treasury belonged to "EVERYONE, AND YET NO ONE IN PARTICULAR." Clearly, fiscal matters were of primary concern to member Phillip Zito when he presented the board with a series of resolutions in August to prevent the merger from happening.[57] Even before the general membership meeting, Zito was prepared with his own options to deal with the pending merger. He argued that for the "good and welfare of the entire membership of the Local 174," one or more of his three resolutions should be passed. Local 174, "rich both in money and in property," faced a significant potential loss with the mergers being compelled nationally "due to race laws or not in their respected states." The first resolution assembled a plan to disperse nearly all of 174's assets, particularly its properties, before the forced merger. The second, more drastic,

56.   Ibid.

57.   Letter from Phillip Zito to Board of AFM Local 174, 6 July 1965; Minutes, 1965, Board Minutes (Local 174), 1944-1966, AFM-HJA.

proposed rescinding current by-laws and allowing for the immediate dissolution of the local without a 9/10th vote. The third resolution, by far the most mild, simply demanded a new accounting of all assets of the Local 174.

Zito managed to procure eight additional signatures for his resolution petition, but one redacted his name by crossing it out and two others sent letters to the members of the board requesting their names be removed. Much to Zito's consternation, the resolutions were rejected by the Board for being "too ambiguous, vague, indeterminate and unconstitutional."[58] Johnny Repak, an initial signatory, requested removal citing his own loyalty to the local, the potential of a civil rights lawsuit, and the general incomprehensibility of the resolutions themselves. While Zito may have been the lone wolf willing to push resolutions forward on this issue, his concern over fiscal matters was not singular.[59] As he continued to push resolutions through the end of 1965, he gathered a level of support indicative of an overall anxiety over not the issue of race, but rather of money. As it happened, 174 members were not the only ones concerned about the potential fiscal fall-out of a merger.

For the 496, the second half of 1965 was filled with merger discussions, plans, debates, and suggestions, all indicating that the group was similarly unsettled by the possibility of being required to join forces. In regular membership and board meetings the issue was discussed extensively. Members brought up examples of mergers in other cities, the president appointed a merger committee that convened its first meeting in September, and a special merger committee

58.   Minutes, 1965, Board Minutes (Local 174), 1944-1966, AFM-HJA.

59.   Journalist Charles Suhor praises Zito for "doggedly [objecting] to numerous moves by Musicians Union President David Winstein" who he argues was "not a tyrant" but had almost "complete control" over the group. He goes on to say that "at union meetings Zito would plow in with contrary ideas that ranged from sound to absolutely silly, creating and then breaking tension, and bringing some perspective and humor to the situation." Suhor, *Jazz in New Orleans,* 130.

report was presented to the entire membership. The report sought to "explain the effects of a merger" and focused on such issues as "distribution of assets, "possible target date," and "representation."[60] Members even voted to increase the pay for officers and board members given that "many special meetings" would be "necessary to negotiate the merger of Locals 174 and 496, involving much time and study."[61] Two years passed with little to no action. Merger agreements were sent back and forth from one local to the other and no consensus on the overall terms of the integration was achieved between them.

By 1968, now into the fourth year of the process, President Winstein—who was also now an active member of the International Executive Board—was understandably defensive on the issue of New Orleans's failure to merge. Responding to a note and clipping about an Alabama merger, in which the writer inquired "are we going to keep up with the times—and soon?" Winstein replied tartly that the writer was "typical of a member who does not attend Local 174 meetings."[62] He argued that the merger negotiations had been underway since 1966, and that 90 percent of the issues had been agreed upon quickly and easily. The impasse lay, in his mind, in the insistence of the Local 496 in extending the transition period. As with many other African American locals in the same situation across the country, the members of 496 were concerned with losing their voice on local, regional, and national platforms. Winstein argued to his critic that eventually the national organization would have to step in, which would ultimately be worse for the 496. He essentially

60.   *Jazz Bulletin*, October 1965, Local 496, AFM-HJA. Again, the contents of the report have unfortunately been lost.

61.   *Jazz Bulletin*, January 1966, Local 496, AFM-HJA. The 174 did the same.

62.   Mrs. Walter Sablinsky to President David Winstein, with attached clipping and reply from Winstein June 1968, folder, "Correspondence 1968," box 20, "President's Correspondence, 1968-1975," AFM-HJA.

laid the blame on the 496:

> There is, has been, and will be no tendency to deny
> their members full and equal rights. Just for your
> information, the Local 174 has on many occasions
> processed claims for 496 members working on 'white'
> jobs for white employers. This is discrimination? Who
> knows, maybe Local 496 may soon be up with the
> 'times.'[63]

With the end of the decade drawing near, Winstein and others
in the 174 realized that the AFM would eventually force the
merger upon them, with potentially damaging effects to
both locals. Still, several members of the 174 continued their
campaign against what they saw as the unconstitutional and
undemocratic move by the AFM to force them to merge.
However, it was not necessarily the racial animosity between
the two separate locals that slowed the process to a near halt.
Rather, concern over Local assets and autonomy in the face of
a mostly musically integrated landscape ruled the day.

To Local 496, the call to "keep up with the times" seemed to
portend a loss of fiscal autonomy and representation on local,
regional, and national levels. While the 174 overcame most
of their internal objections to integration by August 18, 1969,
when they passed a merger resolution by a margin of thirty
to five, the 496 clearly had not.[64] After the August approval
by the white union, 496 members soundly rejected the
agreement.[65] Reporting on the situation, a *Downbeat* magazine
contributor noted that it was "ironic" that the 496 were the
ones to reject the merger.[66] According to the short report, 496
President Louis Cottrell had cited economic reasons rather

---

63.   Ibid.

64.   Minutes, 1969, Board Minutes (Local 174), 1944-1966, AFM-HJA.

65.   Correspondence 1969, box 20, President's Correspondence, 1968-1975,
AFM-HJA.

66.   *Downbeat,* January 8, 1970; Winstein's response in ibid.

than racial relations, which, according to the reporter, had been "traditionally harmonious" in New Orleans. While the reporter's generalization about race in the city was a stretch, he indicated the significance of the altered context of color lines within the musical community and the failure of both locals to keep pace with the changing times.

The many testimonies of musicians and club owners demonstrate that there was a significant degree of integration in the music scene in the early 1960s, even if the locals steadfastly resisted a merger. However, union meeting notes indicate that the two often worked together, albeit not always in the most harmonious of manners. As many clubs and record companies employed members of both unions, coordinated efforts were often necessary. For example, in January 1961 a member of the 496 filed a claim against a venue called Caruso's, and the 174 was duly informed. A June 1962 issue regarding overtime pay brought both locals together to protest Minit Records's failure to appropriately pay session players. Board members of both locals voted unanimously in favor of the musicians.[67] Often murky agreements between clubs and musicians invoked similar issues; in 1963, Albert French of the 496 got embroiled in a conflict over false signatures by bookers on contracts. As the majority of the musicians employed in this case were from the 174, the local delivered the admonition to French and the others "not to do any business whatsoever" or "pay any commission to the Hardy Agency."[68] Moreover, when addressing issues of wages from clubs under their jurisdiction, the 174 consistently demanded owners and bookers pay full scale to members of both locals.[69] On occasion, the 174 would refer musician requests to the 496, but only if they deemed the venue appropriate. February 1961 board meeting minutes

67.   Meeting of Members of the Board of Locals 496 and 174, 26 June 1962, Meeting Minutes 1962, AFM-HJA.

68.   Minutes, 1963, Board Minutes (Local 174), 1944-1966, AFM-HJA.

69.   Minutes, 1966 and Minutes, 1967, Board Minutes (Local 174), 1944-1966, AFM-HJA.

indicated that while "[t]he request of [historically black] Dillard University was referred to Local 496, due to allocation being exhausted," requests from Louis Berndt of [all white] Tulane University and the Tulane University Fine Arts Committee were denied, "due to allocation being exhausted."[70]

Still, more often Local 174 expressed concern over what they saw as the infringement of the African American musicians on territory they deemed their own. In 1964, clearly seeing the writing on the wall, the board of Local 174 called a meeting with its bandleaders and the Committee on Wages regarding "the matter of colored bands encroaching on what was once entirely the property of members of this Local." Complaints had been building for some time, as early that same month, the president of 174 sent a letter to Local 496 reminding them of their violations of "minimums," or the minimum amount to be paid musicians on a given gig. The board voted to approve a second letter to ensure that changes had been made in what they viewed as the 496's undercutting of their efforts to maintain gig standards, and they continued to go after violators in their opposing local throughout the decade.[71] The 496 countered. During a regular member meeting in January 1966 members voted down a directive from the international requesting that they increase their initiation fee in order to "avoid competition with Local 174."[72] Working together in a venue was one thing, but sharing resources was clearly quite another.

Yet despite the occasional animosity that ran through the union structures, musicians themselves recall a gradual shift in the socialization among their ranks in the periods immediately before and after the 1964 civil rights legislation. According to *Downbeat* reporter Charles Suhor, integrated bands began to

70.   Minutes, 1961, Board Minutes (Local 174), 1944-1966, AFM-HJA.

71.   Minutes, 1968, Board Minutes (Local 174), 1944-1966, AFM-HJA. For instance, in May 1968 charges were brought against Local 496 member Saltifor-maggio for not employing the minimum number of players on a gig.

72.   *Prelude,* April 1966, Local 496, AFM-HJA.

appear more frequently by the mid 1960s due in part to the softening of formal segregation laws.[73] While New Orleans arch-segregationists continued to wage a bloody battle against integration, several venues began quietly yet forcefully employing bi-racial bands. Such efforts were not without resistance from the city's segregationists. Jazz historian Bill Russell indicated in a memorandum to Richard Allen that Allan Jaffe had found it impossible to obtain a parade permit in early 1962.[74] Apparently, a television segment with David Brinkley that had aired in late 1961 had angered the White Citizens' Council because it featured Jaffe and Preservation Hall and depicted "colored and white parading together." According to journalist Iris Kelso, the Council had viewed it as "terrible publicity for New Orleans" and had exerted their considerable pressure on City Hall to deny Jaffe's request. Yet Jaffe continued his efforts and integrated parades remained a regular feature of Preservation Hall's weekly line-up throughout the early 1960s.

The cancellation of the 1965 American Football League all-star game as a result of racial discrimination served as a wake up call for many individuals in the city who had been working hard to promote it as a cultural destination *par excellence*. As Charles Suhor reported at the time in *Downbeat*, collateral damage from the embarrassment was the subsequent postponement/cancellation of the planned Jazz Festival for that same year. Suhor indicates that it "sent a chill through the community."[75] Norman Francis, then assistant to the president at Xavier University, tended to agree. In an editorial in the *Louisiana Weekly*, Francis left little to doubt that the city's reputation had suffered a serious blow.[76] "We cannot

73.   Suhor, *Jazz in New Orleans*, 236-37.

74.   Memorandum from Bill Russell to Richard Allen, 23 April 1962, vertical files, "Preservation Hall," HJA.

75.   Charles Suhor, "Jazz in New Orleans in the 1960s."

76.   Norman C. Francis, "Racial Team Work Needed to Make N.O.," *Louisiana Weekly*, January 16, 1965, 2.

be cosmopolitan by simply saying we are," he noted, adding that serious "biracial teamwork" was necessary in order to rework the city's image.

Within several of the city's clubs, such bi-racial teamwork was afoot. Jazz curator and historian Bill Russell noted that "officially" Preservation Hall held the first integrated session in May 1964. Russell said the Thursday night set, "is believed to be the first time local white musicians have played for pay with a local colored band." He added, unceremoniously that "Allan has asked Paul and Raymond [the white musicians] to play with Punch [Miller's] band again on Sunday May 31 and Thursday June 4."[77] Similarly, under the musical leadership of Al Beletto, the Playboy Club in the French Quarter began regularly hosting musicians from both sides of the color line in single gigs. As Beletto recalls, Playboy's owner Hugh Hefner cared little for the details of segregation law in the South. In recounting the decision to integrate in October 1964, it appears as a moot point: "Richie [Richard Payne] was by far the best bass player. And I called Hugh Hefner and asked if there was going to be a problem because of Louisiana state law. And he said, 'If that's the guy you want, yeah, hire him. I have better lawyers than the state of Louisiana.'"

Suhor argues that "Playboy brought good jazz musicians together in integrated settings and advanced the image of jazz as listenable contemporary music in New Orleans."[78] Similar integrationist moves happened under Don Suhor's direction at Sho'Bar in 1966 and Santo Pecora's Dream Room in 1968, all helping to boost music and its role in making New Orleans a premier cultural destination.[79]

In general, the discussion of race, while still maintaining its dichotomous structure of black and white, shifted among musicians during the decade. As one member of the 496 told Jack Buerkle and Danny Barker, players were better judged

---

77.   Notes from BBR, 29 May 1964, vertical files, "Preservation Hall," HJA.

78.   Suhor, "Jazz in New Orleans in the 1960s," 21.

79.   Suhor, *Jazz in New Orleans,* 237.

by their skill rather than their skin color.

> We all have soul. Some of us may have a little more
> soul than others. I know. I've played with some of the
> finest white musicians in the city. I don't know what
> soul is. I can't say that I have more soul than they have.
> I don't think there is any difference between black and
> white music. If you are a good jazzman, you're a good
> jazzman. Some guys say, "he's a good colored jazz
> trumpet player." I just say he's a good jazz trumpet
> player, period! I don't want somebody to single me out
> for anything but the way I play trumpet.[80]

While the mid- to late 1960s brought a trickle of integration,
the momentum seemed to pick up in earnest by the early 1970s
when "more black and white artists were getting to know
each other as peers. The creative exchange Mac Rebennack
pursued in the 1950s had become a social reality to a number of
whites."[81] But it was, as the story of the merger indicates, also
a process of acceptance among African American musicians.
Forced into segregated facilities and sub-par treatment, they
sought equitable enforcement of conditions, but also held
tightly to the institutional structures that had supported them
and their music. The process of cultural integration in the
music scene in New Orleans clearly indicates that there was
much to gain—and lose—on either side of the racial divide.

    With the 496's refusal to sign the merger agreement in the
late summer of 1969, international AFM President Herman
Kenin intervened and mandated integration for November
1, 1969. As predicted by 174 President Winstein, this caused
serious concern for members of both locals. For the 496,
concerns centered on fiscal matters and representation. While
496 President Cottrell may have expressed concern about

80.   Jack V. Buerkle and Danny Barker, *Bourbon Street Black; the New Orleans Black Jazzman* (New York: Oxford University Press, 1973), 120.

81.   Berry, Foose, and Jones, *Up from the Cradle of Jazz*, 241.

economics to the *Downbeat* reporter, he and other members also worried about representation. Even before the August meeting, Vice President Isadore Crump wrote directly to Kenin seeking a resolution to what he argued was a major concern.[82] Having enjoyed direct representation to national conventions since their formation, minority groups, Crump argued, were poised to lose their national voice after the brief interim period of transition lapsed. Crump requested a proposal "to increase by 2 the number of representatives for five years after the interim period," with these two being "former members of the minority groups, elected by the general membership."

Immediately following the national mandate, the 496 sought out legal advice from local consul. Attorney Ralph F. Jackson responded to a request for an explanation of their legal options by saying that his firm saw no alternative for the 496:

> We feel very strongly that the Local 496 faces no choice but to comply with the order or suffer expulsion from the AFM. We do not believe that the officers of the Local would be legally justified in doing anything that would result in the union's disaffiliation with its parent organization. Taking legal action against the merger would involve this risk and we advise against it.

Seeing no other options, the board of the 496 informed its membership that it would accede to the order from the AFM. They argued that they had exhausted all negotiation tactics and faced the possibility of expulsion. Attempting to soften the blow, they told members that they had "no intention of exposing this membership to such a fate, so we will yield to the desire of the Federation."[83]

Sociologist Jack Buerkle and musician Danny Barker argued

82.   Correspondence 1969, box 20, President's Correspondence, 1968-1975, AFM-HJA.

83.   Ibid.

in 1973 that while some of the "family-like" warmth of the 496 may have been lost as a result of the merger, the changing times indicated that it "simply outgrew its usefulness as a distinct entity."[84] According to one 496 member they questioned about the amalgamation, the real issue was perhaps why it did not happen sooner.

> Many of us have been friends across the two Locals — We grew up together. Sometimes, a big hotel would have two bands playing on the same night; one white, the other colored. They'd be playing on one side of the hotel, and we'd be on the other. When it was all over the money (for the union) would go back to two different Locals. Two different plants to keep going. And, besides our strength as a brotherhood was diluted. We just decided it was stupid to go on like that. 'Specially since we were friends.[85]

While not everyone was bound to agree that the membership of either local "just decided" to merge, evidence clearly indicates that the friendship component of this musician's statement was true. Musical collaborations across the two locals had been occurring since the 1950s. Moreover, the cited "inevitability" of the move, as noted by both Buerkle and Barker and the musician, indicates that the process clearly dragged out far too long and was resolved in a less than organic fashion, despite the fact that places like Preservation Hall had been actively encouraging integration throughout the decade.

By early 1970, the formally divided locals had combined to form the AFM Musicians' Mutual Protective Union, Local 174-496. It had been a long, drawn out process that tested the patience of many, despite the fact that members of both locals consistently worked together on artistic endeavors in the

84.   Buerkle and Barker, *Bourbon Street Black*, 101.
85.   Ibid.

city's various clubs and music venues. While the musicians of the newly joined local saw the merger as inevitable, or, more positively, as a gain for their careers, others resented the process which had been forced upon them from upper levels of the AMF. The fact that the process was, as Al Bernard wrote, undemocratic, highlights the ways in which organized labor, despite its underlying efforts at solidarity, frequently accepted a racialized separatism within the labor force. As Bruce Raeburn points out, the New Orleans music scene testifies to the fact that interest in the city's culture and its practitioners "could engender activism against segregation."[86] While individuals like Judge Babylon may have continued to inveigh against "baggy pants Northerners," by the early 1970s, it was more than just a bunch of musical pilgrims from outside the South who saw value in adding "cream" to the city's "coffee."

86.   Raeburn, *New Orleans Style and the Writing of American Jazz History*, 254.

7

"Just Like Ole' Mammy Used to Make": The History of the New Orleans Praline Woman

CHANDA M. NUNEZ

"After Emancipation, the selling of sweets became
a time-honored way of earning a small but honorable living."
-Jessica B. Harris,
The Welcome Table: African-American Heritage Cooking

During the early 1900s, a praline vendor named Mary Louise served as a regular presence on the campus of H. Sophie Newcomb College in New Orleans.[1] She typically stationed herself at the front gate asking "you wan' praline?" to faculty and students and all other passers-by. Sometimes she would not have to ask because crowds, which often included Newcomb College President B.V.B. Dixon, would flock around her to purchase her deliciously popular pecan-filled sweets. Mary Louise always sold all of her pralines before the end of the day.

Known around campus as the "praline mammy," Mary Louise cooked large batches of candy each morning in the kitchen of her St. Antoine Street home which was located nearby in the Uptown section of the city. (figure 1) An enterprising woman, she made sure she had several variations of pralines. She sold not only the traditional pecan pralines, but also several other types, including peanut, pink, and white coconut. Her "office" extended beyond the Newcomb and Tulane campuses. Mary Louise also sold pralines at school-

---

1. Beginning in the late 1800s, Newcomb College served as the women's college for Tulane University.

related events. In November 1900, when Tulane's football team played Louisiana State University (LSU), the Newcomb administrators told the students, "Girls, save up your nickels. Pass by Mammy without looking at her or her pralines, for Tulane is to play L.S.U. . . . "[2]

Mary Louise, Praline Woman, circa 1917, Newcomb College Archives.

When Mary Louise died, her daughter Azelie became the "praline mammy" who sold the confections to Newcomb and Tulane students. A white woman once offered her $5.00 a day plus expenses to make pralines in her kitchen in order that she could give the candy as Christmas gifts.[3] Azelie declined her offer. Perhaps the notion of working in a white woman's kitchen was off-putting for her, or, possibly the self-determined Azelie generated enough income selling pralines

2.   *New Orleans Times-Picayune*, November 17, 1900, 3.

3.   *New Orleans Times-Picayune*, March 21, 1920, 51.

that she did not need the additional revenue. Another sign of Azelie's independent streak is captured in a newspaper account that stated if the Newcomb girls bothered Azelie too much "she would leave the college craving for sweets for a week until she considered them punished sufficiently."[4] That Azelie readily and easily removed her pralines suggests she was fully aware of the role she and her pralines played on the campus. By discontinuing candy sales, she exercised power over the white college students and was likely able to sell her treats in other locations. While Azelie was able to replace the income from the Newcomb girls, they were never able to replace her sweet, delicious pralines.

Like the many black women who made a living as washerwomen in the South after emancipation (rather than as domestic servants), Azelie may have prized her status as a self-employed person, free from the surveillance that working in white households brought with it. Her independence reminds one of the washerwomen described in Tera Hunter's study of 1800s and early 1900s Atlanta; Azelie, too, sought "to achieve freedom, equality, and a living wage against tremendous odds."[5] Like her mother, Azelie did not limit herself to college campuses. She stationed herself in front of the St. Charles Hotel, selling her sweets to New Orleans visitors. Azelie's "baskets of lusciousness drew tourists as thickly as flies about honey."[6] Though Mary Louise, Azelie, and many other enterprising women took to the streets to sell pralines in an effort to support themselves and their families financially, they were not viewed as businesswomen; they were instead stereotyped as mammies. This is evident from the numerous newspaper articles, short stories, and drawings referring to them as a "praline mammy."

Dating back to seventeenth-century France, the praline

4.   Ibid..

5.   Tera W. Hunter, *To 'Joy My Freedom: Southern Black Women's Lives and Labors After the Civil War* (Cambridge, MA: Harvard University Press, 1997).

6.   Ibid.

was named for Marchel de Plessin-Pralin, who suffered from indigestion and ate almonds to alleviate the pain; his butler suggested that he cover the almonds with sugar. Sugar-coated almonds soon became a treat in France. When the French settlers came to Louisiana, they brought the praline with them.[7]

More than simply vending sweets, African American women also were responsible for creating the New Orleans praline, which continued to be sold in France as sugared almonds. African American cooks replaced the almonds with pecans, which were abundant in New Orleans. They also added large amounts of Louisiana sugar as well as milk to thicken the candy.

The candy held very different meanings for the customer and the vendor. "Pralines," as white consumers often referred to them, were a treat. They symbolized a piece of the Old South, lovingly prepared by someone depicted as a faithful "mammy." Generally known as "Pecan Candy" or "Plarines" by African Americans, the candy represented a path to economic freedom and additional income for many of its sellers. Mary Louise turned over to her daughter what can be described as a family business; white commentators on the other hand, praised the candy while typically reducing the women to demeaning caricatures. This paper examines the heritage of entrepreneurship long hidden behind the "mammy" image during the Antebellum and Jim Crow eras. This study also surveys the prominence of praline street vendors in New Orleans from the colonial period until the rise of early twentieth-century praline shops that marketed the "mammy" image to tourists while employing African American candy makers in commercial kitchens. It then considers the return of a more prominent, entrepreneurial role for African American praline vendors in the later part of the twentieth century.

7.   *The Picayune's Creole Cook Book* (New York: Dover Publications, 2002), 375.

New Orleans Markets

The tradition of African Americans selling goods in the New Orleans community dates from the colonial period. Enslaved Africans initially took part in the market economy to provide financial relief to their masters and to earn additional income to provide their own food, clothing, and shelter. While New Orleans was under French rule, the *Code Noir* was established in an effort to control the slave population. Article V of the code excused slaves from work on Sunday; as a result, slaves used this day to their economic advantage by selling goods in the market. The laws of the Code Noir were loosely enforced because the slave merchants sold goods that were considered necessities to the white population of New Orleans. According to historian Jerah Johnson, "by the end of the French Period slaves regularly held a Sunday market on the edge of the city at the end of Orleans Street."[8] The slave market continued under Spanish rule and when the Americans took control of New Orleans, the slave market was maintained. This area would eventually be known as Congo Square.

Slaves, free people of color, Native Americans, and whites congregated on Sundays, and Congo Square acted as an open-air market. During the eighteenth century, "only a handful of slave peddlers occasionally sold goods up and down New Orleans's few short streets and along its riverfront, which served as the city's main food market."[9] When enslaved Africans arrived in New Orleans, they encountered an already existing Native American market, which sold bear grease, game, fish, and baskets. According to Gwendolyn Midlo Hall, "two-thirds of the slaves brought to Louisiana under French rule

8.   Jerah Johnson, "Colonial New Orleans: A Fragment of the Eighteenth-Century French Ethos," in *Creole New Orleans: Race and Americanization*, ed. Arnold R. Hirsch and Joseph Logsdon (Baton Rouge: Louisiana State University Press, 1992), 42.

9.   Jerah Johnson, *Congo Square in New Orleans* (New Orleans: Louisiana Landmarks Society, 1995), 9.

came from Senegambia." Known as merchant princes, these vendors specialized in the buying and selling of goods.[10]

Coming from a long mercantile tradition, the West African women were the stand-out vendors. Enslaved African women and free women of color soon dominated New Orleans markets. In port cities around the Atlantic World, the idea of working outside of the home was attractive to these women because they were able to escape the watchful eyes of their white masters and generate additional revenue. For example, in Savannah, "bondwomen and a smaller number of free African American women virtually monopolized the vending of cakes and confectionery" in the city's public market.[11] During the Spanish period, these women would be in a position to purchase not only material necessities; they would be able to procure their freedom through the Spanish legal system *Coartacion* ("freedom purchase").[12] One historian argues that "African American women became perhaps the most influential buyers and sellers of food in New Orleans," a position they would hold for centuries. [13]

In 1784, the Cabildo vowed to build a market especially for the street vendors in an effort to tax the increasing number of New Orleans street peddlers. In exchange for market stall usage, the Cabildo would receive rent from the vendors.[14] According

10.   Ibid.

11.   Betty Wood, *Women's Work, Men's Work: The Informal Slave Economies of Lowcountry Georgia* (Athens: The University of Georgia Press, 1995), 86.

12.   For more regarding the freedom purchase, see Kimberly S. Hanger, "Landlords, Shopkeepers, Farmers, and Slave-Owners: Free Black Female Property-Holders in Colonial New Orleans," in *Beyond Bondage: Free Women of Color in the Americas*, eds. David Barry Gaspar and Darlene Clark Hine (Chicago: University of Chicago, 2004), 218-36 and Gilbert C. Din and John E. Harkins, *The New Orleans Cabildo: Colonial Louisiana's First City Government, 1769-1803* (Baton Rouge: Louisiana State University Press, 1996), 12 and 161*n*.

13.   Daniel Usner, *Indians, Settlers, and Slaves: The Lower Mississippi Valley Before 1783* (Chapel Hill: The University of North Carolina Press, 1992), 202.

14.   Hanger, "Landlords, Shopkeepers, Farmers, and Slave-Owners," 218-36. See Robert Olwell, "'Loose, Idle and Disorderly': Slave Women in the Eigh-

to Kimberly S. Hanger, very few enslaved and free African American women rented stalls from the Cabildo, yet they continued to sell their goods on the streets. The street vendors remained an important part of New Orleans under American rule. Merchants peddled an array of food items, in addition to pralines: calas, cakes, ice; waffles, pies, and coffee were also sold. The New Orleans City Council began to regulate "the extent to which a slave could barter or sell any commodities, goods, wares, or articles in excess of $5" in 1817. [15] According to African American historian and poet Marcus Christian, any slave found in violation, had to pay fines ranging from $10 to $25.[16] Enslaved Africans continued to control the New Orleans market well into the nineteenth century. The financially independent slaves were not only a threat to their white owners, but they were also competition to local shop owners.

The Treme Market, which opened in the late 1830s, proved to be tough competition for Congo Square. The newness of the Treme Market lured away many of the Congo Square merchants. A sparse number of street vendors, both enslaved and free women of color, remained "to peddle gingerbread, rice cakes, and pralines to the Sunday afternoon crowds."[17] According to one account, "a few aged black women on the outskirts of Congo Square, sold "pralines . . . to the few tourists."[18]

After Emancipation, African American and white women sold sweets and desserts on New Orleans streets. Evidence shows that many of these women were heads of their household, financially supporting children and sometimes

---

teenth-Century Charleston Marketplace," in *More than Chattel: Black women and slavery in the Americas*, eds. David Barry Gaspar, and Darlene Clark Hine (Bloomington: Indiana University Press, 1996), 97-110.

15.   Marcus Christian, "Street Vendors and Street Cries," in The History of the Negro in Louisiana, (unpublished manuscript), 1938-1976, Louisiana and Special Collections, Earl K. Long Library, University of New Orleans.

16.   Ibid., 4.

17.   Johnson, *Congo Square*, 41.

18.   Ibid.

husbands. As street vendors, these women had to secure business licenses to sell their goods. However, due to limited finances, many were not able to pay for the necessary permits; in such instances, they had to apply for a fee waiver. According to Police Inspector Records housed at the New Orleans Public Library, in March 1899, G. Porteous wrote the following letter to D.L. Gaster, Supervisor of Police: "Sir, the applicant Mrs. E. Murphy residing at 3906 Magazine near Austerlitz St. is doing small business in cakes, pies, and bread at above numbered residence. I would recommend a Free Permit [fee waiver] granted her."[19] Mrs. Murphy is one of several small businesswomen to receive fee waivers. Laura Anderson applied for a fee waiver in May 1899. A resident of the Third Precinct, Anderson worked as a washerwoman and ice cream vendor to generate extra income to take care of her invalid husband. Mrs. E. Hogan lived in the Fifth Precinct and applied for a fee waiver in May 1899. A widow with two children to support, Mrs. Hogan worked as a cake vendor. Valle Astor of the Fourth Precinct applied for a fee waiver in May 1899; she worked as a street vendor selling ice cream. Mrs. Edward Raymond of the Fourth Precinct, applied for a fee waiver in May 1901. She was a widow who sold bread and cake on the streets. Josephine Bourgeois also applied for a fee waiver in order to sell candies and cakes. Two of the four women were widows, which underscored the importance of additional wages to support their families.[20] Many of the women listed are presumed to be white, because if they were African American or Creole, it would have been indicated as such.

Praline women left behind few written records; however, their presence was such that observers often wrote about them. In her short story entitled *The Praline Woman* (1899), African American writer Alice Dunbar-Nelson describes a day in the

19.   New Orleans Police Department Collection, Office of Inspector of Police Correspondence, 1899-1913, box 1, March 1899, New Orleans City Archives, New Orleans Public Library.

20.   Ibid., box 1, May 1899-May 1901.

life of a praline vendor. The *praliniere* (one who sells pralines) is described as sitting "by the side of the Archbishop's quaint little old chapel on Royal Street."[21] The "praline woman," named *Tante Marie*, is described as speaking a dialect mixed with French and what was probably the local African American vernacular; this suggests that she may have been Creole. Tante Marie could be heard calling out to potential customers:

> "Pralines, pralines.
> Ah, ma'amzelle, you buy?
> S'il vous plait, ma'amzelle,
> ces pralines dey be fine, ver' fresh."[22]

Marcus Christian wrote of the pralinieres as well. In his unpublished manuscript entitled "The History of the Negro in Louisiana" (1938-1976) Christian describes the "rich basses and shrill trebles, whining, pleading, cajoling, screaming" voices of the street vendors. He also remembers that the praline vendors were perhaps "the best known of all the street-vendors of New Orleans" and standing out among them was Zabet, a praline vendor who "sold her cakes and pecans in and around Jackson Square, and Moreau Lislet, Livingston, Mazareau, Grymes, and Judge Francois-Xavier Martin stopped" to buy pralines. The State Supreme Court was located in the adjacent Cabildo building, so Zabet came in frequent contact with prominent judges and lawyers.[23]

Mammy

The idea and myth of "mammy" dates back to the pre-Civil War South. But who was a mammy, and why was she

---

21.   Alice Dunbar-Nelson, "The Praline Woman" in *Southern Local Color: Stories of Region, Race, and Gender,* eds. Barbara C. Ewell and Pamela Glenn Menke (Athens: University of Georgia Press, 2002), 300.

22.   Ibid., 299.

23.   Christian, "Street Vendors and Street Cries," 5.

so desirable to white customers? In the minds of southern whites, mammy was the enslaved and loyal servant who tirelessly cooked, cleaned, and cared for their families. Working primarily in a domestic capacity, mammy encountered and interacted more with the women of the family. As a result, white women were often the ones who wrote about mammy. Historian Deborah Gray White states that "Mammy was a woman, who could do anything, and she could do it better than anyone else" and "Mammy is especially remembered for her love of her young white charges."[24] According to historian Grace Elizabeth Hale, "at the turn of the twentieth century, mammy became an important part of popular culture as they appeared in books, magazines, and films, in advertisements, on menus, in the names and iconography of restaurants and cookbooks . . ."[25] Consequentially, many artistic interpretations of the "praline mammy" emerged. Some recall the delicious, sweet praline; most chose to interpret the women who sold the candy as either nostalgic connections to their own childhood memories of nannies or the embodiment of the antebellum period. Whites most frequently referred to the praline vendors using some variation of the term "mammy." One New Orleanian recalls as one of her most precious childhood memories in the late 1890s that she had "bought a pecan praline from an old Negro Mammy on the banquette with a basket."[26] In *Social Life in Old New Orleans*, Eliza Ripley "remember[s] the colored *marchandes* who walked the streets with trays, deftly balanced on their heads, arms akimbo, calling out their dainties," which included pralines.[27] In a 1910 edition of *The Newcomb Arcade*,

24.   Deborah Gray White. *Ar'n't I a Woman: Female Slaves in the Plantation South*. (New York: W.W. Norton & Company, 1999), 47.

25.   Grace Elizabeth Hale, *Making Whiteness: The Culture of Segregation in the South: 1890-1940* (New York: Pantheon Books, 1998), 98.

26.   Marion S. O'Neal, "Growing up in New Orleans: Memories of the 1890's," *Louisiana History* 5, no. 1 (Winter 1964) http://www.jstor.org/stable/4230746 (accessed June 5, 2010).

27.   Eliza Ripley, *Social Life in Old New Orleans: Being Recollections of my*

Lois Janvier comments that "Mammy will take her place by the gate and remain there with her basket of pralines."[28] The author of a 1917 piece in a Newcomb publication does not neglect the candy and asks "have you ever tasted pralines? I do not mean the kind you find wrapped in oil paper under the glass case of the candy shops! I mean the real kind, the kind that used to be on Newcomb's steps hidden under that purple stripped bandana in the big old basket, carefully guarded by 'old black mammy.'"[29] One cannot trace the exact moment that the pralines became associated with the mammy figure, but the connection was long lasting. Over centuries, these women served as a prominent part of the city's economic and cultural history, selling their sweets to tourists and New Orleans locals.

Herbert Gutman notes that mammy was an older black woman "who remained in her antebellum place out of loyalty to a white family."[30] According to the mythos, the perfect mammy was so loyal to her white charges, she would never, under any circumstances leave them and did everything in her power to make them happy. In "Cracker Prayer," Harlem-Renaissance poet Langston Hughes writes of a poor white man's final appeal before his impending death:

Lord, Lord, dear Lord, since I did not have a nice old colored mammy in my childhood, give me one in heaven, Lord. My family were too poor to afford a black mammy for any of my father's eight children. I were mammyless as a child. Give me a mammy in heaven, Lord.[31]

Girlhood (New York: D. Appleton and Company, 1912), 24-25.

28.   Lois Janvier, "In the Shadows," *The Newcomb Arcade* (1910): 18.

29.   "Mammy," *The Newcomb Arcade* (1917): 210.

30.   Herbert G. Gutman, *The Black Family in Slavery and Freedom, 1750-1925* (New York, 1976), 632.

31.   Langston Hughes, "Cracker Prayer," in *Simple's Uncle Sam* (New York: Aeonian Press, 1965), 124-25.

This man does not wish to see his birth mother in heaven; instead, he is consumed with the idea of having a mammy to take care of him in his afterlife. Some mammy, any mammy will do for this "mammyless" man.

Like praline recipes passed through generations, the tasks of domestic workers or "mammies" were handed down, too. African American mothers often allowed their daughters to work on a part-time basis in their employers' homes to produce supplementary income. In addition to being caretakers, the younger women were allowed to serve food and beverages at the parties in the homes of whites. To become skilled at serving parties was invaluable because such work would always be available.[32] This tradition of "working parties" was also common of domestic workers of other races as well.

Despite these essential roles, the salaries of domestic workers were often inconsistent. Some women were paid a decent wage; others were sometimes paid partially in cash and the other portion of their wages would be paid to them as food or clothing. This did not sit well with the employees because they had financial responsibilities that required cash payments. By contrast, the praline woman was able to earn cash each day selling her candies. Some would add to their wages by selling dolls and other small items. Some of the domestic workers often worked for white families until death and literally carried the title of "mammy" with them to the grave. In a southern cemetery, domestic worker Malinda Battle James is buried under a tombstone that lovingly reads "Our Mammy."[33]

Artistic Rendering

Perhaps because they were poor, African African, and female, the importance of the praline woman in New

---

32.   Susan Tucker, *Telling Memories Among Southern Women: Domestic Workers and Their Employers in the Segregated South* (Baton Rouge: Louisiana State University Press, 1988).

33.   Tucker, *Telling Memories*, 279.

Orleans history has been overlooked. However, her physical image—dark-skinned, heavyset, and dressed in mammy-attire remained visible within white New Orleans society. The 1904 volume of *The Jambalaya*, Newcomb College's yearbook, contains a picture of a praline vendor. Not buried in the back pages of the book, her image appears in the front of the book among other prominent Newcomb College images, including college president Professor B.V.B. Dixon. This speaks to the praline woman's prominent role on the college campus. A similar depiction of a "praline mammy" serves as a page border throughout the 1923 issue of Tulane University's yearbook. Complete with a *tignon* (a scarf tied around her neck) and a basket filled with pralines, her image is on every other page of the yearbook. Yet another artist interpretation of the "mammy" appeared at the Fine Arts Club of New Orleans Annual Luncheon. Amidst the elite, lunching ladies and crisp linen table clothes covered with carnations were ". . . place cards [that] contained the delightful representation of the well-known Creole mammy vending her pralines."[34]

The Works Progress Administration (WPA) program in Louisiana helped to document at least three praline women through black and white photographs. Founded by President Franklin D. Roosevelt in 1935, the WPA and the Farm Security Administration (FSA) were branches of the New Deal policy whose wide variety of projects were carried out by local and state governments.

The clothing of the women in the photographs is almost identical. Yet, each image tells a different story. In the first image the praline woman stands in Jackson Square smiling, hands on her hips, and a corn pipe in between her lips. She is holding a basket filled with pralines that feature the following notice: *"Creole Pecan Pralines. 3 for $.25."* This raises several issues. There are several types of pralines, including coconut, peanut, and pecan. Pecan pralines were the most costly variety and were usually purchased by the wealthiest customers. This

34.   *New Orleans Times-Picayune*, November 30, 1909, 7.

Praline vendor in front of Jackson Square, 1940, State Library of Louisiana.

vendor seems to be catering to a specific clientele. She seeks to conduct business with a class of people who would have no problem paying her asking price. This sign not only let potential customers know what variety of candy she offers; it also lets potential customers know whether they could have afforded her treats. Market vendors were renowned for bartering; however, this sign is an indication that this praline woman did not compromise. Possibly she had some of the cheaper ones, such as coconut, for those unable to meet her price. Though she was dressed in "mammy" attire, her impish grin, hand-on-the-hip stance, and pipe tell a tale of independence and pride that differs from the loyal mammy stereotype. One also cannot know if this woman was one of the few remaining independent vendors or if she was working for one of the praline shops. The printed sign suggests the latter. Through research, approximately five images of this particular praline vendor have been found. All of the photos were taken by different photographers on various occasions. None of the images mention her name, but all five refer to her as a "mammy." The popularity of this particular praline vendor suggests several things. Firstly, it puts forward the commonality of the New Orleans praline woman. Next, this particular praline woman seems to have been employed selling pralines over the course of many years. This idea alone suggests that she was earning a steady income selling pecan candy. Lastly, she was always willing to pose for a photograph, in all likelihood in exchange for a monetary tip from the photographer.

The praline women's choice of clothing reflected how most working-class African American women dressed. For example, Azelie, the Newcomb College praline vendor, dressed in a similar fashion to her mother Mary Louise: tignon and an ankle-length skirt and apron. Presumably, Mary Louise's mother dressed the same way. Therefore, the style of clothing worn by these women represented a part of their working-class culture and not a gimmick, according to Raphael Cassimere. Growing up in early 1940s New Orleans, Cassimere remembered his older women relatives wearing the same style of clothing.[35] This manner of dress may have appealed to white tourists who believed they were purchasing a piece of the "Old South" from "mammy." On the contrary, they were buying candy from entrepreneurs who dressed like their mothers and grandmothers before them.

Collectively, these Great Depression-era images establish that when jobs were likely scarce, African American women decided to work for themselves. The street vendors had husbands, children, and perhaps even grandchildren to care for and took to their own kitchens out of necessity to make ends meet. The ingredients were items readily available even in the barest of cupboards: milk, sugar, and butter. In

---

35.   Raphael Cassimere Jr., interview with the author, April 2011.

addition, pecan trees were abundant in many of the African American neighborhoods of New Orleans. As a result, pralines may have been the obvious choice when the decision was made to sell something that was delicious and in high demand, yet inexpensive enough to turn a quick profit.

The Marketing of Mammy

The mammy caricature played a prominent role as the tourist industry developed in the early twentieth century and white business owners began to take over the praline business. In an effort to capitalize upon the "mammy" image, New Orleans businesses used it to assist with the sale of their commercialized pralines. Katz and Bestoff, a New Orleans drug store during the twentieth century, placed an advertisement in a 1918 issue of the *Times-Picayune* boasting of delicious Creole pralines "Just Like Ole' Mammy Used To Make."[36] (figure 2) Later that same year, Grunewald Caterers enticed customers with "Real New Orleans old-fashioned Pralines, like Mammy used to make."[37]

In addition to advertisements in newspapers, many candy shops used a mammy image on their packaging. Praline vendors were being displaced by small and large businesses that contributed to the further distortion of these street-level entrepreneurs. Located at 300 Royal Street, Kate Latter's candy shop used a praline package that depicted a smiling African American woman dressed in a tignon, long skirt, and apron seated beside a basket of pralines.

Nearby at 433 Royal Street, the more popular Aunt Sally's Creole Praline shop engaged in the same manner of "mammy marketing." Their box of pralines depicted an overweight African American woman dressed in "mammy garb." The front of the box reads "Look For Mammy With The Blinking Eyes." The tipped lid of the box reads "On The Site Of The

36. *New Orleans Times-Picayune*, February 17, 1918, 6.

37. *New Orleans Times-Picayune*, December 22, 1918, 35.

Katz & Bestoff advertisement, 1918, New Orleans Times-Picayune

Old Slave Box," which refers to the former site of the St. Louis Hotel and Exchange. By devaluing the praline vendors with old South phrases such as mammy and slave, the praline stores sought to appeal to white tourists with images of a faithful servant and a time when African Americans "knew their places." These depictions continued well beyond the early twentieth century. In a November 1974 *Times-Picayune* advertisement entitled "Pralines Shipped in Cotton Bales," Aunt Sally's Praline's recommends that customers send pralines as a Christmas gift. The ad also states that pralines are made fresh daily at 9:00 a.m. in front of an open window and invites readers to come to the store and "See how Mammy does it!"[38] This advertisement appeared a minimum of seven times within that month. These and similar advertisements were printed in the *Times-Picayune* throughout the 1970s. Over

38. *New Orleans Times-Picayune*, November 21, 1974, 6.

one hundred years after emancipation, the term "mammy" remained appealing to many white business owners and customers. The "See how Mammy does it" articles were discontinued in the 1970s; however, Mammy remained a part of Aunt Sally's promotional efforts well into the 1980s. As of 2011, Evans Creole Candy factory is the one praline company yet to discontinue the offensive image. A praline store located in the French Quarter, Evans continues to use a smiling, African American woman with a tignon as a part of its logo. Their mammy also bears the name "Dixie."[39]

Once corporations took over and the praline women were no longer seen on the streets of New Orleans, their images moved not only to the praline boxes but also to the storefront. Many praline shops placed life-sized mammy dolls in front of their establishments. In 1941, Aunt Sally's Canal Street location offered a fifty dollar cash reward for the return of the praline mammy that had been stolen.[40] On a separate occasion, a child saw a praline mammy in front of a shop on Chartres Street and was "so charmed by it that she threw her arms around it, put its arms around her neck, and tried to lift it from the sidewalk."[41]

The store front praline mammies became such a phenomenon that white tourists commonly took pictures posing with the life-size dolls. This is evident in a set of 1957 photographs taken of five-year-old Yvonne Benoit. A trio of photographs document the child posing with three different praline mammies in a single day, which speaks to the abundance of praline store dolls in New Orleans. The first and second images show Yvonne lazily leaning against a smiling black mammy.[42] Ironically, the mammy in the second photo is

39.   Several of the images in this paper are also a part of a museum exhibit I curated, entitled "Pecan Candy." Southern Food and Beverage Museum, New Orleans, Louisiana. February 2011.

40.   *New Orleans Times-Picayune*, April 1, 1941, 25.

41.   Ibid.

42.   1957 photograph taken from the personal collection of Michelle Benoit.

chained to the store.[43] The chains may symbolize slavery and the South's tourist economy being "chained" to the past. The main reason, however, was to ensure that the doll would not be stolen. The next photograph shows Yvonne standing next to a "praline mammy" holding her hand.[44] Ten years later in 1967, Yvonne's ten-year-old sister Michelle was photographed twice with life-sized mammy dolls. The first photograph shows the smiling child, standing next to a dark-skinned, red-lipped, store-front mammy. The second photograph shows Michelle standing next to a grotesque, paper-mache mammy with a menacing grin on her face.

Pralines as a Commercial Enterprise Controlled by Whites

By examining classified advertisements in newspapers, the relative decline of the African American praline vendor can be traced to the maturation of the tourist industry from the early 1900s until the 1940s. African American women continued to sell candy to family, community members, and co-workers to supplement their income; one woman remembers that in the 1930s her grandmother regularly made pralines to sell to her co-workers at the Haspel Clothing factory.[45] While African Americans never lost control of the business within their community, the rising tourism industry caused more white-owned businesses to cater to visitors. As the entrepreneurial praline women became less common, French Quarter praline shops began to hire praline makers.

Many stores placed advertisements in the *Times-Picayune*. In February 1941, a local candy store placed an ad for a "colored mammy, experienced praline maker."[46] In May

43.   Ibid.

44.   Ibid.

45.   Berenice D. Moret, interview with the author, March 2011.

46.   *New Orleans Times-Picayune*, February 19, 1941, 26.

1964, Kate Latter's candy shop placed an advertisement for a "colored girl to learn to make pralines and candy."[47] The newspaper advertisements calling specifically for African American women demonstrate they were hired to be the face of the white-owned businesses while cooking pralines in industrial kitchens instead of their own.

Aunt Sally's Creole Pralines is one of the oldest companies in New Orleans. It was founded in the 1930s by a Creole French couple, Pierre and Diane Bagur. They were said to have purchased a praline recipe and business from an old Greek man who sold the candy around the French Quarter. It has also been stated that Aunt Sally had been a family servant. Extremely creative, Diane Bagur, along with her sister, Yvette Rolufs, made miniature dolls to sell with the pralines, according to Mary McDonald, granddaughter of the Bagurs. The dolls depicted such historic figures as Marie Laveau and Jean Lafitte; nevertheless, it was the praline mammy dolls that were her biggest sellers.[48]

Mary McDonald acknowledges the significant position that mammy held in the development of her family's business. She remembers the racist images on the praline boxes in the 1960s, when she worked at Aunt Sally's as a teenager, and states that a store manager who was not a family member ordered those boxes. In the midst of his being ousted from his position, the manager ordered a large number of the stereotypical mammy designs on their gift boxes. Unable to absorb the financial loss of ordering more boxes, McDonald explained that the family continued to use the praline boxes. Regardless of how accurate or inaccurate the family's explanation might be, the present-day owners acknowledge the damaging role their company's marketing played for decades. As recently as the 1980s, McDonald would give pralines to friends as gifts, but she was so embarrassed by the image of the mammy that

47.   *New Orleans Times-Picayune*, May 20, 1964, 12.

48.   Mary McDonald, interview with the author, November 2010.

she would remove the candy from the box.[49] Her sister, Pat McDonald-Fowler, designed the current store logo, which features just the name "Aunt Sally's Creole Pralines" in red letters. Nevertheless, the term "Aunt Sally" alone conjures images of the days of slavery when the terms "Aunt" and "Uncle" were often tied to the enslaved.

McDonald believes that African American women were "rock solid" within Aunt Sally's and essentially the "true history of the company."[50] Throughout the store's past, the family employed only African American women in the kitchen. McDonald-Fowler suggests that is because of Aunt Sally's hiring process. When looking for additional staff, Bagur asked the kitchen employees if they knew of any experienced praline makers. As a result, the employees' relatives and friends, who were other African American women, joined the company. Additionally, "coming off of the end of the Depression, women were working more than ever before."[51]

McDonald and McDonald-Fowler recall one of the praline makers who was "key to the success in Aunt Sally's."[52] Iola Francis, also known as "Doll Baby," was a "backa-town" resident who worked in Aunt Sally's kitchens for over thirty years. McDonald remembers Doll Baby as an outgoing, petite woman with a beautiful heart-shaped face. She would give candy samples to children, often remembering tourists who had visited the previous summers, and received additional income from the tips she collected from the vacationers by chatting them up and posing for photographs. Referred to as a "candy artist" by McDonald-Fowler, Doll Baby worked in the Aunt Sally's kitchen from 1938 until 1969. According to McDonald-Fowler, the praline makers employed in her commercial kitchen had the potential of additional earnings by

49.   Ibid.

50.   Ibid.

51.   Mary McDonald, interview with the author, December 2010.

52.   Ibid.

posing for pictures with tourists. In a sense, the actual candy makers could function as human props for photographs, much like the life-sized mammy dolls.[53]

The company's kitchen consisted of a tight-knit society of sisters, cousins, and friends. The African American women showed a form of resistance by stating openly they "did not want to work with white girls" and no white woman ever penetrated their close circle. In the 1980s, a Hispanic woman was hired to make pralines but she "did not last long amongst the Black sisterhood" of the kitchen. The African American women tended to be employed by the store for many years. According to McDonald-Fowler, this could be in part due to the benefits the company offered the women. The praline makers received transportation to and from work, medical and dental benefits, and assistance with opening bank accounts.[54]

As with the Newcomb College praline vendors, Mary Louise and Azelie, the tradition of praline making passed down in Aunt Sally's kitchen. Doll Baby's daughter, Edna Francis worked along-side her mother in the kitchen. Francis did not like candy making, and she worked hard to make sure that she would not remain in the kitchen. Francis earned a position in management, pushing back against the "mammy" myth in an individual way. She remained an Aunt Sally's employee from the late 1940s until her death in 2002.[55]

Post-Mammy Praline Entrepreneurs

A less radical and jarring type of change, yet a significant one nonetheless, was the more recent transformation of the praline vendor into entrepreneurs unencumbered by the mammy image. Pralines still hold a place in the hearts and minds of many African American New Orleanians; most grew up with pralines the way kids in other parts of the country

53.   McDonald-Fowler, interview with the author, January 2011.
54.   Ibid.
55.   Ibid.

grew up with cookies and milk. If a family member did not make the candy, then a neighbor did. Mrs. Parline Brent, also known as "Pearly," was a resident of the New Orleans suburb of Harvey.[56] She sold her homemade pralines and pies during the 1960s, 1970s, and 1980s. Mrs. Brent catered only to locals since few tourists traveled across the Mississippi River to Harvey. In contrast to the long skirts and tignons worn by the "praline women," Pearly always wore neat dresses, carrying her purse and basket full of goodies. Although her style of dress differed, her method of advertising in post-civil rights New Orleans beckoned back to the traditional street vendors. In the market, Pearly would call out to potential customers, almost begging them to buy her candies. Through her entrepreneurial efforts, she was able to accumulate enough money to care for her blind husband and four children. Over the years, the sale of her pralines made it possible to send her youngest daughter, Sherika, to nursing school. Pearly took her job as a praline vendor very seriously; selling candy was her only means of income.[57]

Nannan B., whose real name is Beatrice Gibbs, was originally from Port Allen, Louisiana, but eventually settled in New Orleans's Gert Town area (a section of the Carrollton neighborhood). Nannan B. sold pecan and coconut pralines out of her home during the 1960s and 1970s. According to Efrem Scott Sr., who was a regular customer of Nannan B.'s, she placed a sheet pan covered with wax paper on the kitchen table and the pralines would be put on it to cool. An enterprising woman, she also sold frozen cups and coconut candy that "would melt in your mouth."[58] Nannan B. knew

---

56.   Harvey is a suburb of New Orleans, located "across the river" in Jefferson Parish.

57.   Shenna Scott, interview with the author, April 2010. Ms. Scott was a former neighbor of Mrs. Brent.

58.   Frozen cups are paper cups of frozen fruit juices that are a traditional and inexpensive treat for New Orleans children on a hot summer day. Efrem Scott Sr., interview with the author, April 2010.

how to get repeat customers. She would wrap a quarter in a piece of foil and place it on the bottom of a few select cups before she poured the juice in. When neighborhood children would come to buy the frozen cups, they would be none-the-wiser until they got to the very bottom and found a shiny circle of foil remaining. Scott remembers the kids would almost immediately run back to Nannan B.'s house for another frozen cup or praline.[59]

Present day praline vendor Judy Lambert has been making and selling pecan candy for almost thirty years. The forty-two-year-old businesswoman learned to make the confection when she was in the seventh grade. Later, as a freshman at Warren Easton High School, Lambert wanted spending money but was too young for a job, so she began to make and sell pralines. An older relative who had a pecan tree in her backyard gave her the pecans and Lambert sold pralines at school to classmates and teachers for fifty cents per piece.

Lambert never sold candy as a street vendor and did not take the praline business seriously until 2006, when she made candy for a cousin. This cousin gave the candy as gifts to her daughter's teachers. Soon after, the teachers began to request the pecan candy on an almost daily basis, and this prompted Lambert to start a small business. She has become creative in marketing; in 2010, when she took orders for Mother's Day, her customers were pleasantly surprised when they received cellophane-covered pecan candies on a stick, placed in an inexpensive vase, so that they would resemble a bouquet of flowers. On Valentine's Day of 2011, Lambert used moldings to create heart-shaped pecan candy. The candy was placed in a red container decorated with yellow, pink, and white hearts.

Instead of the street cries from the days of old, Lambert has kept up with technological advances in marketing and advertising. She uses emails, text messages, and Facebook to reach customers. A typical message from her might read: "Celebrate Mother's Days in an especially sweet way . . . treat

59.   Ibid.

her to some good ole creamy pecan candy from Ms. Judy. Sold in bouquets of 3 @$10, 6@ $20 or Mini order of candy for $5, Small-$8, Medium-$14, Large-$20. Deadline to order is May 4, 2010."[60]

Loretta Shaw Harrison is the embodiment of an African American praline entrepreneur, and she certainly defies the stereotype of the "mammy." The owner of Loretta's Authentic Pralines, Harrison started making the candy when she was eight years old. Like many of the pralinieres from the days of old, she uses a formula passed down from an older female relative—in this case, her great-grandmother. Harrison surmises that "all poor black people had [to pass down to their children]" was a recipe.[61] Similar to the praline women at Newcomb College, Harrison initially sold her candy to college students. While working as a night-shift librarian at the Louisiana State University School of Medicine's library, she made pralines and sold them to the students. Within a few years, Harrison began taking classes at Tulane University to learn strategies for running a successful business. One class in particular helped her to redevelop the marketing of her candies; she selected more effective colors and a new box design as well as an improved company name. Harrison sees no need to use mammy to market her candies. Her company logo consists of her first name "Loretta" and a parade of pralines second-lining.[62]

In the early 1980s, Loretta's Authentic Pralines made its debut at the New Orleans Jazz and Heritage Festival. In one weekend the company made a profit of $1,500, which was more than double what Harrison made selling the pralines to the college students in one month. Shortly after the Jazz Fest, Harrison opened her first store in Jackson Brewery in the French Quarter. Decades later, Loretta's Authentic Pralines are known world-wide. She has shipped pralines

60.   Judy Lambert, personal Facebook communication, April 2010.

61.   Loretta Shaw Harrison, interview with the author, July 2010.

62.   A second-line is a traditional New Orleans dance.

to Switzerland, Paris, and Afghanistan and has made her delicious candies for the likes of such iconic African American actors as Denzel Washington and Danny Glover. Each year, she sells her confections at the city's most important festivals, including Jazz Fest, French Quarter Fest, and the Essence Festival. Additionally, Loretta appeared in a 2010 Superbowl Commerical.

Conclusion

For centuries, African American women dominated the New Orleans markets selling items desired by white consumers; this kept them in business post-slavery. At the beginning of the twentieth century, the New Orleans praline women were the most popular of the street vendors, selling pralines to locals and tourists alike. These women made the independent decision to work for themselves in an underground economy to support their families, rather than endure the domestic work which was likely their only other option. They were such a success at selling pralines, that when the praline stores were opened in the French Quarter, their image was used to sell and market the candy. Their likeliness could be found on praline boxes and praline store fronts. In an effort to downplay their significance in New Orleans history, the praline women of New Orleans were referred to as "praline mammies" by whites. Despite this, they were able to forge their own identities as successful and independent entrepreneurs.

Dating back to the early twentieth century, the praline women saw a need and filled it with their candies. The vendors and their pralines could be found on college campuses, at neighborhood bus stops, and at several French Quarter locations. It is also difficult to ignore the relevance the praline woman had on the New Orleans tourist economy. Visitors came to the city in hopes of tasting a sweet praline. They were doubly rewarded if they were able to catch a glance at and perhaps get a photo taken with a real live "praline mammy."

Creating and distributing a product once tethered to the Old South and a mammy image, Loretta Harrison represents the most successful African American praline entrepreneur in New Orleans history. Located in the same Jackson Square vicinity where African American women once could only sell items in the street, Loretta's Authentic Pralines is sited at the center of the city's tourist economy. Harrison's achievement, along with that of other modern praline vendors, represents a triumphant statement regarding African American entrepreneurialism in the culinary arts.

8   Sex, Drugs, and Violence, Just Another Night on Bourbon Street in Joe Longo's "S.I.N.ners"

NANCY DIXON

Although many contemporary literary works include service industry workers as minor characters—Amanda Boyden's *Babylon Rolling* and Fatima Shaik's *The Mayor of New Orleans: Just Talking Jazz* come to mind—very few actually center on the industry itself. One recent work that does focus on the service industry and whose main characters work on world famous Bourbon Street is Joe Longo's short story, "S.I.N.ners." Joe Longo's short story, first published in *French Quarter Fiction* in 2003, is populated by characters that editor Joshua Clark describes in his introduction to the collection: "Every year the French Quarter chews up and spits out a stream of eight million tourists, real estate investors, gutterpunks, and celebrities . . . [f]rom the world over . . ."[1] Longo's turn-of-the-twenty-first-century French Quarter is not populated with wide-eyed young waiters and bartenders—nor wide-eyed tourists, for that matter—but rather with minor characters, like the pompous Australian real estate developer, the tightfisted Arab restaurant owner, the underage, drunk frat boy who wishes he were black, and the homeless Moses who sleeps on a stoop in the French Quarter. To understand the context for Longo's short story, we must acknowledge the longstanding and complicated history of the service industry in New Orleans and its literature.

---

1.   Joshua Clark, introduction to *French Quarter Fiction: the Newest Stories of America's Oldest Bohemia* (New Orleans: Light of New Orleans Publishing, 2003), 9.

In much of post-slavery and even post-Reconstruction New Orleans literature, the labor force, particularly the service industry, is comprised of African Americans, as we can see in the works of Kate Chopin, Grace King, Ruth McEnery Stuart, Sallie Rhett Roman, and other turn-of-the-twentieth-century writers. Even in prominent later works, like Sheila Bosworth's *Almost Innocent* and John Kennedy Toole's *A Confederacy of Dunces*, black characters make up the majority of the service industry workers. Toole's Burma Jones, though a lowly barroom janitor, is one of the wisest and funniest characters ever depicted in New Orleans fiction. It is no accident that the service laborers in these literary works are African American. According to Toni Morrison, African American characters in literature seem to "hover at the margins of the literary imagination," often playing minor roles, like maids, servants, butlers, and the like.[2] Historically, the evolution of the service industry in New Orleans is much more complicated. Arnold R. Hirsch and Joseph Logsdon write that "newcomers [to nineteenth-century New Orleans] from the South as well as the North recoiled when they encountered the prevailing French language of the city, its dominant Catholicism, its bawdy sensual delights, or its free black population." Such distinctiveness sets the city apart from its southern and northern counterparts still today.[3]

In "The Foreign French," Paul F. Lachance examines the role of the foreign French citizens in New Orleans from 1804-1819 and notes that they, along with the refugee population from Saint Domingue (now Haiti), were more active than their white Creole counterparts in the service sector.[4] Joseph G.

2.   Toni Morrison, *Playing in the Dark: Whiteness and the Literary Imagination* (New York: Vintage Books, 1993), 5.

3.   Arnold Hirsch and Joe Logsdon, eds., *Creole New Orleans: Race and Americanization* (Baton Rouge: Louisiana State University Press, 1992), xi.

4.   Paul F. Lachance, "The Foreign French" in *Creole New Orleans: Race and Americanization*, eds. Arnold Hirsch and Joe Logsdon (Baton Rouge: Louisiana State University Press, 1992), 122-23.

Tregle in "Early New Orleans Society: A Reappraisal," further examines the large free black population in antebellum New Orleans and its stake in the city's thriving service industry:

> The free persons of color . . . enjoyed a status in Louisiana probably unequaled in any other part of the South. Members of this class were often to be found as owners of cabarets . . . and gaming houses. . . . Many were artisans, barbers, and shopkeepers, and became so prosperous as to own slaves of their own and to acquire large holdings of real property in the French Quarter.[5]

Tregle goes on to say that free women of color, "[m]any, of course, burdened by age, ugliness, or a sense of righteousness, contented themselves with modest shops or presided over oyster, gumbo, or coffee stalls along the levee."[6] But Tregle claims that the real money to be made by these women of color lay in capitalizing on the licentiousness of the wealthy white men in the city.[7] Hirsch and Logsdon note that the majority of the Americans who migrated to antebellum New Orleans did so from the Northeast and that the local "Creole businessmen were no match for the Yankee entrepreneurs."[8] Tregle points out the allure of the city to the "Kaintucks," who stormed New Orleans "from their river flatboats and barges to carouse in the waterfront dives of the city," an allure that the city still holds today for millions of tourists.[9] By 1850, he adds, most of the menial jobs, including chambermaids and waiters, were held by American immigrants to the city, and in

---

5.   Joseph Tregle Jr., "Early New Orleans Society: A Reappraisal," *Journal of Southern History* 18 (Feb. 1952), 34.

6.   Ibid.

7.   Ibid.

8.   Hirsch and Logsdon, *Creole New Orleans*, 92.

9.   Joseph Tregle Jr., "Creoles and Americans," in *Creole New Orleans: Race and Americanization*, eds. Arnold Hirsch and Joe Logdson (Baton Rouge: Louisiana State University Press, 1992), 135.

the early-to-mid-nineteenth century, immigration in the city exploded.[10]

Naturally, in the aftermath of the Civil War, New Orleans was not the same city. Racial tension spiked. Yellow fever was still a problem, as was the heat. The port of New Orleans, once thriving but now under Republican rule, became seriously in debt, and it took decades for the city to recover. But New Orleans has never regained its pre-Civil War status as the commercial center of the Mississippi Valley. According to J. Mark Souther, the city's civic leaders, while concentrating on ways to attract northern investors, at the same time put forth the effort to lure tourists to New Orleans by showcasing Mardi Gras and hosting the 1884 Cotton Centennial. Despite such efforts, Souther claims that "Americans more often viewed New Orleans as a place to indulge weaknesses for drinking, gaming, and whoring," a view of the city that is still held by many tourists today and one that the city has done little to change.[11]

In fact, the real push to capitalize on New Orleans as a tourist destination came at the turn of the twentieth century. According to the writers of *Louisiana: A History*, the reasons for this boom vary widely: the red light district Storyville and the birth of jazz; the improvement in public education and healthcare; the move from an agricultural economy to one profiting from natural resources, such as timber and oil; and the city's exoticism all played a role in transforming this city into the tourist destination it remains today.[12] However, according to Don Doyle, while other southern cities, such as Atlanta and Nashville, were moving forward and embracing the industrial New South, New Orleans, like two other southern port cities, Charleston and Mobile, was "bent on preserving the remnants of the Old South and . . . slow to adapt

10.   Tregle, "Creoles," 163.

11.   J. Mark Souther, *New Orleans on Parade: Tourism and the Transformation of the Crescent City* (Baton Rouge: Louisiana State University Press, 2006), 5.

12.   Bennett H. Wall, *Louisiana: A History* (Baton Rouge: Louisiana State University Press, 1984), 274-75.

to the 'new order of things.'"[13] And like Mobile, which Doyle claims to have "retreated into a pleasure-loving way of life that expressed a sublime indifference to the sober earnestness of the New South," New Orleans remained content to rely on its sex trade and Mardi Gras to fuel its economy as it struggled behind its southern metropolitan neighbors until well into the twentieth century.[14]

The New Orleans shipping industry expanded during World War II with Higgins Industries and other shipyards making boats for the U.S. military, and as a port city, New Orleans received an influx of soldiers and sailors, which in turn meant an uptick in business in the local bars, restaurants, and brothels. Up until the war, most of the city's bartenders, like those in Longo's short story, were male. According to two brief articles in the *Daily Picayune*, as early as 1902, the city's bartenders began to unionize; however, these unions only included "the men behind the drinks," not the women.[15] As in all trades during war time in this country, women moved in earnest into the hospitality business while the men were off fighting.

In the 1950s, Louisiana saw its biggest increase in industrialization ever, thanks to the oil and petrochemical industries, and New Orleans capitalized on that growth up to the downturn of the mid-1980s. However, it was not until the civil rights era that city leaders understood the urgency of repealing the Jim Crow laws that hamstrung the city's tourism and sports industries as well as its African American labor force. Until then, as Souther states, "[b]lacks cooked famed Creole delicacies in French Quarter restaurants, sold pralines in the French Market, carried flambeaux in night [carnival] parades, threw coconuts from the Zulu floats, blew

13.   Don H. Doyle, preface to *New Men, New Cities, New South: Atlanta, Nashville, Charleston, Mobile, 1860-1910* (Chapel Hill: University of North Carolina Press, 1990), xv.

14.   Ibid.

15.   "Bartenders Unite," *New Orleans Daily Picayune*, October 30, 1902, 7.

horns for second-line processions, conjured spells in voodoo demonstrations, and drove mule-drawn tour buggies around Jackson Square."[16] Since then African Americans have become more visible in the hospitality industry, but as Souther goes on to note:

> In a city that is nearly two-thirds African American, very few black workers enjoy better paying [service industry] jobs such as manager, waiter, clerk, concierge, or bellman. Most are relegated to cleaning hotel rooms, janitorial work, or cooking or washing dishes in the grimy kitchens of French Quarter restaurants and dives.[17]

We see this ring true in "S.I.N.ners," in which the only African American character, Ivory, washes dishes in the funky Cajun Cookhouse. All the white characters in the story work the front of the house and interact with the primarily white tourists.

When I waited tables at Restaurant Jonathan in 1976, my African American colleagues never rose above back waiter, even those with more experience than I. At Tyler's Beer Garden Uptown, some three years later, if they weren't on stage playing jazz or shucking oysters, African Americans cleaned up after hours, but were never seen behind the bar. The same goes for the other places I tended bar, like Johnny Matassa's until it was shuttered in the 1980s, and the Abbey on Decatur Street, Old Absinthe House on Bourbon, and 4141 on St. Charles Avenue in the 1990s.

In the early 1970s, the Superdome was built. Although mired in controversy and way over budget, the building of the dome and nearby hotels paved the way for New Orleans as a burgeoning convention center of the South. The city became not only a destination for sporting events — New Orleans has hosted the Super Bowl more than any other city — but also for

16.   J. Mark Souther, "City in Amber: Race, Culture, and the Tourist Transformation of New Orleans, 1945-1995," (PhD diss., Tulane University, 2002), 189.

17.   Souther, "City in Amber," 364.

conventions, concerts, even honeymoons. With the growth in visitors to the city, naturally the hospitality industry also grew. When I began working in the service industry in 1976, no longer were the bartenders unionized; rather, most of the service industry workers in the French Quarter were college students from one of the half a dozen local universities—unskilled workers willing to work for ready cash—alongside career bartenders and waiters.

Longo, as well as the characters he writes about, worked Bourbon Street about a generation later, in 1999. As vital as the history of the service industry is to his narrative, just as significant is the role that service industry workers play in New Orleans literature, particularly that of the twentieth century. Many other writers have worked in the hospitality industry over the years. Lafcadio Hearn owned and cooked at a restaurant for a while and even published a cookbook, *La Cuisine Creole* in 1885. However, Hearn was destitute for much of his time in the city, and most nineteenth-century writers, like George Washington Cable, M.E.M Davis, Grace King, and Kate Chopin, would have found working in the service industry unsuitable. In the twentieth century however, that all changed. More recent writers, such as Seth Morgan, Amanda Boyden, Sarah Inman, Charles Cannon, and Jarret Lofstead, all served time in the French Quarter hospitality industry, and the list of writers who drank in and wrote about the city's bars is too long to print, but there are some notable works that serve as historical context for Longo's "S.I.N.ners."

George Washington Cable's *The Grandissimes* (1880) is set in the city immediately following the Louisiana Purchase and includes women working in the Quarter in many facets of the service industry—from selling *callas* (rice cakes) to Voodoo—but these are all women of color. Clotilde Nancanou, one of the novel's central female characters, laments the fact that she and her mother, Aurora, who are in desperate need of some sort of income, are not permitted to make a living serving others:

[W]e are compelled not to make a living. Look at me:
I can cook, but I must not cook; I am skillful with the
needle, but I must not take in sewing; I could keep
accounts; I could nurse the sick; but I must not. I could
be a confectioner, a milliner, a dressmaker, a vest-maker,
a cleaner of gloves and laces, a dyer, a bird-seller, a
mattress-maker, an upholsterer, a dancing teacher, a
florist—.[18]

According to Tiffany Duet, Aurora and Clotilde "as Creole
ladies and members of society . . . must uphold the image of
the idly rich Southern lady expected of Creoles living in New
Orleans, which . . . is a patriarchal ideal."[19] On the other hand,
the feckless callas vendor, Clemence, is free to roam the city
with her wares, ironically because she is a slave. In another
of Cable's works, "'Tite Poulette," little Poulette's mother, a
free woman of color, must resort to b-dancing at the quadroon
balls in order to keep a roof over their heads.

Not until Kate Chopin's *The Awakening* in 1899, do we
see a white female character in a prominent work of New
Orleans fiction ensconced in the hospitality field. Madame
Lebrun owns the Grand Isle resort hotel where the Pontelliers
spend their summer vacation, and she caters to the needs of
the wealthy New Orleans businessmen and their wives. A
lesser known contemporary of Chopin's, Sallie Rhett Roman,
included the requisite black maids and servants in her short
fiction as well as the dutiful, tightlipped bartenders of the
bachelors' men's clubs, but she also depicted the Italian fruit
vendor, La Misere, who tried in vain to hide his tortured past
while hawking his wares on the streets of the French Quarter,

18.   George Washington Cable, *The Grandissimes* (1880; repr., New York:
Penguin, 1988), 255.

19.   Tiffany Duet, "'Do You Not Know That Women Can Make Money?':
Women and Labor in Louisiana Literature," in *Songs of the Reconstructing South:
Building Literary Louisiana, 1865-1945*, eds. Suzanne Disheroon-Green and Lisa
Abney (Westport Connecticut: Greenwood Press, 2002), 160.

and the melancholy La Fortune, the Latino seller of lottery tickets, one of which seals his young ward's fate. All these characters seem more representative than actually realized, and almost all are people of color.

By the middle of the twentieth century, entire texts were centered around French Quarter bars and restaurants, like the renowned *Dinner at Antoine's* (1947) by Frances Parkinson Keyes, a mystery novel which begins and ends with a dinner at the famed restaurant. In fact, Keyes mentions Antoine's in at least four more of her novels: *Once on Esplanade*, *Crescent Carnival*, *The River Road*, and its sequel, *Vail D'Alvery*. In other mid-century works, the portrayal of the city's bar and restaurant scene is a little less savory, like the seedy bars in William Burroughs's *Junkie* (1953) or Madame Beckley's famous emporium, the "Function," near the seaman dives of "Wharf Street" in Thomas Sancton's *Count Roller Skates* (1956). But perhaps no writer captures the down-and-out New Orleans bar scene better than Nelson Algren in his novel *A Walk on the Wild Side* (1956). As Russell Banks writes in his 1989 foreword to Algren's novel, the characters on old Perdido Street "are pimps and prostitutes, con-men, drug addicts and alcoholics, homeless wanderers, illiterate whites and blacks trying to make an honest dollar in a crooked sort of way," and he goes on to ask about these characters, ". . . what's that got to do with American in the go-go 1980s and '90s?"[20] Naturally, he answers that question by telling us that the truth that Algren sets forth through his marginal characters, like Dove Linkhorn and Kitty Twist, is the truth about us all, and where better to expose that truth than in the dive bars of downtown New Orleans.

By the more tumultuous 1960s, the look of the French Quarter and its denizens in literature reflected the decade's optimism. That decade brought Walker Percy's Binx Bolling "spinning along the Gulf Coast" in his MG with one secretary

---

20.   Russell Banks, foreword to *A Walk on the Wild Side*, by Nelson Algren (New York: Thunder's Mouth Press, 1989), vii.

'king actor William Holden on his way to ⎍nch in *The Moviegoer* (1960). And drinking and play a large part in the protagonist Joan Mitchell's ⎍ctional family in Shirley Ann Grau's *The House on ⎍seum Street* (1961). Joan cannot be sexually intimate unless she is high, and her stepfather, Mr. Norton dies on a bench in Jackson Square after drinking himself to death. Although neither of these novels is truly uplifting, and both treat the very serious issue of mental illness, both are also humorous at times. Aurelie, Joan's mother, lets her daughters have sex — even helps Joan get an abortion — and has been married five times, yet will not let her daughters curse in the house. However, not until John Kennedy Toole's *A Confederacy of Dunces*, published in 1980, over a decade after his death in 1969, do we begin to see the side-splitting depiction of the French Quarter so similar to that in Longo's "S.I.N.ners."

Toole's novel was written in the 1960s, and many of the concerns of that decade — race relations and the civil rights movement, law enforcement, modern psychology, liberal politics, modern commerce — are all parodied by Toole, but his focus on the French Quarter bar, Night of Joy, a front for a child pornography ring, seems especially pertinent to Longo's story. Like "S.I.N.ners," Toole's novel involves several characters loosely connected by complicated subplots that all seem to collide by the end of the book.

Thanks to John Kennedy Toole's mother, Thelma, and her dogged persistence, Walker Percy finally agreed to read the novel, and it was published in 1980 by LSU Press. The following year it won the Pulitzer Prize. In his foreword, Percy writes of the book: "By no means a lesser virtue of Toole's novel is his rendering of the particularities of New Orleans . . . its odd speech, its ethnic whites — and one black in whom Toole has achieved the near impossible, a superb comic character of immense wit and resourcefulness without the least trace of Rastus minstrelsy" (8). Indeed, Burma Jones is a marvel, an oppressed black man in 1960s New Orleans who remains unbeaten, savvy, streetwise, and to some extent even a savior, not unlike Longo's Ivory in "S.I.N.ners." In the hilarious culminating scene of Toole's novel, Jones jumps into the street in front of the Night of Joy to save Ignatius Riley from the oncoming Desire bus, but moreover, his plan to sabotage the club and ruin its owner Lana Lee also ends up exposing the child pornography ring she has been running from behind the bar.

Longo's Ivory, like Burma Jones, is an opportunist. While working as a dishwasher at the Cookhouse in the French Quarter, the bank bag with the night's receipts literally lands at his feet, and he simply picks it up and walks out with it, as there is only one witness, Sal, but he keeps quiet about what Ivory later calls "the felony":[21]

> Ivory was the kind of black dude who had always scared Sal the most. You couldn't tell for a long while if he was a man or a woman. Heavy work outfit. Rolls of fat that could pass for tits. Two earrings. Afro thick but tight. Blacks like Ivory, growing up looking like that, wherever they grew up, you know they're battle tested.[22]

Sal's discretion pays off later in the short story when he is mugged while walking his roommate's dog. Turns out that Sal is not the only one who finds Ivory intimidating, and Sal's assailants take off at the mere sight of him. Like the interconnection between characters in Toole's novel, Sal and Ivory cross paths near the end of the narrative, and similarly, the African American character acts as liberator.

Joe Longo moved to New Orleans in the mid-1990s to attend the University of New Orleans creative writing program. While studying for his MFA degree, Longo worked

---

21.   Joe Longo, "S.I.N.ners," in *French Quarter Fiction*, ed. Joshua Clark (New Orleans: Light of New Orleans Publishing, 2003), 174.

22.   Ibid., 173.

in the service industry as do so many college students in the New Orleans area. Longo was employed as a bartender in the French Quarter, and his two-year gig on Bourbon Street is the inspiration for "S.I.N.ners." He takes the title from the *Service Industry Night* (S.I.N.) at the local House of Blues, an event they have since trademarked. As the title suggests, Longo's portrait of Bourbon Street is not unsullied; however, that is what makes this story so absolutely credible and readable. In fact, Longo said of this story, "every now and then a service industry vet will get in touch with me and say how much they liked it"[23] Having worked as a bartender on Bourbon Street myself, I concur; he nails it.

My last bartending job was on Bourbon Street at the Old Absinthe House in the early 1990s. Except for being a Houlihan's girl in the late 1970s, I had not worked at an outright tourist bar before, and the money was incredible, but so were the characters who visited the bar. We had the requisite tourists in for the current sports match-ups, whom Longo describes in his story as, "Virginia Tech hicks, Florida Gator rednecks, and their wives who have too much enthusiasm for college football," all in town for the Sugar Bowl.[24] But we also had the locals who had been coming into the bar for decades, like Old Jesse (not to be confused with the bartender, Young Jesse), who one day came in when it was hailing outside to tell us "It's sleekin' out dere!" My one-time boss at the Abbey, Mike Zimbauer, in the early 1990s started a rather macabre "murder pool," along the lines of a football pool, in order to bring attention to the spiking New Orleans murder rate at the time, and in Longo's story, Moses takes bets on whether or not his friend Chicken Man — real life Fred Staten, who died in 1998 — will live out the year. In other words, Longo knows the French Quarter and the bar scene on Bourbon Street.

The story follows four main characters at work on New Year's Eve night in 1999: sexually ambiguous, drug-dealing

23.   Joe Longo, interview with the author, January 12, 2011
24.   Ibid., 162.

Ivory, from the Iberville Projects and dishwasher at the Cajun Cookhouse; sex-crazed, Tulane business school drop-out Matt, bartender at Kiwi Cruz Daquiris; pill-popping, bulimic, failed Olympic gymnast Garnet, employee of Waikiki East; and her roommate and Pizzazz bartender, Sal. The names of all these fictional Bourbon Street establishments sound familiar. There is no Cajun Cookhouse on Bourbon, but there is a Cajun Cabin, a Club Razzoo instead of Pizzazz, and daiquiri shops abound now in the French Quarter. Longo traces the decline of the always decadent but once much more fashionable and locally friendly French Quarter scene in his portrayal of these generic businesses and their denizens, and by doing so we see that this is no longer the French Quarter of legends like Louis Prima, Al Hirt, or Evangeline the Oyster Girl. Instead he offers a much more realistic if utilitarian picture of the Quarter, a place where tourists can have fun while service industry workers and business owners make money off of them. Like Sal's boss tells him, "We're in Sin City. It's a new millennium. We're making money."[25] That could be the mantra for almost all of the characters in this short story.

The first character we meet in the story is also the only local character, Ivory, who laments "the poor hand he's been dealt as a child of the [nearby] Iberville Projects."[26] He also wonders "[w]hat brothers are doing running around with a name like Ivory" and wants to know "who put the notion in his momma's head. . . . Was it her ambition that he whiten up?"[27] Ivory's identity crisis, while humorous, not only concerns his name. Almost every night after work, Ivory takes his shift pay straight to the Faubourg Marigny lesbian bar, Rubyfruit Jungle (a lesbian bar that has since moved to the French Quarter and is now housed in the 1135 Decatur bar), in search of "something in the range of warmth, hugs and nuzzles, something the skeleton rock whores can't put up

25.   Ibid., 169.
26.   Ibid., 156.
27.   Ibid., 158.

on the market. Quality time with some warm ass flesh, thirty seconds of soft."[28] Ivory is big enough and dangerous looking enough that folks get out of his way. Even at Rubyfruit, Longo writes that "dykes mistake him for one of their own, for a Queen Latifah gone hardcore instead of R&B. . . . Ivory's got a kind of Shirley Hemphill thing going on."[29] Longo's story is not politically correct, and to some readers would be downright offensive, but it is also wildly humorous and real.

Ivory is not the only character trying to be what he is not. His struggle with his identity foreshadows the young white frat boy who Longo calls "wigger boy."[30] Ironically, Sal seems to be the most tolerant and level headed character in the story, but when "wigger boy" tells him "Thanks, nigger" after Sal served him his free kamikaze, Sal jumps over the bar, throws the drink in his face, and throttles him, before the bouncers at Pizzazz peel him off. Sal is a racist who is wound tight, but more than he hates blacks he hates "these Limp Bizkit Kid Rock motherfuckers."[31] Longo also includes Sal's racist philosophy surrounding the annual African American gridiron clash, the Bayou Classic, which he compares to military conflict:

> Sal has done three tours of duty at The Bayou Classic. A Thanksgiving weekend football tradition. Grambling vs. Southern, two black colleges vying annually to see who has the cheapest and most ignorant student body in Louisiana. This past year Pizzazz tried to close, "catch up on some maintenance," but the NAACP threatened a lawsuit. Sal loved the logic of their crusade. We will force you to take our money, it is part of our civil rights to be overcharged for piss liquor and treated

28.   Ibid., 164.
29.   Ibid., 158-59.
30.   Ibid.,168.
31.   Ibid, 169.

like shit by a resentful service staff. We'll sue you if you refuse to screw us like you screw white tourists.[32]

Sadly, African American visitors to New Orleans are discriminated against in local bars, and on New Year's Eve 2004, twenty-six-year-old Levon Jones, in town for a flag football game associated with the Sugar Bowl, was killed by bouncers at Club Razzoo, prompting then mayor C. Ray Nagin to order "a study of how Bourbon Street clubs treat black patrons" and Coroner Frank Minyard telling television news stations that the bouncers "killed that man."[33]

Longo also draws on real life in portraying Sal's girlfriend/ roommate—it's unclear which—Garnet, a failed gymnast. Longo's wife is a gymnast and aerialist currently working in New Orleans. But that is where the similarities end. Garnet is a sad sack pill freak who moved to New Orleans from Houston, where she trained in "Bela Karloyi's Auschwitz" until she broke her leg in an awkward landing.[34] She and Sal even have a dog named Oksana, "after Oksana Baiul, reckless driver, Olympic princess."[35] Like Matt, Garnet moved to New Orleans to attend college—in her case, Loyola, from which she quickly dropped out, and since then—"her apartments have marked a steady slide down the neighborhoods along the Mississippi River," not unusual for service industry workers, nor is Garnet's substance abuse. In fact, Matt is the only character purposefully working on Bourbon Street. It's all part of his fifteen-twenty-year plan.

Matt came to the city to attend Tulane business school, and during carnival in his senior year, while looking for a way to cash in on the Mardi Gras madness, he landed at the daiquiri bar, Kiwi Kruz, where he is still working a year later:

32. Ibid, 169.

33. Gwen Filosa, "Charges dropped against two remaining Razzoo bouncers," *New Orleans Times-Picayune*, nola.com, October 20, 2008.

34. Joe Longo, "S.I.N.ners," 162.

35. Ibid., 171.

"So Matt takes his cash, lives off half and hands the rest over to Merrill Lynch. He plans to be drunk for the next fifteen or twenty years, wake up one day and be a millionaire."[36] He doesn't want to get stuck in "a bitch job in a germ-controlled building" like so many of his college classmates, the same classmates who "bitched about the 'quality of life' down here. . . . The roads are so not smooth. The produce is gross. I'm way over the drinking thing. And off they went to Houston, Austin, New York, San Francisco. Law school and med school."[37] Like Garnet, Matt remains in an altered state most of the time, drunk, while continuously struggling to get laid. In one of the most comical yet disgusting scenes in the novel, Matt, in order to achieve sexual satisfaction, takes matters into his own hands, literally. While on the roof of Kiwi Kruz mixing up a batch of piña coladas, Matt masturbates into the vat while fantasizing about a woman who rejected his come-on at Molly's the night before. He tries to hit on Garnet, again unsuccessfully, later that night. In fact, most of the characters' paths cross only briefly during this long night, but the night itself is even more significant.

Longo sets this story on the most hyped and anticipated night in a hundred years, New Year's Eve 1999. As Garnet tells Matt, "I thought the millennium was something special, something we were privileged to be alive to see. Some great reckoning."[38] But of course it is just another night on Bourbon Street with "no glitches, no terrorism, no anarchy. [j]ust fireworks and warmth."[39] He even includes that dangerous and longstanding New Orleans tradition of shooting guns into the night sky on New Year's Eve, and Ivory, for one, wants no part of it: "Fuck tonight's millennium action, bullets in the

36.   Ibid., 175.
37.   Ibid.
38.   Ibid., 167.
39.   Ibid., 161.

sky."[40] Instead he heads to Kiwi Cruz Daiquiris next door.

In the end, these characters are tired and bored, bored with their shift work, their lives, and even with Bourbon Street. This is an industry plagued with age, race, and sex discrimination along with substance abuse. I, for one, was sexually harassed by nearly all of my male bosses in my twelve plus years of bartending. And like Garnet, I too was falling down the rabbit hole of substance and alcohol abuse and got out of the business just in time. And Longo captures all that in his very droll short story. However, as funny as it is, he fails to capture the outright fun that can be had as a service industry worker. Nonetheless, Longo skillfully captures just another "night in the life" of these service industry workers. The New Orleans he describes here is not "The Big Easy" or "The City that Care Forgot." His is a decadent drug and sex-fueled French Quarter populated by drunken tourists, desperate criminals, and service industry workers who seem to take it all in stride. Tennessee Williams, in his essay "Amor Perdido," referred to such characters—himself included—as "Quarter Rats," and in reading Longo's "S.I.N.ners" we too can see "[l]ife getting bigger and plainer and uglier and more beautiful all the time."[41]

I turned to teaching English after working at the Old Absinthe House on Bourbon Street, not to be confused with the Old Absinthe Bar, one of the city's premier jazz venues that was shuttered in the 1990s and is now one of the all-too-ubiquitous daiquiri shops in the Quarter. The Old Absinthe House is a sports bar, which used to attract big name athletes, agents, sportscasters, who wanted to escape the madness of Bourbon Street in its "locals" back bar. By the looks of the current online reviews of the Old Absinthe House, its heyday is long gone, and so is the back bar, but it is still one of the French Quarter tourist joints that offers beverage discounts

40.   Ibid., 157.

41.   Tennessee Williams, "Amor Perdido," in *Where I Live: Selected Essays* (New York: New Directions, 1978), 5.

to locals.

Joe Longo no longer works in the French Quarter either. He talks about his French Quarter bartending history and its influence on his short story: "Through grad school I had a series of bottom-barrel bartending jobs, culminating in a Bourbon Street gig where I worked for two years. That combo of aggressive clientele and cynical hospitality is not an environment where people are at their best, and as bad as people can be externally they're often worse inside their own heads. I think that accounts for the rhythm and tone of the story."[42] He goes on to state:

> I was reading and re-reading Don DeLillo's *Underworld* when I began writing "S.I.N.ers," so I was stupidly ambitious (seventy additional pages follow the original published version), which probably accounts for the best and the worst passages in the story. I was working on another novel when Katrina hit, but now it sits idle. It became more important to write dark-hearted satire for three years. Now I don't write at all, but I can't promise that I've given it up for good.[43]

Let's hope not. Aside from Longo's writing career, Katrina and the ensuing flood wreaked havoc on the French Quarter service industry for a time, even though the Quarter did not flood.

Mardi Gras is now marketed to college students as a premier spring break destination, and some krewes are even looking (not very successfully) into corporate sponsorship. The Louisiana Superdome, its original name since opening in 1975, is now the Mercedes-Benz Superdome; condos, t-shirt and daiquiri shops fill the French Quarter; and Dixieland music is hard to come by outside of Preservation Hall. Souther captures the current tourist atmosphere:

42.   Joe Longo, interview with the author, January 12, 2011.

43.   Ibid.

Indeed, a tourist visiting New Orleans today would be . . . likely to forge memories of navigation on a sea of drunken T-shirt-clad tourists on Bourbon Street sipping fruity, red Pat O'Brien's drinks from souvenir "go-cups," and shouting for other tourists perched on iron balconies to toss beaded Mardi Gras necklaces purchased from gaudy souvenir shops that blared Cajun music through open doorways.[44]

Yes, the French Quarter has changed, and most believe not for the better, but when I began working in the Quarter in the mid-'70s, longtime residents were lamenting the change then. Gone were the high-class (and low-class, for that matter) Bourbon Street burlesque clubs; the Playboy Club had just closed, and Al Hirt's Night Club at 501 Bourbon was less than a decade from closing its doors as well. Longo's story does much to help us recall pre-Katrina French Quarter. As Andrei Codrescu writes in his post-Katrina memoir, *New Orleans, Mon Amour*, if "[y]ou live in a tourist town, you got visitors. You can run, but you can't hide. They are all wonderful, but they are here to have a good time. Bad for your liver. Bad for your work. Good for stories."[45] And Longo has not only made a living serving those tourists, but also written a story capturing their brief visits to the city along with the laborers who make them want to visit again and again.

44.   Mark Souther, *New Orleans on Parade*, 222.

45.   Andrei Codrescu, *New Orleans, Mon Amour* (Chapel Hill: Algonquin Books, 2006), 243.

9 Organizing and Rebuilding a *Nuevo* New Orleans: Day Labor Organizing in the Big Easy

Aurelia Lorena Murga

In early October 2005, just over a month after Hurricane Katrina devastated the Gulf coast region of the United States, New Orleans mayor Ray Nagin asked local business leaders how he should ensure that Mexican workers did not overrun the city.[1] Indeed, in the aftermath of Hurricane Katrina thousands of workers, many of whom were black, evacuated the city, losing their jobs, and as a result their livelihoods. At the same time, the reconstruction of the city attracted a large contingent workforce—a significant part of that being Latino workers.[2] With 80 percent of the city's buildings affected by flooding, a labor force was needed for the clean-up and rebuilding efforts.[3] That need was evidenced in an executive order issued by President George W. Bush on September 8, 2005. The order suspended the Davis-Bacon Act for a ninety-day period following Katrina and allowed employers to pay workers the prevailing wages on federally funded construction projects in the Gulf states of Louisiana and Mississippi, where

1.   "Profile: Ray Nagin," BBC News, accessed March 29, 2011, http://news.bbc.co.uk/go/pr/fr/-/2/hi/americas/4623922.stm.

2.   Judith Browne-Dianis, Jennifer Lai, Marielena Hincapie, and Saket Soni, "And Injustice for All: Workers' Lives in the Reconstruction of New Orleans," 2006, accessed February 14, 2008, http://www.advancementproject.org/reports/workersreport.pdf; Elizabeth Fussell, "Latino/a Immigrants in Post-Katrina New Orleans: A Research Report," in *World On the Move: Newsletter of the American Sociological Association's Section on International Migration* 13, no. 2 (2007): 2-4.

3.   Fussell, "Latino/a Immigrants."

wages were already far below the national average.[4] Moreover, the Bush administration awarded labor contracts that were subsequently subcontracted multiple times over, providing employers with the opportunities to exploit vulnerable reconstruction workers.[5]

Furthermore, only days before the suspension of the Davis Bacon Act, on September 6, 2005, the Department of Homeland Security (DHS) "suspended sanctions for employers who failed to verify the work authorization of their employees as required under federal immigration law. DHS reinstated this requirement on October 21, 2005."[6] Consequently, soon after Katrina, Latino/a immigrants "constituted 25 percent of construction workers."[7]

The experiences of Latino day laborers in New Orleans provide a critical window into the exploitative work situations faced by immigrant workers after Katrina. Years after the storm, the physical reconstruction of the city's structures and the social and emotional reconstruction experienced by its residents continues. This essay focuses on the organizing efforts and resistance strategies used by Latino day laborers — workers seeking employment in open-air spaces throughout the city—as they challenge racism, wage theft, and focus on building their lives in *Nuevo Orleans*.

In particular, this essay illustrates the issues experienced by Latino immigrant day laborers in post-Katrina New Orleans by examining what motivates day laborers, as a disenfranchised community of workers, to organize as reconstruction workers in New Orleans. The following sections will provide a brief overview on Latino and immigrant

4.   Browne-Dianis et al., "And Injustice for All."

5.   Loren K. Redwood, "Strong–Arming Exploitable Labor: The State and Immigrant Workers in the Post-Katrina Gulf Coast," *Social Justice* 35, no. 4 (2008/9): 33-50.

6.   Browne-Dianis et al., "And Injustice for All," 33.

7.   Kevin R.Johnson, "Hurricane Katrina: Lessons from the Administrative State." *Houston Law Review* 11 (2008): 15.

organizing, the methodology used during data collection, and the findings that address issues revolving around day labor organizing in New Orleans. In particular, they focus on how Latino immigrant day laborers identify as reconstruction workers in post-Katrina New Orleans, their participation in community organizing, and their motivation for organizing in the city.

A broad portion of the literature examining Latino and immigrant labor organizing efforts illustrates struggles and successes within union organizing.[8] Unions in the United States are facing shifting balances of power and "recruiting immigrant workers into union ranks has become increasingly central to the larger project of rebuilding the United States labor movement, which has been in a downward spiral for decades."[9] Over the past several decades, union participation by Latino and immigrant workers has been higher among Latinos born in the United States, or by those having secure immigrant status, when compared to U.S. born whites.[10]

Moreover, much of the existing literature argues that immigrant workers are more easily organized than other workers in the U.S.[11] This is partially due to the history of collective action and militancy that immigrant workers may have experienced in their countries of origin.[12] Indeed, some scholars believe immigrants may be the best hope for a

---

8.   Dan Clawson, *The Next Upsurge: Labor and the New Social Movements* (Ithaca, NY: Cornell University Press, 2003); Ruth Milkman, *Organizing Immigrants: The Challenge for Unions in Contemporary California* (Ithaca, NY: Cornell University Press: 2000).

9.   Milkman, *Organizing Immigrants*, 1.

10.   Jake Rosenfeld and Meredith Kleykamp, "Hispanics and Organized Labor in the United States, 1973 to 2007," *American Sociological Review* 74 (2009): 916-37.

11.   Milkman, *Organizing Immigrants*.

12.   Miriam J. Wells, "Immigration and Unionization in the San Francisco Hotel Industry," in *Organizing Immigrants: The Challenge for Unions in Contemporary California*, ed. Ruth Milkman (Ithaca, NY: Cornell University Press, 2000), 109-29; Milkman, *Organizing Immigrants*.

revitalized labor movement.[13] Consequently, immigrant labor organizing has proven to be a central focus in communities throughout the United States. For instance, community projects and organizations have seen the importance of building strong community membership and leadership among immigrant workers. These efforts have centered on the collective power of workers, focusing on workers' team building efforts and their leadership toward social and economic justice.[14]

More recent research has examined day labor organizing, which has become a central focus in communities around the country. The academic literature on day labor organizing has primarily addressed the obstacles faced in organizing immigrant day laborers around the creation of day labor centers, or hiring halls. Michelle Camou finds that workers and organizers often have different motivations for, and understandings of, the creation of worker centers.[15] For instance, immigrant workers tend to understand worker centers in terms of material rewards (e.g., employment, resolution of work grievances), while organizers often frame worker centers around issues related to collective action, justice, and solidarity.[16] In Baltimore and Denver, the cultural systems in which day laborers operate are guided by self-reliance and material well-being.[17] Consequently, "solidarity

13. Clawson, *The Next Upsurge*; Saru Jayaraman and Immanuel Ness, "Models of Worker Organizing," in *The New Urban Immigrant Workforce: Innovative Models for Labor Organizing*, eds, Saramathi Jayaraman and Immanuel Ness (Armonk, NY: M.E. Sharpe, 2005), 71-84.

14. Saru Jayaraman, "La Alianza para la Justicia: A Team Approach to Immigrant Worker Organizing." in Saramathi Jayaraman and Immanuel Ness eds. *The New Urban Immigrant Workforce: Innovative Models for Labor Organizing*. (Armonk, NY: M.E. Sharpe, 2005), 85-104.

15. Michelle Camou, "Synchronizing Meanings and Other Day Labor Organizing Strategies: Lessons from Denver." *Labor Studies Journal* 34, no.1 (2009): 39-64.

16. Camou, "Organizing Strategies."

17. Michelle Camou, "Capacity and Solidarity: Foundational Elements in the Unionization Strategy for Immigrant Day Labourers," *International Migration* 50, no.2 (2012): 41-64.

is not immediate and, in some day labor communities, organizers may lack access to the types of personal social networks that historically have facilitated immigrant organizing."[18]

Organizers and immigrant workers in the Deep South face a particular set of obstacles. The Deep South has experienced changing demographics over the last several decades sparking interest in the changing social and political dynamics of communities experiencing new influxes of Latino immigrants. Beginning in the 1890s, as a result of amendments made to the Immigration and Nationality Act, parts of the Deep South, Midwest, and West, became new destination areas for immigrant populations—specifically Latinos.[19] These amendments allowed for post-1965 immigration to the United States by people of Latin American and Asian origins.[20]

With the influx of Latino immigrants to the South, social justice activists have had to reexamine their organizing efforts. Barbara Ellen Smith writes that organizers and social justice activists in the South are unfamiliar with some of the issues faced by immigrants. In fact,

> when immigration to the South began to escalate sharply in the 1990s, many social justice organizations were ill prepared to respond. Unfamiliar with the issues facing new immigrants—legal status, access to driver's licenses, language barriers, etc.—organizations both large and small were in many cases also preoccupied

18. Camou, "Capacity and Solidarity," 3.

19. Manuel A. Vásquez, Chad E. Seales, and Marie Friedmann Marquardt, "New Latino Destinations," in *Latinas/os in the United States: Changing the Face of America*, eds. Havidán Rodríguez, Rogelio Sáenz, and Cecilia Menjívar (New York: Springer, 2008), 19-35.

20. Charles Hirschman and Douglas S. Massey, "Chapter 1: Places and Peoples: The New American Mosaic," in *New Faces in New Places: The Changing Geography of American Immigration*, ed. Douglas S. Massey (Russell Sage Foundation: New York, 2008), 1-21.

with fundamental questions of political direction and financial viability.[21]

Consequently, in a time of heightened racist and xenophobic sentiment in a post 9/11 United States, community organizers and workers in the South experience various obstacles in their organizing efforts.

Methods

In July 2008, I moved to New Orleans, Louisiana, to conduct fieldwork with post-Katrina Latino day laborers. I became an active, full-time volunteer with the Congress of Day Laborers — El Congreso de Jornaleros — a project of the New Orleans Workers' Center for Racial Justice (NOWCRJ). El Congreso is a grassroots membership organization of reconstruction workers formed in the weeks following Katrina. Unlike other organizations that may provide specific services — such as health care or resource information — the Congreso focuses on organizing workers, although assistance with interpretation and wage claims are also provided. The organization focuses on building leadership and agency, so workers may advocate for their rights as reconstruction workers.

My initial research was to last four months; however, my participation in day labor organizing, which was not a proposed aspect of my academic research, called for a longer stay in New Orleans. As a result, my ethnographic experience lasted for a period of twenty-three months (July 2008-July 2010). Before moving to New Orleans I had no experience with community organizing, much less organizing focused on workers' and immigrant rights. My participation within the Congreso was voted on by day laborers. During my

21.   Barbara Ellen Smith, "Across Races and Nations: Social Justice Organizing in the Transnational South." in *Latinos in the New South: Transformations of Place*, eds. Heather A. Smith and Owen J. Furuseth (Burlington, VT: Ashgate Publishing Company, 2006), 237.

first week in New Orleans I was introduced to workers by day labor organizers. Members then voted on whether my research and participation with the workers was something they supported or not. This vote reflected the experiences day laborers had previously encountered with researchers and journalists in post-Katrina New Orleans. Following Katrina, workers participated in various interviews with researchers and journalists and saw little in the way of reciprocity. Indeed, part of the organizing goals created within the Congreso center around the importance of day laborer narratives—how and where their knowledge and experiences are recorded and what is done with them.

The findings in this chapter are based on ethnography as well as a series of thirty-one in-depth, semi-structured interviews with day laborers in post-Katrina New Orleans. Participants were primarily from Mexico and Central America, with the majority migrating from Honduras. Interviews were conducted in Spanish, audio-recorded, and ranged in length from one to two hours. Interviews were then transcribed and analyzed in Spanish and the portions of the responses cited in this essay were subsequently translated into English. I use pseudonyms throughout the essay in order to protect the identity of participants.

Volunteering with the Congreso meant I participated in daily morning outreach with day labor organizers throughout *las esquinas* (day labor corners) of New Orleans during the week. Outreach consisted of several things: speaking with day laborers about worker and immigrant rights; issues of wage theft; answering questions about the organization; and scheduling rides to doctor's visits and municipal and traffic court appearances where I would also translate for them, if necessary. I also participated in labor actions, marches, and protests. My experiences with day laborers also consisted of days when we just spoke about home—their native countries— families, stories about working in New Orleans, and in other places, soccer games, and everyday life events.

I spent hundreds of hours with day laborers, and as a result, many, but not all, of the experiences and interviews (both formal and informal) I gathered were completed with members of the Congreso. Membership in the Congreso fluctuated. For the most part, all day laborers were "members" of the Congreso if they looked for work in las esquinas. Still, there were some day laborers who played a more active role in the organization with much of this depending on availability related to work schedules. Likewise, some day laborers participated in Congreso meetings depending on their needs or desire to participate in day labor organizing.

Research Findings

Hurricanes Katrina (August 2005) and Rita (September 2005) impacted an area of ninety thousand square miles and attracted Latino immigrant workers, along with U.S.-born workers, to the Gulf areas. During this time there was an abundance of work.[22] As Don Nicolas points out:

> The city was like a cemetery . . . and you couldn't walk a block without it being like a *subasta* (auction block). We made a lot of money . . . "come on, come on" employers would tell us. My friend would say, "the man says he'll pay us one hundred per person for demolition work." And as we were returning home from one job there would be another five employers asking us to work. We'd get home around 10 p.m. *El patron* (the boss) would say, "I'll come for you at 7 tomorrow." If there was another employer there he'd say, "How much is he paying you? I'll pay you 150." They needed workers. They were nice to us—even the National Guard—*te hechaban la mano* (would give you

22.   Kai Erikson, foreword to *The Sociology of Katrina: Perspectives on a Modern Catastrophe*, eds. David L. Brunsma, David Overfelt, and J. Steven Picou (Lanham, MD: Rowman & Littlefield Publishers, Inc., 2007), xvii-xx.

a hand). Today, it's not like that.[23]

Many workers speak of the first weeks and months after Katrina as a time when they did not have to look for work, the work or employer came looking for them. Workers did not have to worry about being harassed by employers or by the police or National Guard during that time. As a matter of fact, day laborers explained to me that, at first, day labor corners did not exist. However, as reconstruction work began to slow down Latino workers began to meet at Lee Circle in the City's Central Business District (CBD). And when the city began attracting tourists again, those looking for work on Lee Circle became an uncomfortable blemish, leading to raids on Lee Circle by Immigration and Customs Enforcement (ICE). Consequently, day laborers created and began meeting on different *esquinas* throughout the city.

Day Laboring in New Orleans

New Orleans day laborers are under constant surveillance by authorities and frequently experience harassment. For many, just standing on the corner creates anxiety. There is looming intimidation and fear of deportation among day laborers in New Orleans. Adrian expressed some of these issues as we spoke about his experiences when looking for work on the corner during a time when day laborers are no longer welcomed in the city. Below he speaks of the pressures and consequences of being a day laborer in New Orleans.

The army . . . they would arrive and run people off. Once as I was arriving at the corner, a *poli* (officer), I don't know his rank, but he had a lot of stripes here (he points to his arm). "You," he told me. I saw that people were running, and I asked myself "But why are they running?" "*Diablos* (damn)," I said to myself. He

23.   Don Nicolas (pseud.), interview with author, March 2010.

told me, "You, come here." He was at a distance from me (pointing to the trash can in the room to note the distance). I said to myself, "I'm not afraid of this guy." He said, "You come here, don't try to run because I will run after you." I knew that those guys in the army are good at running. I said, "*¡No, pues ya me clavaron!*" ("Well, they got me now!"). So I went to him, and he told me "put your hands behind your back." And I said, "But why? I just got here." He responded, "Well, that doesn't count, you'll have to tell that to the judge."[24]

As New Orleans day laborers began meeting on different corners of the city, the responses from home improvement stores, convenience store managers, community residents, the police, and National Guard varied. However, the overarching sentiment and actions toward day laborers were negative and unwelcoming. During the time I volunteered with the Congreso we would receive constant phone calls from day laborers requesting assistance—either in the form of translating for workers during their interactions with law enforcement or in advocating for the release of workers who were being detained by police or the National Guard.

The need to organize

In those first few weeks of meeting with workers and organizers I began to understand the importance of taking ownership of the dignity of the work process and the issues of justice tied to it. It became apparent that day laborers are reconstruction workers and many of them spoke with great pride of the work they had done in order to rebuild New Orleans. For many workers New Orleans was now their home, too. As a result, workers felt the need to organize and mobilize as a collective.

Some day laborers were familiar with organizing practices

24. Adrian (pseud.), interview with the author, March 2010.

since they had participated in *sindicatos* (unions) in their countries of origin. However, the majority of workers were new to community organizing. The most obvious reasons for organizing or participating in the Congreso were to build collective action and power for fighting against poor working conditions, harassment, and wage theft. Moreover, the undergirding issues of social, racial, and economic justice resonated in the organizing activities of the Congreso. Don Jaime, an active member of the Congreso, was motivated to join when he witnessed the harassment of day laborers on the corner.

> Look, [giggles] there are many motives as to why I began to participate in the Congreso. Many motives. I decided to participate when I saw a day labor organizer defending workers on the corner against the military. They were chasing us off the corner and they were arresting others, they would hit workers, you know? I noticed that she (the day labor organizer) was arguing with authorities, and she asked us to stand on the sidewalk. They (the officers) were satisfied but didn't think she would be able to keep us on the sidewalk because they thought we were a bunch of . . . how do I want to say it . . . the police wanted to say that we were a bunch of animals, you know?[25]

Certainly, many day laborers were inspired by the support and advocacy efforts provided by organizers. Workers often expressed feelings of anger and frustration as they were being harassed by authorities. Day laborers are particularly vulnerable in these spaces. Indeed, they did not only experience harassment from police or the National Guard, but also experienced yelling from drivers driving by day labor corners in their cars. However, day laborers are resilient and remain steadfast in their efforts toward protecting their

25.   Don Jaime (pseud.), interview with author, February 2010.

corners. Many felt like they were not doing anything wrong —
no estamos hacienda nada malo. They simply look for work in a
city that received them and supported their work efforts at the
very beginning. Yet, as time passed, workers began to feel the
pressure of "immigrant" and "Latino" status in New Orleans.
Indeed, many began to feel, see, and experience persecution
because they were identified as such.

During a time when day laborers were being physically
harassed by police and the National Guard they knew there
were day labor organizers advocating for them. As tensions
grew on the corners between workers and the authorities
many began to see the supportive response and actions of
day labor organizers. As a result, more day laborers began
participating in Congreso meetings and were motivated to
advocate for their rights as reconstruction workers.

Organizing and building community

The Congreso became a staple among Latino day laborers
on the corners of New Orleans. When speaking with Adrian
about his participation in community organizing and why he
chose to participate in the Congreso he said:

> I liked the Congreso. The day labor organizer, you
> all, all of you, the Congreso has helped me. And it is
> a family as well, do you know what I mean? One sees
> things and that the Congreso worries about Latinos
> and wants them to learn, that people will open their
> eyes to the issues affecting the Latino community.[26]

I asked Adrian to elaborate on this and he added:

> To learn about all sorts of experiences, wage theft, to
> learn about work situations and open up to learning.
> To learn about others' experiences. And well, I have

26.   Adrian (pseud.), interview with the author, April 2010.

liked participating with the Congreso de Jornaleros a lot. What do I like? I like everything. And thanks to them, to everyone, I hope this will continue.[27]

El Congreso provided workers with opportunities to build community among Latino day laborers. Day laborers also participated in other organizations, such as churches, but, for the most part, knew that the Congreso was a steadfast advocate of their efforts and that it facilitated the creation of leadership among workers. Moreover, in response to racist experiences, day laborers joined actions, marches, and protests throughout the city — advocating for their rights as well as the rights of other disenfranchised communities — in particular black New Orleanians.

Some of the day laborers I spoke with planned to adopt and continue to use the organizing practices they learned in New Orleans once they leave the city. Indeed, I believe this is a result of the efforts made by the organizers of the NOWCRJ and their focus on creating strong community building efforts among day laborers. During a formal interview with Agustin I asked him what was one of the best experiences of living in the United States. He responded:

> Agustin: The best experience that I have had is working with the Congreso de Jornaleros.
> Myself: Really?
> Agustin: Yes, because it has always provided us with ideas about how to fight for our rights and how we can represent ourselves when we face discrimination. Only this organization, well, has provided us with ideas, it has provided us with techniques to use so that those that discriminate against us don't manipulate us.
> Myself: Can you give me an example of how they have taught you this?
> Agustin: Well, the direction, toward organizing. The

27.   Ibid.

way in which we can convince people to join a — a great group of people. And, how would I say it, work with a great group of people, and take advantage of different experiences. Unite people, join meetings, and when we are in groups, we begin to share experiences and through the use of this technique we can do something. And that's what I've always liked a lot.[28]

Agustin, and others like him, may not attend all meetings or voice their opinions during meetings, but they have learned how to fight for their rights as reconstruction workers. For instance, for the most part, day laborers learned that they have rights to lost or unpaid wages under the law. This information and the steps to take when claiming stolen wages, I learned, provided workers with a sense of empowerment. Workers also learned where to go when they needed resources or support, for example if they needed assistance with interpretation during traffic or municipal court appearances. They also knew that they were not alone, and that other workers were there to support them.

Some Congreso members, while quiet and unassuming during meetings, were a constant source of support for other workers. For instance, after the Congreso assisted Ismael and six other workers in fighting against an arrest and possible deportation after being accused of theft during the clean-up efforts following Hurricane Ike, he became an active member of the Congreso. Ismael noted that he began to attend meetings because of the assistance he received from the organization and explained his reasons for joining the Congreso:

I can continue to help those who helped me. Thanks to those here, I am in New Orleans, and that is why I like coming to meetings and listening. I don't really speak a lot but I like to learn and, well, I like to tell people what happens here like, like learning about our rights.

28.   Agustin (pseud.), Personal Interview, January 2010.

Ismael continued to invite his friends to Congreso meetings and was supportive of organizing efforts. He, like other workers, learned the importance of solidarity and collective action. Likewise, he and other workers participated in actions because they knew that they, at one time or another, may need the support of others. Throughout their time in New Orleans they have learned and experienced that without collective action change is less likely to occur.[29]

During the end of my two year tenure with the Congreso I witnessed the growth and strength built within membership. Leaders began emerging. Besides their continued participation in protests and meetings throughout the city with council members or with allies, they also became more active facilitators of meetings. The two organizers, who were used to facilitating meetings, began taking a back seat during weekly Congreso meetings. Organizers showed day laborers how agendas were created and assisted them with facilitating meetings, which led to members leading weekly meetings on their own. Likewise, members who emerged as leaders were continuously encouraged to take part in projects and workshops, and encouraged other day laborers to join the Congreso.

Organizing for the Future

One of the motivating factors influencing day labor participation in organizing efforts revolves around the future of other Latino immigrants and workers in New Orleans. Day laborers not only reflected on their own futures—social, economic, and political positions—but also remained socially conscious of the potential situations faced by Latino newcomers to the city. I asked Hector, a long-standing member of the Congreso, why he began participating in day labor organizing. His response reflected the views of many other Congreso members:

---

29.   Ismael (pseud.), interview with the author, November 2009.

I believe that good things, they may not happen right away in a day, maybe not even in a month, or a year, but I think about the future. For example, what we are doing here or what we do today, maybe we'll leave, we may not benefit from our actions, because we may no longer be here . . . but those that come to New Orleans, because they'll keep coming to New Orleans, the way I see it. People will keep migrating to New Orleans, because they always face the same problems, things aren't improving. So we're organizing, for that, so that if we don't last here, someday we'll see something good come out of it. And so that those that arrive after we do, so they won't have to go through what we are going through, so that they will do better. They may be members of our own family, maybe my family member, or that of a neighbor or friend. Someone of our community will be able to benefit, some day, maybe the situation will be better for them, and hopefully, we'll also be able to enjoy them as well.[30]

Indeed, day labor organizing in New Orleans created advocacy and solidarity among workers. Many day laborers expressed the need for looking toward the future—not only their own but that of Latino newcomers. Like Hector, other day laborers realized that they may not benefit from the actions they were taking at the time, but looked toward justice building in the city and hoped for a better New Orleans in the future. They remained steadfast in creating a collective movement whose efforts were grounded in social, racial, and economic justice.

Conclusion

This chapter not only underscores the crucial role that Latino day laborers play as non-standard workers in a racialized labor market, historically organized along a black/

---

30.   Hector (pseud.), interview with the author, December 2009.

white continuum. It also reveals the challenges faced by reconstruction workers building their lives in New Orleans — whether for the short term or if in the long run they ultimately decided to call New Orleans home. Moreover, it reveals some of the resistance strategies used by Latino day laborers living in post-Katrina New Orleans. Day laborers remain a particularly vulnerable population in the New Orleans Metro area. They have faced harassment from National Guard, police, security guards, and people yelling obscenities and disparaging racist and xenophobic remarks from cars. Yet, there is a certain amount of resiliency and dignity that is shown by *jornaleros* on day labor corners. Many have now made New Orleans home, part of their daily life is looking for work in a city they helped rebuild. Many know and feel that they are not doing anything wrong as they take part in day laboring on the corners of New Orleans. As a result, they have begun to organize and advocate for their rights as reconstruction workers

Indeed, the strength of the Congreso has provided day laborers with leadership skills and advocated for their continued participation in actions, protests, and membership recruitment. In some of my first meetings with the Congreso in July 2008 there was a steady participation of fifteen to twenty day laborers at weekly meetings, by the time I left New Orleans in June 2010 members were overflowing the conference room of the New Orleans Workers' Center for Racial Justice. During that time, the walls of the NOWCRJ reverberated with enthusiasm as workers gathered. Their efforts and engagement in day labor organizing have now become part of their everyday lives and efforts toward building a better Nuevo Orleans.

10 Ascriptive Segmentation Between Good and Bad Jobs: New Orleans Restaurants and Construction Workers

AARON SCHNEIDER AND SARU JAYARAMAN[1]

This project explores the nature of work in New Orleans after Hurricane Katrina. Despite creating steady and growing amounts of wealth, the two largest sectors of employment, hospitality and construction, have not created decent livelihoods. These sectors offer a few good jobs, but most of the jobs provided are poor in compensation, conditions, and stability. Part of the explanation for this may lay in long-term regional patterns of antagonism to working-class organization, as well as ongoing processes of deindustrialization and deregulation occurring in all U.S. cities. In addition, the data below show specific patterns of segmentation by characteristics such as race, gender, and immigration-status, in which ascriptive characteristics are used to block some people from decent livelihoods. One of the most striking observations of the current study is that the experience of segmented labor markets is increasingly extrapolated to all workers, as more and more job categories and workers face informality, exploitation, and lack of regulation.

We begin with the construction and restaurant sectors because these were the two most significant sources of employment in the New Orleans economy over the last five

1. The authors are grateful for the suggestions of the editors and the challenges of participants in the workshop, "Working in the Big Easy: The History and Politics of Labor in New Orleans, From Slavery to Post-Katrina." We welcome the comments, critiques, and observations of readers at aaron.schneider@du.edu and saru@rocunited.org.

years, accounting for fully one fifth of all jobs.[2] These also happen to be two especially informalized sectors in terms of the way markets for labor operate, with increasing informality and deregulation as a result of actions taken after Katrina. These sectors are also the main occupational destination for new immigrants, people of color, and workers without formal educational qualifications. The labor market experience of these groups has been segmented into specific kinds of activities within construction and restaurant work.

The study takes advantage of two original sources of empirical material. The first is a survey of workers in restaurants from the greater New Orleans metropolitan area, based on a representative, stratified sample of restaurant workers (See Appendix 1 for description). These observations, conducted by the Restaurant Opportunities Center of New Orleans, include quantitative and qualitative evidence on the conditions of workers within the restaurant sector. The study reveals staggering patterns of generally poor and dangerous lives, racial and gender hierarchies in the allocation of the few decent jobs, and rampant violations of the most basic regulations of working conditions.

The second source of observations is a survey of construction workers conducted over two periods, once shortly after Katrina in 2006 and a second survey in 2009, several years after reconstruction had advanced. The construction worker survey offers a population-based sample of construction sites, randomly chosen on the basis of a stratified sample of homes in New Orleans. The construction worker survey also includes an additional set of respondents selected for convenience at day laborer pick-up sites. Construction worker surveys were conducted with the help of the Loyola Immigration Law Clinic and the Berkeley Institute of Human Rights, and include both quantitative and qualitative evidence on working conditions in reconstruction.

2.   Bureau of Labor Statistics, *Gulf Coast Leisure and Hospitality Employment and Wages* (Washington, D.C.: Bureau of Labor Statistics, 2011).

Like the restaurant worker survey, the construction survey revealed generally poor and dangerous lives for workers, with exaggerated racial and especially immigration-status differences in worker experience, rampant violations of working conditions, and patterns of abuse and exploitation hardening and expanding over time.

Both sectors display a proliferation of low-wage jobs, held largely by people of color, in a high growth hospitality region recovering from disaster. This combination entails growing inequality — low-wage jobs in the midst of plenty — accelerated by Hurricane Katrina but consistent with long term processes that characterize both the region and the urban sector in the U.S. more generally.

Class in New Orleans

This project argues that conditions in restaurants and construction reveal the difficulty of class politics in New Orleans. To begin, it is necessary to explain why we emphasize the concept of making a working class. By using the word "making," we emphasize the role of agency in creating and resisting social structure. Some might understand the nature of work in New Orleans as the inevitable result of market processes. Others might quibble with the notion that apparently unorganized and segmented workers can ever structure lower-class power. Indeed, most portrayals of New Orleans tell a story of Katrina washing away the low-wage and low-productivity population of the city to allow a boom in cosmopolitan sectors such as non-profits, education, and medical research, evidenced by an influx of individuals with high levels of human capital, concomitant increases in average income, and a rising percentage of residents with college degrees.[3]

Yet, cosmopolitan sectors do not exist without infrastructure

3.   Amy Liu and Alison Plyer, *The New Orleans Index at Five* (Washington, D.C.: Brookings Institution, 2010).

and services, and we choose to explore conditions in low-wage, hyper-exploitative portions of the workforce to make sense of how labor markets are restructured in the wake of major disruption. As new dimensions of exclusion are layered upon old, the politics of the working-class experiences obstacles that complicate even further the issues of consciousness, organization, and resistance that make up class formation.

Class formation is never a neutral, apolitical, or even uniform process. It forms out of the prior experience of working people: the nature of the exploitation they face, their self-conscious efforts at organization, and the resulting political and social conflicts in which they engage. Their ability to engage in class politics is not automatic, and there is little guarantee that it will be successful. This project draws no firm conclusions about the prospects for class politics in New Orleans, but it does trace the dimensions along which it would have to form were it to emerge.

This approach to class draws on insights built on experiences that occurred far away and in completely different circumstances. E.P. Thompson explored class identity and organization among U.K. workers at the start of the industrial revolution, and though the time period and context are different, his conclusions hold contemporary lessons:

> The making of the working class is a fact of political and cultural, as much as of economic, history. . . . The changing productive relations and working conditions of the Industrial Revolution were imposed, not upon raw material, but upon . . . the inheritors of Bunyan, of remembered village rights, of notions of equality before the law, of craft traditions. . . . The working class made itself as much as it was made.[4]

Thompson's point is that class formation depends on the

---

4.   E.P. Thompson, *The Making of the English Working Class* (New York: Vintage Books, 194).

active efforts of working people, and their action is informed by the historical, cultural, and political legacies they bring to the workplace from their lived experience. Class formation in factories was not solely an economic imperative of exploitation and shared misery derived from a mode of production; eighteenth-century English workers drew upon the cultural and political action of women, Irish Catholic immigrants, and English Protestant arrivals from the countryside. Each brought with them historical baggage, and interweaving disparate experiences was both pre-requisite and part of making a self-conscious working-class political movement.[5]

The lesson is that class is made, and it therefore must constantly be remade. The modes of production within capitalism evolve, constantly reorganizing the workplace, and with it, the experience of workers. In constant flux are the terms of exploitation, the demographic balance of the workforce, and the organization of capital, both economic and political. Working-class struggles to negotiate the terms of their incorporation into capitalism require constantly reinterpreting and reestablishing shared experience to build political power, a challenge that was only poorly accomplished before Katrina, and now requires redoubled effort.

If working class organization is to emerge, and there is no guarantee that it will, it will draw on prior patterns of organization, memories of norms of legitimacy and justice, and the direct experiences of contemporary exploitation. As part of understanding and encouraging that process, the current project attempts to describe conditions in the most important low-wage sectors of New Orleans, where work is distributed in particular ways to racial, ethnic, and gendered subgroups. The few good jobs are reserved for workers who are generally white, male, and native-born, and the rest of the

5.   "Engels saw the "passionate, mercurial Irish temperament" as the precipitate which brought the more disciplined and reserved English workers to the point of political action," Thompson, *Making of the English Working Class*, 442-43.

jobs are allocated to people excluded on the basis of one or another ascriptive characteristic such as race, ethnicity, gender, and immigration-status. These patterns alone do not make a working class, and in fact probably make class struggle more difficult. Still, there will be no working-class politics without addressing these highly specific patterns of exploitation. The conclusion considers how that working-class politics might look.

Deregulation, Deindustrialization, and Hurricane Katrina

To make sense of labor market structuring in contemporary New Orleans, it is important to consider the disruption caused by Hurricane Katrina in 2005. In particular, it was not so much the wind and water that altered the city as the political campaign to loosen constraints on employer control over workers. Katrina hit the Gulf Coast as a category 3 storm, with winds over 110 mph and storm surges of five to sixteen feet. While the eye of the hurricane missed the city and the immediate hurricane damage was no more than to be expected, the failure of the levees led to the catastrophic flooding of 80 percent of the city, over 1,800 deaths, and damage to 70 percent of all occupied housing units. As a result of the ensuing displacement, the pre-Hurricane Katrina population of 455,188 dropped by an estimated 225,000 shortly after the storm, and had recovered only 75 percent of its original level in 2009, to 343,829.[6] Many of those who could not return were poor and black, and the percentage of African Americans in the city dropped to 61.3 percent from 66.7 percent.[7] At least in part

6.   U.S. Census Bureau, *U.S. Census 2010*, http://www.census.gov/2010census/, accessed 04/01/2012.

7.   While Hurricane Katrina affected all neighborhoods and homes, block-by-block analysis suggests that half of the city's white residents experienced flooding as compared to three quarters of black residents, Donna L. Brazile, "New Orleans: Next steps on the Road to Recovery," in *The State of Black America* (Washington,

because so many of the poorest residents have not returned, average incomes rose from $39,942 to $45,325, and the poverty rate dropped to 23 percent, its lowest level since 1979.[8] Still, median black household income remains 45 percent lower than white household income, and Latino household incomes are 25 percent lower than white households.

The growth of the Latino population in New Orleans accelerated after Katrina, even above rates of growth in the Latino population in the rest of the country. Prior to Hurricane Katrina, New Orleans had maintained a relatively small Latino population, drawn partially from a Central American middle class connected to the United Fruit company and remaining at 3.1 percent in 2000.[9] By 2010, the percentage had increased to 5.2 percent—a rate of growth that moved Louisiana in the direction of the rest of its southern state neighbors, though it had not yet caught up. Some of these new arrivals came from other parts of the U.S., especially the South, where the Latino population had expanded over the previous decade. When combined with the rapid decrease in the poor and African American population, the increase in the Latino population was particularly felt in portions of the workforce without

---

DC: National Urban League, 2006), 233-37. This is consistent with other studies which show a disproportionate impact of the hurricane on African American residents, see David L. Brunsma, David Overfelt, and J.Steven Picou, *The Sociology of Hurricane Katrina: Perspectives on a Modern Catastrophe* (Lanham, MD: Rowman and Littlefield, 2007); James R. Elliott and Jeremy Pais, "Race, Class, and Hurricane Katrina: Social Differences in Human Responses to Disaster" *Social Science Research* 35 (2006): 295-321; William W. Falk, Matthew O. Hunt, and Larry L. Hunt, "Hurricane Katrina and New Orleanians' Sense of Place: Return and Reconstitution or 'Gone with the Wind'? *DuBois Review* 3, no. 1 (2006): 115-28; Chester Hartman and Gregory D. Squires, *There Is No Such Thing as a Natural Disaster: Race, Class and Hurricane Katrina* (New York: Routledge, 2006); K. Lavelle and J. Feagin, "Hurricane Katrina: The Race and Class Debate," *The Monthly Review* 58 (2006): 52-66.

8.   Liu and Plyer, *The New Orleans Index at Five*, 2010.

9.   Nicole Trujillo-Pagán, "Hazardous Constructions: Mexican Immigrant Masculinity and the Rebuilding of New Orleans" in *Neoliberal Deluge*, ed. Cedric Johnson (Minneapolis: University of Minnesota Press, 2011).

formal training.

The increased need for workers in construction and food services after Hurricane Katrina coincided with a systematic weakening of workplace protections. For the express purpose of "faster and more flexible responses to hazards facing workers involved in the cleanup and recovery," the federal government suspended Occupational Safety and Health Administration (OSHA) standards, reinstating them in January 2006 for most of the Gulf Coast, though not Orleans Parish.[10] The Davis-Bacon Act was also suspended, eliminating requirements for federal contractors to pay prevailing wages, and though the Act was reinstated on November 8, all contracts already entered remained grandfathered into the suspension. Further, employers were not required to maintain strict records on wages paid, nor did they have to verify eligibility to work or identification documents.[11] Finally, the requirement of open competition for federal contracts was eliminated, with the suspension of the Competition in Contracting Act, as were affirmative action requirements.[12]

In practice, the weakened regulatory environment has continued long after the temporary period ended, perhaps due to the general weakness of institutions meant to enforce workplace standards. There had already been a long-term trend of decreasing resources and actions by the Department of Labor, as Department actions decreased by one third from

10.   "OSHA Resuming Regular Enforcement Along Most of the Gulf Coast," *News Release*, Occupational Safety and Health Administration, January 20, 2006. http://www.osha.gov/pls/oshaweb/owadisp.show_document?p_table=NEWS_RELEASES&p_id=11805

11.   Ruth Ellen Wasem, *Hurricane Katrina-Related Immigration Issues and Legislation*, CRS Report for Congress, order code RL23091, September 19, 2005.

12.   Congressional Research Service, *Emergency Contracting Authorities*, order code RS22273, September 20, 2005; Charles V. Dale, *Hurricane Katrina Relief: U.S. Labor Department Exemption of Contractors from Written Affirmative Action Requirements*, CRS Report for Congress, order code RS22282, Sept 27, 2005.

2001 to 2007. Enforcement hours by the Wage and Hours Division fell by approximately 100,000, and the number of cases concluded fell from 38,051 to 30,467 over the same period. Hurricane Katrina closed the New Orleans Department of Labor's Wage and Hour Division for four months, and the number of investigations fell by 37 percent in the following year. The hurricane was particularly crippling as it allowed many post-hurricane violations to delay beyond the two-year statute of limitations on Wage and Hour jurisdiction claims, making it impossible to pick them up again even after the division reopened.[13]

Some might suggest that conditions in New Orleans after Hurricane Katrina were unusual and do not necessarily represent long-term or broader trends. For several reasons, the lessons from New Orleans are both analytically useful and of substantive concern.[14] First, the large number of poorly treated workers in New Orleans is not a temporary phenomenon but rather has stabilized as an enduring characteristic of the local workforce. Second, the pattern of segmentation facing different categories of immigrant, African American, women, and other workers has not improved in five years since Hurricane Katrina. Instead, abuses have become the norm, and workers in all kinds of jobs are increasingly suffering mistreatment.

None of this is to say that conditions before Katrina were fantastic. They were not, and New Orleans had already experienced a thirty-year stagnation in wages, expanded insecurity in service jobs, and a decline in traditional

13.   Annette Bernhardt and Siobhán McGrath, "Trends in Wage and Hour Enforcement by the U.S. Department of Labor, 1975-2004," *Economic Policy Brief*, no. 3 (September 2005) Brennan Center for Justice, NYU School of Law.

14.   In formal terms, a study of undocumented workers in the construction sector in New Orleans is an example of "extreme-case design." The study of cases with extreme values on an independent or dependent variable demonstrates clearly the tendencies which might be obscured by studying cases closer to the population average, see John Gerring, *Case Study Research: Principles and Practice* (Cambridge: Cambridge University Press, 2006).

manufacturing. Yet, post-Katrina patterns give particular pause in the context of ongoing crises and disasters, such as flooding in the Midwest, severe weather across the U.S., and the oil spill that hit the same coast as Hurricane Katrina. In the aftermath of disaster, the most vulnerable were forced to pay the greatest costs, and conditions did not improve over time. While conditions before Katrina were certainly not good, the post-Katrina environment appears to have become even worse. The next section describes the design and results of original surveys of conditions for restaurant workers and construction workers in New Orleans.

Working in New Orleans
Means Building and Serving

Workplaces in New Orleans are disproportionately restaurants and construction sites. Together, jobs at these places make up almost 20 percent of total employment, a percentage that has increased steadily over time and experienced a spike when reconstruction intensified and other sectors experienced downturn immediately after Katrina.

The Greater New Orleans metro area is home to over 2,500 food service and drinking places, a number that has steadily grown since the 1990s.[15] The restaurant industry makes up over half of the jobs in Greater New Orleans tourism and contributes greatly to the state's economy. State sales tax revenue generated by the Louisiana restaurant industry is more than $134 million annually.[16] In Greater New Orleans alone, the gross domestic product by metropolitan area from the accommodations and food services sector was $2.6 billion

---

15.   Bureau of Labor Statistics, *Quarterly Census of Employment and Wages*, available at http://www.bls.gov/cew; Kerri McCaffety, *Etouffée, Mon Amour: The Great Restaurants of New Orleans* (Pelican Publishing Company, 2002).

16.   Louisiana Restaurant Association, available at http://www.lra.org/lra/about/about.asp, accessed 04/01/2012.

in 2008.[17] Tourists generate more than $5 billion in spending and up to $300 million in tax revenues.[18]

A similar dynamic of growth is evident in construction, for slightly different reasons. While new home and building construction grew during the early part of the decade as a result of rising real estate prices, Hurricane Katrina provided a different kind of boost in the reconstruction of damaged property. Significant private and public investment grew the sector by 158 percent in 2006 and produced 34,185 jobs.[19] In total, this contributed between $2.8 and $2.9 billion towards local gross product in each of the years since the storm, with an increasing shift towards publically subsidized investment in infrastructure since 2008.[20]

As indicated in Table 1, the "Food Services and Drinking Places" sector (hereafter "food services sector") provides over 44,000 jobs per year in the New Orleans metro area, and is the largest private sector industry in all of Orleans Parish. In fact, the food services sector contributed to 65 percent of employment in the category of "Leisure and Hospitality."[21] Construction follows closely behind; with 31,200 workers, it is the third largest private sector industry.

17.   Bureau of Economic Analysis, *Regional Economic Accounts. Gross Domestic Product by Metropolitan Area*, available at http://www.bea.gov/regional/gdpmetro/action.cfm.

18.   New Orleans Convention and Visitors Bureau, *Hospitality Industry Report, Fourth Quarter 2009*, December 9, 2009, available at http://www.neworleanscvb.com/.

19.   Amy Liu, Matt Fellows, and Mia Mabanta, *Special Edition of the Hurricane Katrina Index: A One-Year Review of Key Indicators of Recovery in Post-Storm New Orleans* (Washington, D.C.: Brookings Institute, 2006).

20.   Bureau of Economic Analysis, *Regional Economic Accounts. Gross Domestic Product by Metropolitan Area*, available at http://www.bea.gov/regional/gdpmetro/action.cfm.

21.   The "Leisure and Hospitality" supersector includes 1) arts, entertainment, and recreation, 2) food services and drinking places, and 3) hotels and other accommodations. See Table 1 for food services and drinking places as a subsector under "Leisure and Hospitality." Data available from: www.bls.gov/ces.

Table 1. Employment in the Food Services Sector, Construction, and Other Select Industries, Greater New Orleans, 2009

Industry	Employment (in 1000s)	Share of Total Employment
Total Greater New Orleans Employment	519.5	100%
Leisure and Hospitality	68.6	13.2%
Health Care	58.1	11.2%
Food Services and Drinking Places	**44.8**	**8.6%**
Manufacturing	35.5	6.8%
Construction	**31.2**	**6%**
Hospitals	15.9	3%

Source: Bureau of Labor Statistics, Current Employment Statistics, July 2009.[22]

After Hurricane Katrina, the Greater New Orleans economy declined, as evidenced by a sharp decrease in employment (see Figure 1). Hit subsequently by the recession and the BP oil spill, employment growth lagged in all sectors, though the restaurant industry has not suffered nearly as much, and even grew through 2007.[23] Construction, which suffered some losses in the 2008 recession, recuperated almost to 2007 levels as a result of subsequent stimulus and infrastructure investment. While these two sectors did relatively well and continued to drive the regional economy, the workers who produced this wealth did not, as the next sections display.

22.   In this table, Greater New Orleans refers to the New Orleans metropolitan statistical area (MSA), which includes Jefferson, Orleans, Plaquemines, St. Bernard, St. Charles, St. John the Baptist, and St. Tammany parishes.

23.   See the National Restaurant Association's Restaurant Performance Index (July 2009). Available at: http://restaurant.org/pressroom/pressrelease. cfm?ID=1838.

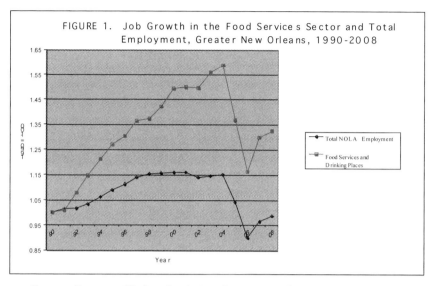

FIGURE 1. Job Growth in the Food Services Sector and Total Employment, Greater New Orleans, 1990-2008

Source: Bureau of Labor Statistics, *Current Employment Statistics* (2009)[24]

Serving New Orleans

While the number of jobs in the Greater New Orleans restaurant industry has grown, restaurant workers' earnings have not. Average annual earnings in the restaurant industry lagged behind that of the entire private sector. In 2001, private sector annual earnings averaged $37,469 but only $15,435 in restaurants; and by 2008, private sector earnings had increased to $44,272 a year while wages in the restaurant industry increased to only $16,870.[25]

Our survey data is consistent with government statistics

24.   In this figure, Greater New Orleans refers to the New Orleans metropolitan statistical area (MSA), which includes Jefferson, Orleans, Plaquemines, St. Bernard, St. Charles, St. John the Baptist, and St. Tammany parishes. Bureau of Labor Statistics, *Current Employment Statistics* (2009)

25.   In interviews, workers told us how low wages force them to work all the time. One fast food restaurant manager told us, "Because I don't work a salaried job I have to go to work every day to make money. If I work 20 hours, that's like $200. I try to go to work as much as I can because it pays off in the long run. . . . They try not to let us have overtime . . . but when you put in more people less people get paid."

that show restaurant work to be primarily low-wage. As can be seen in Table 5, the vast majority of workers in our sample (87%) reported earning low wages, and almost one-third (31%) reported earning wages below the poverty line.

Table 2. Restaurant Wages

Wages Earned by Restaurant Workers	Percent of Workers
Less Than Federal Minimum Wage (< $6.55)	3%
Below Poverty Line ($6.55 – $8.45)	28.1%
Low Wage ($8.46 - $18.30)	55.6%
Livable Wage ($18.31 and higher)	13.2%

Source: Restaurant Industry Coalition survey data

Also, the majority of restaurant workers surveyed reported that they do not receive basic workplace benefits. The data in Table 3 shows that the vast majority of workers surveyed do not have health insurance through their employers (84.5%); over half (53.2%) reported not having any type of health insurance coverage at all; a third (32.2%) went to the emergency room without being able to pay; and a quarter (26.3%) of workers pay for health care out of their own pocket. Some workers reported that they cannot afford insurance even when it is offered by the restaurant. A veteran female bartender stated, "Even if I had an option to get health benefits, I wouldn't be making enough to afford them. . . . It's nice to have that option, but if people can't afford it, then what's the point?"

An overwhelming majority reported that they do not get paid sick days (88.6%) or paid vacation days (74.2%). As a result, 72.3% of the workers we surveyed reported working while sick. A server who has worked in fine dining for ten years explained that "people are more likely to try and work through contagious illnesses" rather than stay at home. One male server reported, "I've seen broke down servers, bartenders, who just keep working because they can't afford not to and they got a sprain or whatever or pulling their back, and they have some condition of some kind and they just work through it." A female server reported, "There [are] times when I call in and tell them I'm sick. . . They don't care! You gonna be sneezing over peoples food and stuff like that and if you wanna put a mask on or try to cover yourself up or whatever then it's bad for the business. . . . That's how it is right now [though]; they just don't care."

Table 3. Jobs and Benefits

Job Benefits and Health Reported by Restaurant Workers	Percent of Workers
Employer does not provide health insurance	84.5%
Do not have any health insurance coverage	53.2%
Gone to ER without being able to pay	32.3%
Do not get paid sick days	88.6%
Do not get paid vacation days	74.2%
Have worked when sick	72.3%

Source: Restaurant Industry Coalition survey data

While conditions are generally poor for all, patterns of division are also evident, with the worst conditions allocated according to racial and gender hierarchies. White workers are more often in the front of the house serving and bartending, while workers of color are in the back, preparing and cooking food and washing dishes. Survey data showed three-quarters (78.4%) of all white workers worked in the front-of-the-house while three-quarters of the workers in the back of the house were either African American (62.5%) or Latino (10.5%).

One worker observed, "Definitely there are Hispanics working back there, and it's interesting because they are the ones in the back; they're the ones doing the hard work and this is a . . . Mexican restaurant, but there wasn't a single Mexican or Hispanic server. All Caucasian, all college kids, all white, uppity on top of that. But everyone in the back . . . to them it's almost like a favor, 'Be grateful we even give you this job' kind-of-thing, so they kind of took a lot of abuse in like verbal and a lot of racial slurs."

An African American worker reported, "At [fine dining establishments in the French Quarter], you can be as smart as this book right here but they won't hire people like me for certain positions," and a fine dining owner confirmed, "Well, I don't have any black people working here. They never came to apply. The black people have their thing and the white people have their thing. It is strange."

These hierarchies translate into differences in earnings, benefits, opportunities for training and advancement, and working conditions (see Table 4). Front-of-the-house workers generally earn higher wages and have greater opportunities to increase their earnings through tips. One quarter (24.5%) of all front-of-the-house workers reported a living wage (more than $18.31 per hour) compared to only 2.1% of back-of-the-house workers. Additionally, back-of-the-house workers are more likely subject to unsafe working conditions where they put both themselves and the public at large at risk. They are also less likely to be afforded benefits such as health insurance and sick and vacation days, or receive health and safety training, even as they experience a greater percentage of unsafe working conditions and workplace injuries, such as exposure to toxic chemicals (41.2%), cuts (42.2%), and burns (50%).

Table 4. Race Breakdown by Restaurant Job Type

	African-American Workers	White Workers	Latino/Hispanic Workers	Asian Workers	All Workers
Front-of-the-house Workers	32.1%	78.4%	55.6%	83.3%	57.4%
Back-of-the-house Workers	67.9%	21.6%	44.4%	16.7%	42.6%

Source: Restaurant Industry Coalition survey data

The stark differences in job quality between front-of-house and back-of-house positions are compounded by a general lack of mobility between the two types of positions. Of all workers surveyed who never received a promotion, more than three-fourths (76.7%) were workers of color. Once hired in back-of-house positions, workers are essentially trapped there, experiencing worse conditions, lower wages, and little chance of advancement.

The front and back divide good jobs from bad within individual restaurants, and good and bad jobs are also separated across segments of the industry. High-end restaurants, known as "fine-dining," tend to include the largest number of higher paying jobs; "family-style" offers fewer; and, "quick-service" or "fast-food," almost none.[26] Once again, ascriptive characteristics assigned workers to different portions of the sector. Over half (57.1%) of the survey respondents working in the fine-dining segment were white, and 58.7% of all African Americans were concentrated in quick-service jobs. Women of color were doubly concentrated, with 70 percent of all black women in the quick service segment. This was expressed in wage differences, as 26.7 percent of men and 73.3 percent of women reported earning minimum wage or less.

New Orleans restaurants, one of the largest and most lucrative sectors in the city, show a shocking pattern of poor pay, dangerous conditions, limited benefits, and absent opportunities for advancement. The sector is marked by extreme inequality, with a few good jobs in the front of the house in fine dining restaurants and a host of bad jobs in the back and in family style and quick serve sectors. Workers were allocated to jobs not based on skill or experience, but rather according to racial, gender, and immigration-status

26.   Fine-dining workers averaged $13.40 per hour, while workers in family-style averaged $12 per hour and quick-service $8.50. There were even some respondents among the fine dining servers who reported earnings over $100,000 annually.

differences, making it difficult to advance from bad to good jobs. The conclusion also reflects on what this might mean for working-class organization. In the next section though, we explore similar patterns of segmentations in construction.

New Orleans Construction Workers

These patterns of exploitation and inequality are also evident in the construction sector, though two additional observations are relevant there. First, while conditions are bad for all, the most significant segmentation would appear to be along the lines of ethnicity and immigration status, with the worst pay, danger, and benefits reserved for undocumented Latino workers. Second, while these conditions may be worse for undocumented Latinos, conditions are deteriorating for an increasing number of workers in an increasing variety of job categories. This section describes these trends by drawing on responses from construction workers surveyed at a random sample of worksites in 2006 and 2009 and a non-random sample of pick-up site workers surveyed in 2009.

With respect to working and living conditions, the survey research indicates a set of disturbing trends. The first set of results attest to the fact that workers in construction in New Orleans live precarious lives with limited income, dangerous work, and difficult living situations. These conditions were present in 2006, and they remain all too evident in 2009. Second, while these conditions are evident for all workers, the undocumented suffer more intensely on a number of indicators; responses were polarized in 2006, and they remain polarized in 2009. Third, and perhaps most striking, some of the conditions and abuses that were endured by undocumented workers in 2006 have now become generalized to the rest of the construction worker population.

Within the randomly sampled population, we attempted to characterize these trends precisely by comparing proportions of documented and undocumented workers experiencing different conditions across time periods. We distinguished among trends using Pearson chi-squared statistics to test the significance of differences in proportions of documented and undocumented workers experiencing each condition. The tables below present the proportions of documented and undocumented workers experiencing each condition and the statistical significance of the differences between group proportions. For each condition, we also present the proportion of the workers at day laborer pick-up sites.

Table 5 displays the difficult working and living conditions faced by all construction workers, regardless of immigration status. There were some statistically significant differences between undocumented and other workers, but more striking is the general inadequacy of working conditions for all workers on these items of the survey.[27]

This situation has not improved in five years since Hurricane Katrina. In 2006, 9.4 percent of undocumented workers had health care and in 2009 only 10.7 percent. Other workers fared better, but far below what might be acceptable, with access to health insurance at 59.4 percent in 2006 and 50.7 percent in 2009.[28] Slightly less than two thirds of undocumented workers (62.3%) lacked access to medicine when they needed it in 2006, and this problem persisted into 2009 when 53.6 percent reported lacking access. Once again, while other workers did slightly better, no workers did well, with 16.2 percent lacking access to medicine when they needed it in 2006 and 19.7 percent in 2009. Access to treatment was even lower, with 92.3 percent of undocumented workers lacking treatment for a reported medical problem in 2006, 84.0 percent lacking treatment in 2009, and 69.8 percent of pick-up site workers lacking treatment.[29]

27.   Although there were some improvements over time, this may have been partly structural, as fewer medical facilities were available in 2006.

28.   Only 7.5 percent of pick-up site workers had access to health insurance.

29.   Among other workers, only one-quarter sought treatment for their medical problem in 2006 and 41.4 percent in 2009. While the difference between docu-

Table 5. Difficult Living and Working Conditions for All, (%)

	2006			2009			
	Undoc	Other	Diff	Undoc	Other	Diff	Pick-Up Site
Have health insurance or medicare	9.4	59.4	50.0**	10.7	50.7	40.0**	7.5
Have medicine when needed	37.7	83.8	46.1**	46.4	80.3	33.9**	45.3
Sought treatment if needed	7.7	25.2	17.5**	16.0	41.4	25.4**	30.2
Harmful substances/ chemicals	20.8	32.5	11.7	30.4	44.9	14.5	42.0
Dangerous conditions	41.5	41.3	.2	53.6	56.3	2.7	36.0
Received general training	39.6	48.6	9.0	54.7	68.6	13.9**	44.0
Illness/accident resulting injury	11.5	12.4	.9	37.0	39.1	2.1	44.9
Physical abuse	1.9	0.0	1.9	11.1	10.4	.7	20.4
Receive extra pay when working >40 hours	30.2	28.2	2.0	37.5	34.8	2.7	20.8
Sometimes	5.7	2.4	3.3	5.4	10.1	4.7	7.5
No	64.2	69.4	4.8	57.1	55.1	2.0	71.7

**Difference in group proportions significant at p<0.01; *Difference in group proportions significant at p<.05

---

mented and undocumented was statistically significant at p<.001 on these indicators, the rates of insurance, access to medicine, and access to treatment was so low for all workers that it made sense to put this indicator in this category.

The health challenges faced by undocumented and other workers are even worse in the context of the dangerous work inherent in reconstruction of residences after a storm, conditions which remained difficult and even deteriorated over time. Self-reported exposure to harmful chemicals or substances was high for all workers, though documented and native-born workers were more aware of the hazards, as 44.9 percent reported exposure in 2009 compared to 30.4 percent among the undocumented. Both groups reported dangerous conditions, ranging from 36 percent among pick-up site workers and 56 percent among documented and native-born. No workers were consistently trained, with only 54.7 of undocumented workers reporting training, 68.6 percent of other workers, and 44.0 percent of pick-up site workers. Perhaps as a result, all workers reported high rates of illness or incidents resulting in injury on the job—37 percent of the undocumented workers, 39.1 percent of other workers, and 44.9 percent of pick-up site workers in 2009.[30]

In addition, workplace violations would appear to affect both undocumented and other workers, as 11.1 percent of undocumented workers reported physical abuse at work, a level matched by documented and native-born workers at 10.4 percent, and 20.4 percent among the pick-up site workers. Further, despite the difficult and dangerous work they undertook, neither undocumented nor other workers were consistently paid overtime for work beyond forty hours in a week. In both 2006 and 2009, documented workers actually reported slightly higher rates of overtime nonpayment some or all of the time, at 65.2 percent in 2009, compared to 62.5 percent among undocumented and 79.2 percent among pick-up site workers.

30.   Within the randomly sampled population, this represents a statistically significant increase (p-value <0.00) from 2006 when only 11.5 percent of undocumented workers and 12.4 percent of other workers reported injuries on the job. Still, the rising rate of illness and injury seems surprising, as it was in the immediate aftermath of the storm that the most dangerous debris removal and remedial work on unsafe buildings occurred, so some of the increase could have been a result of reporting.

While the figures above portray the general difficulty of life as a construction worker, other indicators suggest that distress is meted out particularly on the undocumented. In the indicators presented below, differences in proportions across groups were all statistically significant, with notably high rates for undocumented workers and less prevalence among others. The results from these comparisons are displayed in the table below.

Table 6. Worse Conditions for the Undocumented, (%)

	2006			2009			Pick-Up Site
	Undoc	Other	Diff	Undoc	Other	Diff	
Own their residence				0.0	49.3	49.3	2.0
Have partner or spouse	58.5	59.4	.9	57.1	52.1	5.0	44.2
Partner in N.O.	29.0	61.8	32.8**	37.5	81.1	43.6**	30.4
Have Children	69.2	68.4	.8	67.9	72.9	5.0	60.4
Children in N.O.	43.4	20.0	23.4*	15.8	64.0	48.2**	9.4
Informed of risk of mold	37.7	67.1	29.4**	35.3	65.7	30.4**	28.0
Informed of risk of asbestos	35.8	64.9	34.1**	43.6	62.0	18.4*	30.0
Informed of risk of unsafe building	19.2	58.7	39.5**	29.6	65.7	36.1**	46.0
Deportation threats	7.7	1.6	5.1*	21.8	3.6	18.2**	16.3

**Difference in group proportions significant at p<0.01; *Difference in group proportions significant

While 54.1 percent of all workers had a spouse or long term partner, undocumented workers were much more likely to be separated from their families. Among undocumented workers with a long-term partner, 37.5 percent report that their partner is in New Orleans compared to 81.1 percent of other workers, and this number was only 30.4 percent of pick-up site workers. Likewise, 64 percent of other workers with children have them in New Orleans, while only 15.8 percent of undocumented worksite sampled workers and 9.4 percent of pick-up site sampled workers do. Instead of living with their families, undocumented workers and pick-up site sampled workers were much more likely to live with a large number of roommates, 4.43 and 4.75 respectively, as compared to 2.77 in the households of other workers.

These conditions can be considered indicative of the absence of family networks, and they were matched by other types of vulnerability, such as the inability of undocumented workers to accumulate assets as a reserve for slow times. Roughly 84.5 percent of documented workers report having access to a vehicle, compared to only half of undocumented workers and 44.0 percent of the pick-up site sampled workers. Also, though home ownership was relatively low among all construction workers, at 28.1 percent, no undocumented workers and one pick-up site sampled worker owned their own home, while 49.3 percent of other workers owned their residence. When we explored the data by race, it became further evident that only 8.7 percent of foreign-born Latinos overall owned their own homes while 64 percent of Caucasians and 58.3 percent of African Americans owned their own residence.

Vulnerability in living circumstances was exacerbated by dangerous and risky work. Fully 64.7 percent of undocumented workers reported not being informed about the risk of mold; 56.4 percent were not informed about the risk of asbestos; and, 70.4 percent were not informed about the risk of unsafe buildings. This is significantly less preparation than other workers ($p < 0.05$), though even they did not receive adequate warnings about risks. For example, 38.0 percent of documented workers were not informed about the risk of asbestos. None of these indicators had improved since 2006, with no statistically significant change in the proportions of workers suffering these conditions of dangerous and risky work. The numbers were similar among the pick-up site sampled workers, who reported 72 percent not being informed about the risk of mold; 70 percent not informed about the risk of asbestos; and 64 percent not informed about the risk of unsafe buildings.

Another example of the enhanced vulnerability of undocumented workers was the rate at which employers threatened to deport workers in the event they complained. The rate was predictably higher for undocumented workers and worsened over time for all groups.[31] Among undocumented worksite sampled workers, threats of deportation affected 7.7 percent in 2006 and 21.8 percent in 2009, compared to 16.3 percent among pick-up site sample workers.[32]

One of the starkest workplace differences was evident in wages and income, which were significantly less for undocumented workers in both 2006 and 2009. On average, wages were $10.88 per hour for undocumented workers in 2006 compared to $16.35 among documented workers, with the difference spreading to $11.16 and $17.30 in 2009.[33] Differences in wages were highly statistically significant, and this difference remained even when we controlled for the type of work. Skilled workers, those reporting more sophisticated work such as electrical, plumbing, and carpentry, still showed a statistically significant $7.08 wage tax for undocumented workers.

31.   The non-zero result for native-born and documented immigrant workers suggests that employers used this threat whenever they perceived an opportunity to use national origin as a means of intimidation, whether or not the workers had documentation to work legally.

32.   Among documented workers, threats of deportation were not absent, at 1.6 percent in 2006 and 3.6 percent in 2009.

33.   Pick-up site workers averaged $10.31. In this case, significance tests used the t-statistic and accounted for the possibility that group means are non-homogeneous, as indicated by the Levene's test for equality of variances. Still, results are practically indistinguishable from those under the assumption that variances are equal.

Table 7. Poor Conditions Generalized from the Undocumented to All, (%)

	Undocumented			Other			Pick-Up Site
	2006	2009	Diff	2006	2009	Diff	
Receive less than promised	37.7	48.2	10.5	25.4	33.3	7.9	62.3
Unfair treatment by employer	15.4	34.5	19.1*	9.7	30.4	20.7**	60.8
Problems being paid for work	32.1	41.1	9.0	20.8	38.6	17.8**	57.1
Problems with payment	21.2	50.9	29.7**	11.4	31.9	20.5**	57.7

**Difference in year proportions significant at $p<0.01$; *Difference in year proportions significant at $p<0.05$

To determine the overall financial situation of the workers, questions were asked that addressed both wages and average amount of work.[34] When coupled with the fact that undocumented workers report working fewer hours per week (41.20 hours compared to 49.37), the monthly salary was also less for undocumented workers; undocumented workers had a mean monthly salary of $1,536.20, less than half the documented worker salary of $3,380.70.[35]

34.   Wages were calculated using self-reported income per payment, frequency of payment, and average hours worked. Differences between documented and other workers were robust to truncating outliers at a maximum of 1.5 standard deviations above the mean. When outliers were truncated, undocumented workers received a mean hourly wage of $10.75 and documented workers received a mean hourly wage of $15.80.

35.   Income was calculated using self-reported income. Differences between undocumented and other workers were once again robust to truncating outliers at a maximum of 1.5 standard deviations above the mean. With outliers removed, undocumented workers received a mean salary of $1,536.20 and documented workers received almost exactly double that at $3,076.78. These differences are even more pronounced when considering that undocumented workers reported sending remittances to their families, resulting in an even lower living wage.

While the construction sector was characterized by particularly difficult conditions meted out to undocumented workers, it would appear that conditions are getting worse for everyone. Some of the deplorable conditions previously reserved to undocumented workers have now been generalized to the rest of the population. These patterns are displayed in the table above. Unlike the previous tables which measured the statistical significance of differences across group proportions within each year, this table compares within group proportions across years. Differences across groups did not shift considerably, but conditions for both groups appeared to deteriorate over time, with all workers approximating conditions among undocumented workers. Once again, while we hesitate to draw conclusions from the comparison between the random sample of worksites and the non-random sample of workers at pick-up sites, the alarmingly high numbers in the final column give pause.

In 2006, 37.7 percent of undocumented workers received less money than promised at least some of the time, as compared to 25.4 percent among other workers, but this increased to 48.2 percent and 33.3 percent in 2009 and 62.3 percent among pick-up site workers. Based on a question that asks whether workers experienced unfair treatment from an employer, 15.4 percent of the undocumented responded affirmatively in 2006, compared to almost a third fewer, 9.7 percent, among other workers. By 2009, the affirmative response rates had increased and were almost the same, 34.5 and 30.4 percent among undocumented and other worksite sampled workers, and 60.8 among pick-up site sampled workers. The rate of problems with employer payment was 21.2 percent among undocumented and 11.4 percent for others in 2006, but more than doubled among undocumented to 50.9 and almost tripled among others to 31.9 percent in 2009, and stood at 57.1 percent among the pick-up site sampled workers. When the question was asked another way, 32.1 percent of undocumented workers reported problems being paid for work at least some of the time in 2006, as compared to 20.8 percent of documented, increasing slightly among the undocumented in 2009 to 41.1 with others practically catching up at 38.6 percent and pick-up site workers reporting an astounding 57.7 percent.

Several factors could explain these particularly worrying trends. One explanation is that in the immediate aftermath of Hurricane Katrina, employers experimented with mistreatment on undocumented workers. Finding that there was no punishment, they extended mistreatment to other workers in subsequent years. A second explanation is that the construction sector began to filter out by 2009. As more regulated and better paying jobs in public infrastructure projects came online and absorbed native-born and documented workers, more informalized and unregulated work and worse conditions were left in the residential construction sector, where the survey was targeted. A third explanation is that the combination of the recession and the slowdown of rebuilding several years after Hurricane Katrina meant that there was simply less work in residential construction, creating slimmer margins for employers who became more likely to shift the burden to workers. As for why the mistreatment accelerated faster for the native born and documented, it is possible that undocumented workers were already being mistreated at such high rates that there was little more that could be squeezed from them. Whatever the explanation, the implication is worrying — exploitative labor market conditions now affect more workers, in more jobs.

Workers were also victimized in other ways. Construction workers, especially day laborers and undocumented workers, frequently work for cash, making them vulnerable to criminal predation. The results of the survey confirm that crime is a problem, though it is distributed in some unusual ways. Among the worksite sampled respondents, victimization by crime was highest for African Americans, at 41.7 percent, and white respondents reported victimization at 34.8 percent, while Latinos reported victimization at 19.5 percent, similar to the pick-up site rate of 20.8 percent.[36]

Also, although police are the main public authority charged with protecting individuals from crime, survey results suggest that police harassment is an increasing problem for all workers. In 2009, a total of 29.9 percent of respondents reported police harassment, in contrast to 6.1 percent of respondents in 2006. Harassment at the hands of police affected 20 percent of undocumented workers and 38.8 percent of other workers in 2009. When we explored these results by race, we found that police harassment was especially directed at African Americans, with 68.0 percent reporting police harassment, a statistically significant difference from white respondents at 27.3 percent and Latino respondents at 19.8 percent, with pick-up site workers reporting a slightly higher 30.6 percent.[37]

These patterns of abuse, distributed along race and immigration-status lines and worsening for the whole population, are being met in unusual ways. Most workers face difficulties organizing or otherwise forming horizontal bonds to resist exploitation and repression, and few were active in any organizations. Levels of affiliation were above twenty percent only in sports leagues and religious organizations for the worksite surveyed workers. The only area in which there was a statistically significant difference in worker activity was among pick-up site workers active in ethnic and worker organizations. This was particularly notable for worker organizations, with 30.2 percent of pick-up site workers claiming affiliation with a worker organization as compared to only 8.7 percent of the workers surveyed at worksites.

36.   It is interesting to note that the more common type of victimization experienced by undocumented workers, the theft of wages by employers, was not reported nor is it punished as a criminal offence, Southern Poverty Law Center, *Under Siege: Life for Low-Income Latinos in the South* (Montgomery, AL: SPLC, 2009).

37.   This is consistent with the findings of a Department of Justice investigation of the New Orleans police department, Civil Rights Division, *Investigation of the New Orleans Police Department* (New Orleans: US Department of Justice, 2011).

Table 8. Levels of Organization

	Worksite Sample	Pick-Up Site Sample	Difference
Worker organization	8.7	30.2	21.5 **
Ethnic organization	2.0	11.3	9.3 **
Sports league	21.3	34.0	12.7
Religious organization	34.7	41.5	6.8
Community organization	13.3	13.2	-.1
Political party	8.0	5.7	-2.3
Other	3.3	0.0	-3.3
Tenant association	5.3	1.9	-3.4
Neighborhood association	9.3	5.7	-3.6

**Difference in group proportions significant at $p<0.01$; *Difference in group proportions significant at $p<0.05$

This result bears some consideration as it indicates an avenue for further research. What makes people organize? Pick-up site workers suffered the worst conditions of exploitation in the form of non-payment of wages, generally lacked documents, and were out of work when surveyed. In short, these were the most vulnerable members of the construction sector workforce, yet they were the most organized. It is possible that their higher levels of organization are a result of being pushed to their limits, when they can take no more, and when they have nothing left to lose. Alternatively, it is possible that these were workers with the greatest organizational resources on which to draw. They were overwhelmingly Latino; they may have come to the U.S. favorably predisposed to workplace organization; their condition as majorities at pick-up sites might have created additional bonds; and, there has been significant targeting of pick-up site workers by advocacy organizations such as the Worker Center for Racial Justice.[38] Further, it is possible

38.   New Orleans Worker Center for Racial Justice website, http://www.now-crj.org/, accessed 04/01/2012.

that the form in which they organize, as a worker center and not as a union, offers greater flexibility to their organization, even as it limits the kinds of agreements they can enter into and pressure they can bring. Finally, pick-up sites might simply be easier places in which to organize, as worksites may be overseen by contractors or employers hostile to the information-gathering and organization-building of workers. Whatever the explanation, in the context of efforts to understand class formation, it is worthwhile to consider what parts of the New Orleans workforce currently organize, and how other workers can be incorporated into a working-class political movement.

Comparison and Conclusion

The restaurant and construction industries provide two clear windows on the world of low-wage work and inequality in post-Katrina New Orleans. In both industries, expanding economic activity and wealth creation have coincided with a huge and growing underclass of people suffering under deplorable working conditions and earning low wages with little or no benefits. In both industries, this growing underclass has been exaggerated by deregulation after Hurricane Katrina, failure to enforce remaining workplace regulations, and the apparent complicity of public authorities who participated in the general harassment of workers. This has resulted in deteriorating conditions for all workers, as well as patterns of exploitation and inequality marked by clear race, gender, and immigration-status distinctions.

While this general story is similar across both sectors, the dimensions and dynamics of inequality have evolved in unique ways. In the construction industry, inequality would appear to be based especially on immigration status. Undocumented workers experience significantly worse pay, working conditions, and living conditions. One explanation could simply be the degree to which exploitation has progressed in the sector. In the absence of regulation and in the presence of outright repression by public authorities, especially towards African Americans, working conditions for all categories of worker are deteriorating, and more and more categories of work, including some work that requires greater training and credentials, face increasingly bad treatment.

By contrast, the restaurant sector displays a slightly different pattern, in which the sector retains a few good jobs, but reserves those jobs for white workers. The good jobs are characterized by livable wages and decent working conditions, but these jobs remain largely inaccessible to workers of color, especially women of color, who are allocated to back-of-house roles or low-wage segments of the industry according to ascriptive characteristics of race, gender, and immigration-status, with little chance of advancement.

An additional characteristic of restaurants deserves mention; market demand and social practices in restaurants create a particular logic of job segmentation.[39] For front-of-house workers, the fine dining experience and the direct interactions that occur between workers and consumers depend on maintaining the seeming civility of working conditions. Back-of-house jobs or those in family style and quick serve restaurants, by contrast, are either invisible to the consumer or need not retain the fine dining illusion. Perhaps employers, who are generally white, feel more comfortable exploiting marginalized populations. Perhaps customers, who are also generally white, feel less offended if they only see marginalized populations suffering exploitation or if they need not see them at all. Regardless of the cause, racialized and gendered roles in restaurants facilitate segmentation, make it possible for increasing wealth and growth to coincide with inequality and exploitation, and allocate the few good jobs and many bad jobs according to ascriptive characteristics

---

39.   The one part of the construction sector in which there is significant work-place organization is in the unionized building trades that generally mediate conditions on large-scale infrastructure and business construction projects.

that have nothing to do with skill, experience, or any other criteria that might reflect productivity in the workplace.

For those few who currently have decent jobs, the lessons of construction hold an ominous warning. In a remarkably quick amount of time, the few good jobs that were reserved to native-born construction workers have been turned bad. Distinctions remain in some areas, and the sector remains segmented according to immigration status, but poor conditions are no longer reserved to undocumented workers and the jobs they do. There has been a rapid bottoming-out of conditions for all workers, documented and undocumented, skilled and unskilled. There are simply few good jobs and few workers able to create a decent life in the residential construction sector.

These patterns suggest the crucial importance and unique challenges facing working-class politics. First, it is abundantly clear that the lack of regulation and outright hostility from public authorities leave employers with a free hand to segment their workforce and allocate working conditions as they please. Second, worker organization, which seems the only defense, has to face the ascriptive divisions that guide the allocation of jobs and that simultaneously complicate the formation of working class movements. Yet, it is precisely out of the racial, gender, ethnicity, and immigrant histories of workers that a vibrant working-class movement must emerge. Class, as E.P. Thompson observed, must be made, in the sense of workers drawing on prior experience, including rural and communal traditions, to provide bonds of class and tools of organization.[40]

This calls for contextually specific class and extra-class identities around which workers can organize; something Gramsci considered the ideological work of "organic intellectuals."[41] Such intellectuals frame worker identity that

40.   Thompson, *Making of the English Working Class*, 1966.

41.   Antonio Gramsci, *Selections from the Prison Notebooks* (New York: International Publishers, 1973).

bridges structural patterns of exploitation, historical legacies of prior struggle, and cultural contexts, such as those provided by gender, race, ethnicity, and immigration-status. This task lies at the core of organizational and political struggle by workers, but it is beset by real constraints and outright hostility.

Here, social movement theories draw attention to the resource mobilization and political process challenges of mobilizing and organizing workers.[42] With the institutional and market power of employers and the state generally arrayed against workers, working-class politics requires institutional forms that can generate resources, attract members, and secure political access to sustain mobilization in the face of likely setbacks, harassment, and established opposition. The current project does not suggest that working class organization has taken hold in New Orleans. Still, by drawing attention to the patterns of segmentation and exploitation that currently organize labor markets in New Orleans; the project highlights the dimensions of resistance that are necessary to make a working-class movement. While there are no guarantees such a movement will emerge or be successful, the failure to protect the most vulnerable in restaurants and construction has led to everyone becoming worse off.

Appendix 1. Restaurant Worker Survey Methodology

Real wages were determined by either calculating workers' average weekly earnings including tips and dividing by the average number of hours worked per week or, for un-tipped workers, using their hourly wage. Wage groups were then created using the Louisiana State minimum wage at the time the survey was conducted ($6.55), the Department of Health

---

42.   Sydney Tarrow, Charles Tilly, and Doug McAdam, *Dynamics of Contention* (New York: Cambridge University Press, 2001).

and Human Services (HHS) 2008 federal poverty line earnings for a family of three of $17,600 per year, and the Economic Policy Institute's (EPI) Basic Family Budget Calculator. The following six factors were chosen to calculate a livable wage: a) Housing, b) Food, c) Transportation, d) Healthcare, e) Taxes and f) Other basic necessities. Definition of wage groups and distribution of the sample population across groups can be seen in Table 5

Appendix 2. Construction Worker Survey Methodology

We conducted two rounds of surveys among construction workers in New Orleans, including a random sample of all construction workers and targeted sampling of Latinos. Participation was strictly voluntary with informed consent, anonymity, and no financial compensation. Interviewers applied a structured questionnaire with 129 questions, in either Spanish or English, depending on the preference of respondents. The survey was implemented in two separate years, 2006 and 2009, and the questions were largely kept constant across years except questions added to reflect changing circumstances in New Orleans and among immigrant workers.[43]

The random samples aimed at a representative number of respondents, with 212 respondents in 2006 and 150 respondents in 2009. To identify interview sites, we randomly selected a proportionate number of addresses from each census tract in the city based on a comprehensive database of addresses from the City of New Orleans Sewerage and Water Board.[44] In total, 296 addresses were selected, a sample size

43. Results from the 2006 survey appeared in several outputs, see for example, Laurel Fletcher, Phuong Pham, Eric Stover, and Patrick Vinck, "Latino Workers and Human Rights in the Aftermath of Hurricane Katrina," *Berkeley Journal of Employment and Labor Law* 28, no. 1 (2007): 107-53.

44. The database was created by merging the New Orleans Sewerage and

large enough to account for the possibility that no interview would be possible at some of the sites.[45]

Teams of trained surveyors were assigned to the selected sites, with each team trained in the application of the survey, fluent in Spanish, and traveling in groups of two or more. Once the survey team arrived at a designated point, the sampled housing unit, they were instructed to identify the closest construction site within a ten block radius. At each construction site, the survey team would ask the closest worker standing to the left to participate in the study. If that person declined, the team asked the next person to the left until a respondent was found.

The 2009 survey results also include fifty-three responses from workers sampled at pick-up sites for day laborers on street corners and in front of building supply stores. This sampling strategy intentionally over-represented Latino workers, and therefore cannot be used to draw general conclusions about the construction worker population, but does suggest some interesting differences within the Latino population.

Despite the best efforts of researchers to eliminate bias and preserve reliability, there are limitations. Generalizations should for now be limited to the greater metropolitan area of New Orleans, though they suggest an agenda for ongoing research on the national context. Also, the survey addressed sensitive subjects such as discrimination, trauma, immigration status, labor abuse, and abuse by state authorities, and it is

Water Board dataset of addresses with water meters with data from the Census Bureau and the Geographic Information Systems (GIS) Department of New Orleans, and included all addresses in the city of New Orleans with geographic reference points and links to pre-Hurricane Katrina demographic information. The sampling procedure was conducted with the support of the Emergency Operations Center (EOC) of New Orleans.

45.   Based on the minimum sample size formula, the minimum sample size was 97 if we assumed 95 percent confidence, a prevalence estimate of 50 percent, and desired precision of .10. To have sufficient sample size to stratify, we increased the minimum sample size requirement to 150. The minimum sample size formula is given by: $N \geq Z^2 \times (P)(1-P)/d^2$.

possible that respondents did not always answer truthfully. To minimize error, surveyors stressed anonymity in the consent form, never asking or recording names, and repeated promises of anonymity before sensitive questions.[46]

46.   To minimize risk of worker discomfort, surveyors offered respondents information sheets and contact information for non-profits active on worker rights and immigrant rights, and the study was submitted to review by the Institutional Review Board of the author's university.

About the Authors

Thomas Jessen Adams is Lecturer in History and American Studies in the Department of History and the United States Studies Centre at the University of Sydney. His works focuses on the history of American labor, political economy, cities, social movements, and the Gulf South. He is completing monographs on the history of service as a category of labor in the U.S. and the political economy of metropolitan New Orleans from the post-segregation era to the present. He lives in New Orleans and Sydney.

Eric Arnesen is professor of history at The George Washington University. A specialist in the history of race, labor, politics, and civil rights, he is the author of two award-winning books—*Brotherhoods of Color: Black Railroad Workers and the Struggle for Equality* (Harvard University Press, 2001) and *Waterfront Workers of New Orleans: Race, Class, and Politics, 1863-1923* (Oxford University Press, 1991)—and *Black Protest and the Great Migration: A Brief History with Documents* (Bedford/St. Martins, 2003), and the editor or co-editor of four other books. A recipient of fellowships from the National Endowment for the Humanities, the Fulbright Commission, and the Woodrow Wilson International Center for Scholars, he is currently completing a biography of A. Philip Randolph.

Demetri D. Debe is a Ph.D. candidate in Early American, Atlantic, and Caribbean History at the University of Minnesota, Twin Cities where he is writing his dissertation. He holds a master's degree from the National University of Ireland. Demetri's research interests include the African Diaspora, Women's history, American Indian and Indigenous Studies, Food Studies, and Labor history seen through the lenses of race and gender. He has published articles on the history of the Caribbean, of the American South, and of Ireland.

Nancy Dixon, an English professor at Dillard University in New Orleans, has been studying, teaching, and writing about Louisiana literature and culture for over twenty years. Her first book, *Fortune and Misery: Sallie Rhett Roman of New Orleans* (LSU Press, 1999), won the LEH Humanities Book of the Year, 2000. More recently, she is editor of the 2013 Lavender Ink book, *N.O. Lit: 200 Years of New Orleans Literature*.

Saru Jayaraman is the Co-Founder and Co-Director of the Restaurant Opportunities Centers United (ROC-United) and Director of the Food Labor Research Center at University of California, Berkeley. After 9/11, together with displaced World Trade Center workers, she co-founded ROC in New York, which has organized restaurant workers to win workplace justice campaigns, conduct research and policy work, partner with responsible restaurants, and launch cooperatively-owned restaurants. Saru is a graduate of Yale Law School and the Harvard Kennedy School of Government.

Elizabeth Manley is an Assistant Professor of History at Xavier University of Louisiana. She received her Ph.D. in 2008 from Tulane University and in the process fell in love with New Orleans. She now considers herself an adopted native, but also spends time in the Caribbean, where she works on issues of identity politics, authoritarianism, gender, and sexuality in the twentieth century.

Michael Mizell-Nelson's research interests center upon New Orleans and twentieth century US history, and he has collaborated in developing several online database projects and video documentaries. He is a recipient of various scholarships and grants, including a one-year research fellowship from the National Endowment for the Humanities. The latter allowed him to revise and expand his manuscript of working class New Orleans residents in Jim Crow-era New Orleans, which is nearing completion. He is an associate professor in the University of New Orleans History Department.

Aurelia Lorena Murga received her Ph.D. from Texas A&M University and is currently an assistant professor of sociology at the University of Texas at El Paso. Her areas of study focus on racial/ethnic inequality, Latina/o sociology and migration. Dr. Murga is currently working on a manuscript on day labor participation in post-Katrina New Orleans.

Chanda M. Nunez is a native New Orleanian. She holds undergraduate and graduate degrees in history from the University of New Orleans. She currently lives in Atlanta, Georgia, where she continues to research pralines.

Kodi Roberts is assistant professor of history at Louisiana State University. His work focuses on intersections of race, religion, and resistance movements in African American history. His book *Voodoo & the Promise of Power: the Racial, Economic, and Gender Politics of Religion in New Orleans, 1881-1940* (forthcoming from LSU Press) looks at the racialization of Voodoo in Depression-era New Orleans and the parallel inculcation of contemporary local culture into the rituals of Voodoo practitioners. He is also currently working on a project that looks at engagement in religious institutions by the Marxist Black Panther Party in the 1970s.

Aaron Schneider is the Leo Block Chair at the Korbel School of International Studies at the University of Denver. His work focuses on the intersection of wealth and power, and he has conducted research in Latin America, India, and Sub-Saharan Africa. In New Orleans, he has been particularly interested in the political economy of Post-Katrina development: who is in, who is out, and who will enjoy what benefits of recovery. This interest has led to engagement and advocacy for the working people of the city, especially those who are marginalized by multiple forms of racial, ethnic, and gender exclusion.

Steve Striffler is the Doris Zemurray Stone Chair in Latin American Studies and professor of anthropology and geography at the University of New Orleans. He writes on labor, immigration, Latin America, and the U.S. South.

Celine Ugolini is a French native from Corsica, France, who spent five years living in New Orleans. In 2006, she obtained her bachelor's degree in English and American studies from Michel de Montaigne Bordeaux 3 University in France. She went on to graduate with a master's degree in Anglophone studies from that same university in 2008. She has been working on a dual Ph.D. from Bordeaux 3 in Anglophone Studies and from the University of New Orleans in Urban History since 2008.

Index

Symbols

4141 bar, 196

A

Abbey bar, 196, 202
Alabama: AFM merger, 153;
    coal miners, 20, 25-26;
    sharecroppers, 9; steelworkers,
    96
Algiers, La., 71, 108, 113, 126, 131
Algren, Nelson, 199
Al Hirt's Night Club, 209
Allen, Richard, 157
Amalgamated Association of
    Street and Electric Railway
    Employees of America, 69
American Federation of Labor
    (AFL), 12, 31, 69, 71-73; African
    American sub-division 421,
    86, 90; CIO, 147; conductors,
    69, 74-75, 80; Division 194, 71-
    72, 74-76, 80-82, 85-86, 88-89,
    91-92, 94-95; linemen, 81, 85;
    motormen, 69, 74-75, 80; track
    laborers, 81; transit workers,
    95-96; utility company
    employees, 73, 78, 95
American Federation of Musicians
    (AFM), 146-48, 154, 159-60;
    Civil Rights Department, 149;
    Local 174, 133, 146, 148, 150-56,
    159, 161; Local 496 (African
    American), 133, 137, 146,
    148, 149-50, 152-56, 158, 161;
    merger, 149, 151, 153-54, 159,
    161; Southern Conference, 149
American Football League all-star
    game (1965), 157
Ameringer, Oscar, 73

Anderson, Laura, 170
Antoine's restaurant, 199
Appadurai, Arjun, 119
Arnesen, Eric, xii-xiii, 71-72, 133;
    *Waterfront Workers of New
    Orleans*, xii-xiii, 12, 15, 17, 19-
    20, 31
Astor, Valle, 170
Atlanta, Ga., 194; washerwoman's
    strike, 22, 25
Aunt Sally's Creole Pralines,
    178-80, 182-84; Canal Street
    location, 180
Austerlitz St., 170

B

Babylon, Judge Edwin A., 131, 136,
    162
Bagur, Diane, 182-83
Bagur, Pierre, 182-83
Ballard, Frederick, 75
Banks, Russell, 199
Barker, Danny, 158, 160
bartenders union, 195, 197
Bates, Ruby, 7
Bayou Classic, 204
Bayou Manchac, La., 33
Bearden, Bessye J., 5
Behrman, Martin, 74
Beletto, Al, 139, 158
Benoit, Michelle, 181
Benoit, Yvonne, 180-81
Berg, Donnie, 131
Bernard, Al, 162
Berndt, Louis, 156
Berry, Jason, 137
Bienvenu, Gus, 81-83, 86
Bienville, Jean-Baptiste Le Moyne,
    Sieur de, 36